John Stoughton

Windsor: A History and Description of the Castle and the Town

John Stoughton

Windsor: A History and Description of the Castle and the Town

ISBN/EAN: 9783744728768

Printed in Europe, USA, Canada, Australia, Japan

Cover: Foto ©ninafisch / pixelio.de

More available books at **www.hansebooks.com**

WINDSOR:

A HISTORY AND DESCRIPTION

OF THE

CASTLE AND THE TOWN.

BY THE

REV. JOHN STOUGHTON.

LONDON:

WARD AND CO., 27, PATERNOSTER ROW.

WINDSOR: S. COLLIER.

1862.

LONDON:
SAVILL AND EDWARDS, PRINTERS, CHANDOS STREET,
COVENT GARDEN.

TO

THE REVERED MEMORY OF

H.R.H.

THE PRINCE CONSORT,

TO WHOM, IN ITS ORIGINAL FORM, THIS LITTLE WORK WAS

BY SPECIAL PERMISSION DEDICATED:

IT IS NOW,

WITH HUMBLE GRATITUDE AND AFFECTION, INSCRIBED,

BY

THE AUTHOR.

PREFACE.

IGHTEEN years ago the Author published "Windsor in the Olden Time," which was very favourably received, and especially by those best acquainted with the Castle and neighbourhood. That little volume has now for a long time been out of print, and though repeatedly requested to republish it, sensible of its imperfection, he has always refused to do so. At length, however, having collected materials to render the book more complete, and more generally acceptable as a guide to the Castle, he has recast the whole, and now presents to the public a substantially new work.

He sincerely thanks all his friends connected with Windsor Castle and the Royal Service there—particularly Mr. Woodward, the Queen's Librarian—for the valuable assistance which he has received from them in preparing this publication.

CONTENTS.

PART I.

HISTORICAL.

CASTLE.

	PAGE
CHAP. I.—THE FOUNDATION	1
CHAP. II.—FROM HENRY III. TO EDWARD III.	9
CHAP. III.—ORDER OF THE GARTER	27
CHAP. IV.—FROM RICHARD II. TO EDWARD IV.	37
CHAP. V.—THE TUDORS	60
CHAP. VI.—THE STUARTS	87
CHAP. VII.—WILLIAM AND ANNE	138
CHAP. VIII.—HOUSE OF HANOVER	144

TOWN.

CHAP. I.—MEDIÆVAL WINDSOR	149
CHAP. II.—MARTYRS IN THE REIGN OF HENRY VIII.	158
CHAP. III.—AGE OF ELIZABETH	165
CHAP. IV.—TOWN IN THE SEVENTEENTH CENTURY AND SINCE	178

PART II.

DESCRIPTIVE.

CHAP. I.—THE ROYAL PRECINCTS	193
CHAP. II.—THE NEIGHBOURHOOD	228

PART I.

HISTORICAL.

CASTLE.

CHAPTER I.

THE FOUNDATION.

HE antiquities of Windsor carry us back to the time when the Romans were in possession of our island. Traces of their triumphant career are to be found in the neighbourhood. Roman bricks have been found at Old Windsor, and coins and urns at St. Leonard's. At Egham, also, Roman remains have been discovered. One of the great Roman roads passed the first-named place at no great distance. Some antiquaries have supposed that the station called "*Pontes*," mentioned in the ancient Roman Itinerary (called the Antonine Itinerary), was at Old Windsor; but others, with greater probability, have fixed it at Staines. About eight years ago, the neighbourhood of Virginia Water was examined with a view to trace the remains of the Roman road.—"An investigation," says Mr. Edgell, the gentleman chiefly engaged in the research, "was commenced in Mr. Forbes' field, west of Broomhall, near the road leading to Sunninghill, in which situation may be seen a remarkable specimen of Roman road in its most perfect state : whilst in the fields, still more

to the westward, are scattered fragments of Roman bricks, tiles, and lead, affording sufficient indication that a Roman town, which must have been of considerable extent, once existed there. Its course was kept in view for some distance; crossing the western road, it passed north of the clock-case, and terminated on the brow at the extremity of the heath. The remarkable and undeviating line taken by the Roman engineer was observed, bearing to the north side of Ashford church, where, in my recollection, a portion of the Roman road existed perfect; but now it is nearly, if not entirely, destroyed by the plantations, &c. From a bridge crossing the Thames below Staines, from those of the large encampments adjoining the river, together with the bridge at the ford at Ashford, must the station of Pontes have been denominated."*

These antiquarian researches, however, relate rather to the neighbourhood of Windsor than to the place itself. Poetry and tradition have associated with the latter the romance of King Arthur; and, in the preface to the "Black Book," or register of the Garter, we are gravely informed that this deservedly noted and famous prince, "in whose reign the riches and power of the Britons largely increased, began that noble tower at Windsor, and there instituted his Round Table." It need scarcely be remarked, that there is no evidence whatever to support such a statement, and that most, if not all, of what is related respecting that celebrated personage is fictitious.

There can be no doubt, however, that, at a very remote period, the Saxon kings had a palace at Old Windsor. It then bore the name of Wyndleshora, a Saxon appellation,

* "Observations upon certain Roman Roads and Towns in the South of Britain."—Appendix, p. 45.

probably referring to the winding banks of the Thames in that vicinity.* A town of some extent existed there prior to the Conquest, and in the reign of William the Conqueror contained a hundred houses. Though Saxon urns, at different times, have been dug up in the neighbourhood, no one yet has been able to identify the site of the royal palace. Wherever it stood, it seems to have been the resort of the Saxon princes ; and here, it is said, Edward the Confessor held his court. A story is related of him by William of Malmesbury, to the effect that one Wulwin, who was cutting down wood at Brill, in Bucks, fell asleep, and lost his sight for seventeen years, but through a dream he came to the king's court at Windsor, and was cured by the royal touch. In accordance with his saintly character, Edward was a munificent benefactor to the church ; and in an ancient deed of gift to the monks of Westminster, we find the king, "for the hope of eternal reward, the remission of his sins, the sins of his father and mother, and all his ancestors, to the praise of Almighty God, granted, as an endowment and perpetual inheritance, to the use of the monks there that served God, Windsor, and all its appurtenances."

But the brotherhood at Westminster were not permitted long to retain the gift, for William the Conqueror, being attracted by the beauty of the neighbourhood, selected it as a residence. He required the monks to resign it into his possession, and compensated them for the loss by the grant of certain estates in the county of Essex. William ascended the English throne in the year 1066, and pro-

* In the " Annals of Windsor," p. 11, a new derivation is proposed from Windles, a river in Windsor Forest, several miles distant. That Windsor should take its name, not from a large river on which it stands, but from a small one a long way off, is a very strange hypothesis.

bably at an early period of his reign erected a castle on
the site of the present one, since in "Domesday Book,"
which was completed in the year 1086, the edifice is referred to as already in existence, and as containing within
its precincts half a hide of land, parcel of the manor of
Clewer. Being extremely fond of the chase, the king
appropriated for that purpose the forest for many miles
round, and established laws for the preservation of the
game. No description of William's castle remains, but it
was probably of the same character with other Norman
strongholds, of which many remains may be seen in different parts of the kingdom. A high solid rampart, flanked
by salient towers, and defended by a parapet, enclosed an
open space, in which, near the extremity, and on the highest
elevation which could be obtained, stood the keep, the
citadel of the fortification, and, in some cases, the residence
of the lord. The entrance was accessible only by a pre-
cipitous flight of steps exposed to the missiles of the
besieged, or by stairs of studied intricacy. The approach
was guarded by a stockade, or a second rampart and ditch,
dividing the enclosure into two wards or "baileys," called
upper and lower. Sometimes within the ramparts other
buildings were erected, as the residence of the owner of the
fortress, rather more adapted to domestic habitation than the
cheerless keep.* The castle at Windsor, though intended
as a hunting seat for the Conqueror, would, as a matter of
course, in a warlike age, and under circumstances such as
those which attended his accession to the sovereignty of
England, partake of the nature of a fortress. The accommodation it afforded must have been of limited extent, and
therefore the festivities of his court at Windsor, in the

* See Introduction to the Illustrations of Windsor Castle, by Sir
Jeffrey Wyatville.

Whitsuntide of 1070 and 1072, to which authors refer, were most probably held at the old Saxon palace.

William Rufus, wearing his crown, no doubt, in accordance with royal custom at such festivals, was there at the same season in 1095 with all his retinue, except the Earl of Northumberland, whose absence being construed into disaffection, he was besieged at Bamborough, and being afterwards taken prisoner, was conveyed to Windsor, and there confined. The Bishop of Durham, when attending the Christmas court festivities, died here on New Year's day, 1095.

Henry I. enlarged the castle and erected a chapel, and in the year 1110 kept the feast of Whitsuntide at New Windsor, and invited the nobles of the realm to attend the solemnity. This is the first undoubted instance of a court being held in the new palace; and it was on this occasion that ambassadors came to solicit the hand of the Princess Matilda for the Emperor Henry V., to whom the royal maiden, then but five years of age, was solemnly betrothed by proxy,—there being no small disparity in age between the noble pair, for her illustrious suitor had seen more than forty summers. In the reign of the first Henry, scenes of regal festivity and splendour within the walls of the castle were not unfrequent. Here, on the 29th of January, 1121, he was united to his second queen, Adelaide, daughter of Godfrey of Louvain.

"The coronation of this lady," says Speed, "was appointed to be celebrated by Roger, Bishop of Salisbury, the infirmity of palsy so troubling Ralph, Archbishop of Canterbury, that himself could not perform it; yet, because Roger was not appointed by him, he forbad his employment; and the king wearing his crown, saith the monk of Chester, this testy old man could hardly be intreated by the lords to withhold his hands from striking the same from the king's head. Of such spirits then were those spiritual prelates, and jealousy to lose their pompous pre-eminence of honour." *

A similar contention about placing the crown on the king's head arose between the Archbishops of Canterbury and York, at the Christmas festival, in the year 1127, when David of Scotland and the English barons swore fealty to the Empress Maude.

The castle of Henry I. differed but little in point of extent from that part which now forms the middle and lower wards. The king's house occupied "the upper ward, and the hall formed a portion of a line of buildings separating the two courts, and defended on the lower side by a ditch." A few architectural fragments, in the Norman style, brought to light from the excavations made in the castle-yard during the late improvements under Sir Jeffrey Wyatville, are, perhaps, the only existing relics of the palatial buildings of the twelfth century at Windsor, and might probably belong to a chapel which then formed part of the castle, and which is supposed to have covered a portion of the site of the military knights' houses. This chapel was dedicated to Edward the Confessor, and had an establishment of eight secular priests.

In the reign of Stephen, Windsor was considered the most important fortress in the kingdom next to the Tower of London; and in the treaty of peace between him and Duke Henry, afterwards Henry II., it is mentioned as the place of meeting between them. In the year 1170, the latter held his court in the castle, when William of Scotland and his brother David visited the monarch to present their congratulations on his return from Brittany. Five years afterwards, a treaty of peace was concluded on the same

* Speed's " History of Great Britain," p. 459.

spot between Henry and Roderic O'Connor, King of Connaught, by which the coast of Ireland, from Dublin to Waterford, was ceded to the English monarch. In the same reign, expenses were incurred in repairing or improving the royal buildings, of which there are several curious entries in the records of that period. In the nineteenth year of Henry II.'s reign, the expenditure on the castle was estimated at £73 7s. 6d.; and in following years different sums are mentioned as paid by Master Geoffry, who, from the frequent occurrence of his name, seems to have been master of the works. Among the appendages to the royal palace at that time was a vineyard, and the expense of the vintage is specified in the annual charges relating to Windsor.

Every one knows that Henry II. was an unhappy father, and the Chronicler Fabyan relates that the king ordered to be painted on the walls of his apartment at Windsor, an old eagle with four young ones pecking at it. "What means such a picture?" it was asked. "I am the old eagle," said the poor monarch, "and the eaglets are my sons. John, whom I love best, imagines my death." John was represented picking out the old man's eyes.

In the reign of Richard I., Windsor was involved in the troubles of the period. Hugh de Pudsey, the martial Bishop of Durham, occupied it, as regent, during the absence of the chivalrous monarch; but he was compelled to surrender it to Longchamp, Bishop of Ely, a brother prelate, of similar warlike propensities. He retained it for awhile, and then delivered it to the Earl of Arundel; it was afterwards yielded into the hands of Prince John. Subsequently it was besieged and taken by the barons who remained faithful to the interest of their absent sovereign.

It is recorded that John, after his accession, imprisoned in the castle of Windsor the Lord of Brambar and his wife

and children, and starved them to death, because, when
the imperious monarch sent for the baron's eldest son to be
his page, the mother heroically exclaimed, that she would
not surrender her children to a king who had murdered
his nephew.   Within the walls of Windsor Castle the same
monarch afterwards sought security during his perilous
struggle with the barons ; and thither he repaired, after
the charter of England's freedom had been extorted from
him on the neighbouring plain of Runnymede, to brood
over plans of revenge, and to lament, with the fury of a
maniac, over the concessions he had been forced to make.*
Attempting again to invade the rights of his subjects, he
was once more assailed by his powerful barons, who invested
the castle, but were obliged by the garrison to raise the
siege.

* " It is probable that John and his attendants went to the conference (at Magna Charta Island, Ankerwyke) from Windsor in the
morning of each day, and returned to the castle at night."—" Annals
of Windsor," vol. i. p. 53.

CHAPTER II.

FROM HENRY III. TO EDWARD III.

ENRY III., a munificent patron of architecture, soon after his accession to the throne, made very considerable additions to the castle. In the eighth year of his reign, it appears, from existing records, that the sheriffs of London were commanded to deliver one hundred of fir to Master Thomas, for the purpose of making doors and windows, an order which probably relates to some new and stately edifice. In the twenty-third year of the same reign an order was given to the bailiffs of Windsor to paint the queen's chamber, to line or plaster the chamber of the prince, to make a private room contiguous, to put iron bars in the windows, and to form a floor in the turret of the gate, so as to divide it into two stories, and to cover it with lead ; entries which, though trivial in themselves, become interesting as indications of the state of domestic architecture at that early age. In the twenty-fourth year, Walter de Burgh was commanded to make a certain apartment for the king's use in the castle of Windsor, near the wall of the said castle, sixty feet in length and twenty-eight feet wide ; and another apartment for the queen's use, which should be contiguous to the king's, and under the same roof ; and a chapel, seventy feet long and twenty-eight feet wide, along the same wall, so that a sufficient space should be left between the apartments and the chapel to make a grass-plot. Respecting the royal habitation, nothing further can be ascertained than the dimensions. Of the chapel there are other notices, which prove it to have had the appendages of a galilee or porch, a cloister, and a bell-tower. In three years the walls of the chapel were ready for the roof, and a pressing order was addressed to the Archbishop of York to see the works completed. The roof is described as a lofty wooden one, after the manner of that which was then being built at Lichfield; and directions are given that it should be lined and painted, so as to appear like stone; and, also, that it should be covered with lead. The same order directs a bell-tower to be erected in front of the chapel, to be built of stone, and of a size to hold three or four bells. Four gilt images were also to be provided, and placed where the king had previously determined. The cloisters seem to have been partially completed about this time, but some portion was not carried up to the roof until five years later, when six *carrates* of lead for covering it are mentioned, to be provided by the sheriffs of London. An order was also given to enclose the space from the door of the great hall to the galilee with a wall, ten feet high, with a small door near the wardrobe; and, also, to make a wooden barrier round the galilee, to prevent horses from approaching it. While these alterations were going on, the king must have been hard pressed for money, since Madox, in his "History of the Exchequer," relates that in the twenty-ninth of Henry's reign, not having enough to pay the officers of the chapel, he was driven actually to pawn a valuable image of the Virgin, which stood within its precincts.

"Many entries and particulars," observes Mr. Britton, "respecting towers, a new kitchen, an oriel, a private chapel, an oratory, accommodation for the queen, colours, boards, laths, lead, crenellation of towers and walls ; a salting-house, and other offices ; a wardrobe for the queen's clothes, and a chamber for nurses, are specified in the items of accounts and works for this reign.   A fountain, a conduit, a drawbridge, iron chains, a portcullis, a lavatory, a barbican, and many other domestic essentials, as well as military objects, were made and provided."*

In those days, the natural soil rammed down and strewed with litter or rushes, was the only floor of which even the baron's home could boast; but as a special piece of regal luxury, Henry III. ordered a room on the ground floor at Windsor to be "boarded like a ship."

To entertain the poor at certain seasons was deemed in those times no mean virtue ; and in the twenty-fourth year of this reign an order was given to the bailiffs to fill the great hall of the castle, on the Nativity of our Lord, with poor people, and the lesser hall likewise on the days of St. Stephen and St. John, and the Epiphany.   Similar directions are given to fill the hall with poor chaplains and clerks on the day of St. Thomas, and with poor boys on St. Innocents' Day.   Carpenters were maintained in the royal establishment, and minute items of domestic expenditure are preserved, down to one of 15s. to Matilda, the wife of Master Thomas, carpenter, to buy a new gown.†   The lesser hall was in the upper bailey, the large hall in the lower.   A description is preserved of a throne, painted and gilt, which stood in the large hall, with the figure of a king in his regalia on either side.   Mention is further made of stained glass windows, which were not completed till some

* "Architectural Illustrations of Windsor Castle."—By Britton.
† Among the writs issued from Windsor during this reign, is a curious one relating to a white bear, which was kept in the Tower of London, for the purpose of catching fish in the river Thames for the royal table.

years after the erection of the building, but which, together with the other decorations, evince a decided progress in the conveniences and luxuries of life. But little remains of the castle as it was in the reign of Henry III.* The old grey towers, which still flank the western wall—namely, the Salisbury Tower, at the bottom of the hill ; its neighbour, now undergoing "restoration," formerly known as the Garter Tower ; and the old bell tower, often called Julius Cæsar's Tower, are the chief remains of Windsor Castle as it stood in those distant days. In removing some buildings connected with the canons' houses to the south of St. George's Chapel—on the spot where the *Domus Regis* of Henry III. stood—a door in a wall belonging to that period has been brought to light—probably the relic of a chamber for the king or queen, of which a notice is extant in orders given to Walter de Burgh in the 24th of Henry III. It may be added that when extensive alterations were made in Thames-street in the year 1852, the workmen employed in pulling down the houses which stood in the castle ditch discovered a subterranean passage, which has since been kept open by a well-like shaft communicating with the green bank which slopes down from the castle wall, close to the Garter tower. The author was allowed very recently to explore the passage, and found that in one direction it descended towards the lower part of the ditch, where it terminates, and in the opposite direction ascended towards the castle wall. A good flight of stone steps still remains, and the masonry of the roof is perfectly sound. A screen wall is built across the upper part, and this intercepts further access ; but it was stated by one of the castle workmen that the passage takes a bend and turns up to the crypt of the bell tower. It no doubt

---

* The *Domus Regis*, with the larger hall, must have occupied the site of what is now St. George's Chapel.

belongs to Henry III.'s castle, and was possibly a sally-port in the fortification. It is supposed to have been connected with a barbican noticed in the rolls of the 23rd year of Henry III., but there appears no direct evidence to show where that barbican stood. We may notice, that in the thirty-fifth year of his reign, Henry III. made a grant of land in the forest for a Leper Hospital, of which probably we have a memento and a mark of the site in the hamlet of Spital, on the road to St. Leonard's.

Henry III.'s son, afterwards Edward I., was educated at Windsor, for we find in the Issues of the Exchequer the following order:—" Pay out of our treasury to Hugh Giffard and William Brun £200, for the support of Edward our son and his attendants residing with him at our castle of Windsor."

The quietude of Windsor was disturbed by the wars between the king and the barons. Prince Edward during this turbulent period held Windsor Castle, but Henry and his queen chiefly resided at the Tower of London. On one occasion, when her residence was assailed by a mob, she attempted to escape in her royal barge to Windsor ; but the populace endeavoured to sink the vessel, and she with difficulty escaped their violence and returned to the Tower. Not feeling herself safe there, she afterwards removed to the Bishop of London's palace, whence she was privately conveyed to Windsor Castle. The monarch subsequently made the city of London pay dear for the insult which had been offered to his queen. He deprived it of its charters, and summoned the Lord Mayor and some other citizens to appear before him at Windsor, there to affix the city seal to the instrument of their humiliation. On their arrival at the castle, they were treated with the greatest indignity by the officers of the household, and committed to the charge of the constable of the Round Tower, where they were confined till the following day. The mayor and four others were afterwards subjected to strict confinement till they should pay their ransom. Sixty thousand marks was the sum demanded, which, however, was reduced to twenty thousand marks, on the earnest plea of the citizens, who declared themselves unable to raise the larger amount.

During the same reign in which Windsor Castle was disturbed by the civil commotions of the kingdom, the elements also assailed it with violence. Holinshed mentions a remarkable storm in the year 1251, on St. David's Day, when the chamber wherein the queen and her children then were, was beaten down to dust, and the whole building sore shaken. "In the parks oaks were rent asunder and turned up by the roots, and much hurt done, as mills with the millers in them, sheepfolds with their shepherds, and ploughmen, and such as were going by the way, were destroyed and beaten down, the chimney of the nursery thrown down by the shock, several oaks being at the same time uprooted in the parks by a tremendous hurricane."

These scanty fragments, associated with the information which the history of our country at large affords, respecting the circumstances of our monarchs, and the state and habits of society in those remote times, may enable us to form some imperfect idea of the place and its appearance during the reigns of the early Norman sovereigns. The castle was the only building of any importance whatever. A few scattered dwellings around the royal abode, inhabited by the vassals of the king, or the serfs of the soil, were all that constituted the Windsor of that period. It was the age of feudalism, when everything deserving the name of civilization was confined to the prince and the baron, and the great mass of society was in a state of semi-barbarism. Nor could royalty itself, in those days, boast of any other magnificence than such as in our eyes seems most rude and comfortless. The apartments, the banquets, the festivities, the costumes, were all of this description, and the manners of society were of a corresponding character. One can picture the Norman stronghold on the brow of Windsor Hill, its towers and fortifications, its gloomy halls with their oaken rafters, and its large straggling chambers, with narrow loopholes fitted rather to exclude than to admit the light of heaven. We can also fancy that we see the mail-clad lords doing homage to their feudal sovereign, or unbending from the toils of the field amidst the boisterous merriment of the royal feast. The forms of England's queens, and the ladies of their courts, pace along the battlements or wander in the gardens of the castle. Nor can we forget that violence and war often broke in upon scenes which just before were quiet and joyous.

In the reign of the first Edward, brighter days dawned on Windsor. The country being relieved from intestine feuds, and the differences between the king and the nobles of the realm being adjusted, the seat of royalty, no longer exposed to the incursions of war, became the scene of courtly magnificence, and witnessed many of those rude displays of festivity which characterized the age. It had been the favourite residence of his wife Eleanor while he was prince, and here she gave birth to three children, John, Eleanor, and Henry.

In the sixth year of Edward's reign, according to a record preserved among the archives in the Tower, a splendid tournament was held in Windsor Park. Accoutrements were provided for thirty-eight knights; and, from the accounts of the money expended, it would appear that they were clothed in very costly array. " Armour was provided for all the knights. It appears to have been of gilt leather; and various sums, from 7s. to 25s., were paid for making and gilding each suit to the three persons employed, Cosmo the tailor, Salvag' the tailor, and Reymunde de

Burdieus. At the end of this item of the account, there is a memorandum stating that each suit of armour consisted of a tunic, a surcoat, a pair of ailettes (appendages to the shoulders), a crest, a shield, a helmet of leather, and a sword of 'balon,' probably whalebone (*baleen*)."[*]

Among the anecdotes relating to the castle at that period, there is a remarkable account of the preservation of the king from what might have proved a most serious accident. One day, when he was playing at chess with a knight, he suddenly rose from his seat, without having any definite motive for doing so ; and the next instant the centre stone of the groined roof of the apartment fell to the ground on the spot which he had just left.

Stow mentions that in this reign, in the year 1295, a destructive fire broke out in the castle of Windsor, consuming many of the offices, and defacing several "goodly images made to beautify the building."

Edward II. frequently resided at Windsor, and here his renowned son Edward III. first saw the light. He was christened in the then existing chapel, four days after his birth. The uncle of Isabella, and the rest of the French nobles who were at the court of his royal parents, were urgent with the king to allow his name to be Louis ; but the English nobles, always averse to foreign appellations, insisted that the princely boy should be baptized by none other than the name of Edward. The ceremony was performed by Cardinal Arnold, and the prince had no less than seven godfathers. Rude, no doubt, was the splendour of the ceremonial, as high-born dames, noble knights, and mitred priests gathered round the font ; far different from that display of beauty and grandeur which, after the lapse of more than five long centuries,

---

[*] " Annals of Windsor," vol. i. p. 107.

graced the baptism of a regal descendant, who had given him, in addition to the name of Albert, that of Edward, in the spirit of the old nobles at the first Windsor christening.

Astrological studies were usual in those days, and much importance was attached to them. The horoscope of Edward was drawn at the time of his birth; and according to Ashmole, who describes it as painted on a window in the prebend's lodgings belonging to Doctor Hever, it represents the king as "born at 40 minutes after five in the morning" of the 23rd of November, 1312; "the 6th degree of the sign of Scorpio ascending, and the 18th degree of Leo culminating."

Among the relics relating to Edward III. and the town of Windsor, the place of his birth and his favourite residence, is a curious tale in verse, the MS. of which has been discovered by Mr. Hartshorne, and inserted by him in his "Collection of Ancient Metrical Tales." It turns upon the common ballad incident of a king incognito meeting with a peasant—visiting his home—hearing all he has to say—inviting him to the royal castle—and redressing his wrongs.

In the reign of Edward III. Windsor Castle was rebuilt. Amongst the Harleian MSS.* we find a paper in which John Stow, the antiquary, tells us, "The two higher wards were builded by Edward the Third, certainly, and upon occasion, as is reported, of his victory against the French King John, and the King of Scots, David—both of them prisoners at one time in the old castle of Windsor, as is said, where being visited by the king, or riding together with him, or walking together in that ground where the wards be now, as a parcel of his park, the strangers commending the situation, and judging the castle to have been better built in that place than where it was, as being on

* No. 367.

C

higher ground, and more open to see and to be seen afar
off, the king approved their sayings, adding pleasantly, that
it should so be, and that he would bring his castle thither,
that is to say, enlarge it so far with two other wards, the
charges whereof should be borne with their two ransoms,
as after it came to pass." According to this story, France
and Scotland suggested the improvement, and had to pay
for it.

Under Edward III. the old castle was taken down,
with the exception of three towers at the west end of the
lower ward before noticed, which still remain as mementos
of the old feudal fortifications. Ashmole,* whose veneration for all that pertains to royalty and knighthood is
most amusing, begins his account of the rebuilding of the
castle by observing, that to the end it might be *honestly*
and duly performed, King Edward, by letters patent, in
the twenty-third year of his reign, appointed John Peyn-
tour, Richard de Rochell, and Robert de Bernham, and
other surveyors, to *press* hewers of stone, carpenters, and
other artificers ; also, to provide stone, timber, and other
materials. The same historian goes on to repeat the re-
newal and amplification of these powers to other architects,
especially the famous William of Wykeham, to whose
genius and taste the monarch was mainly indebted for the
construction of his favourite edifice. He further tells us
that, in the thirty-fourth year of Edward's reign, there was
then great store of the best diggers and hewers of stone
imprest in London, and out of divers counties of England,†
by virtue of writs directed to the sheriffs, with command to

---

* See his " History of the Order of the Garter."

† The counties mentioned were as follows :— Essex, Hertford,
Wiltshire, Leicestershire, Worcestershire, Cambridgeshire, Hunting-
donshire, Kent, Gloucestershire, Somersetshire, Devonshire, and
Northamptonshire ; each was to supply forty men.

send them to Windsor by the Sunday next after the feast of St. George, there to be employed at the king's wages. The sheriffs were to take security that the workmen should not depart from Windsor without license, under the penalty of £100 : and because some left Windsor clandestinely, proclamation was made to punish the fugitives with imprisonment in Newgate ; and any person who dared to employ them, with the forfeiture of all his goods. The pestilence having swept off a large number of the workmen, fresh writs were issued to the sheriffs,* commanding them to press as many more as were wanted ; and in default of doing this, they were to be fined £200. Parts of the castle, both in the reign of Henry II. and Edward III., were built of Egremont stone, which considering the difficulty and expense of bringing it must have been highly esteemed.†

In the thirty-seventh year of the king's reign, when the building was ready for glazing, twelve glaziers, a very scarce class of artificers (for glass windows were then little used), were also *impressed*. In the same year also the work went on effectually, says Ashmole, as may be guessed from the great store of workmen *pressed* for the service ; and from this time, he adds, to the forty-third year of this king's reign, artificers were yearly *pressed*. Thus men were forcibly brought from all parts of the kingdom to do the monarch's bidding. The circumstance throws a strong light on the condition of the labouring classes of that period. It indicates the imperfection of the personal liberty of the subject, and the unconstitutional assumptions of royal

---

* The places to which the writs were sent, and the number of men each county was to provide, were as follows:—York, sixty ; Derby, twenty-four ; Salop, sixty ; Hereford, fifty ; Nottingham, twenty-four ; Lancaster, twenty-four ; Devon, sixty.

† " Domestic Architecture," vol. i. 25.

authority. It shows that the people were only in a sort of transition state from the villanage of feudalism to the rights of hired freemen. It also affords an illustration of the pecuniary means of our early sovereigns. There had been no necessity to impress workmen, had they been properly paid by their royal master. The fact was, that the revenue of the sovereign was so comparatively trifling, that he had not the means of bearing the expense of costly buildings ; and therefore, if he resolved to have them, his vanity or his taste could only be gratified by a violation of justice. The statute of labourers, passed in the same year which witnessed the commencement of the castle by Edward, sheds further light upon the condition of the artisan. That famous statute recites, that workmen were not willing to serve after the pestilence, which had just proved so destructive of life, without taking excessive wages ; and it enacted that such manner of servants, as well men as women, should be *bound* to serve at such wages as were paid in the twentieth year of the king's reign, on pain of imprisonment. This was quite in the spirit of Edward's impressment of labourers, showing a similar disregard to personal liberty, and must be acknowledged to be a clumsy, as well as unjust mode of legislation, to meet a difficulty which competition among workmen, in the natural course of things, would easily have removed. The same statute shows the wages that were paid ; for the regulation of these was an important part of the enactments. Master carpenters were to have threepence a day ; journeymen, twopence ; master masons, fourpence ; journeymen threepence ; labourers, one penny. Agricultural labourers were to receive, during harvest, threepence a day, besides diet ; or twopence per quarter for threshing wheat. These, it must be confessed, were high wages ; as threepence a day then was equal to five shillings now ; and the fact places the labourer of the fourteenth century, with regard to the means of livelihood, in enviable comparison with his descendants in the nineteenth.*

The rebuilding of the castle occupied eighteen years, during which period large sums were annually expended on the works. In the first half of the year 1363, for instance, the expenses amounted to £3802 17s. 8d., out of which £932 was paid for lead only. In the next year, the outlay altogether was £3031 9s. 9d. The last year or two the sums paid were about £2000 per annum.

The castle was finished in 1369, having been eighteen years in progress. It was built under the direction of the illustrious Wykeham, the favourite of Edward III., who

* The following extract from "Domestic Architecture in England," vol. ii. 28, is interesting in connexion with the works at Windsor Castle:—

"As in earlier times, all the metal work was executed on the spot, and forges and furnaces were built for the smiths and plumbers. These forges and furnaces required fuel, and it had been already discovered that coal was a more efficient material than wood. Owing, however, to the prejudice of the Londoners against that mineral product, no supply of it could be procured in the metropolis, and the king's master of the works was compelled to buy a cargo of it at the pit mouth in Durham. At this time, when thousands of vessels and many lines of inland railway are daily engaged in bringing this important necessary of life to the capital, the narrative of the voyage of a ship chartered to carry coals for the works at Windsor in 1367 may be interesting to the reader. According to the custom of the time the king sent his writ to the sheriff of Northumberland ordering him to buy seven hundred and twenty-six chaldron of coals, and send them to London. The sheriff purchased them by the greater hundred, at Winlaton, in the county of Durham, at 17d. the chaldron. On their voyage to London the colliers met with a 'mighty tempest at sea,' and through that, and by reason of the excess of London measure over that of Newcastle, a loss of eighty-six chaldron and one quarter was incurred, the greater part having been thrown overboard during the tempest. Arrived at London, the coals were put on board 'shutes,' or barges, and taken to Windsor, at a cost of 1s. a chaldron. The total expense of bringing this insignificant quantity of fuel to London, including its cost price, was £165 5s. 2d., to which must be added the barge hire to Windsor."

rose from very humble origin, to fill the highest offices in church and state. His architectural genius shed a lustre around the age in which he lived. He was not only an architect, but a wit and a courtier, as one might judge from the round, comely, and good-humoured face of the effigy on his tomb at Winchester. His social qualities probably contributed to raise him to his elevation ; and saved him on one occasion, as tradition says, from the displeasure of his royal master. When he had finished the castle, he wrote the famous inscription, "*Hoc fecit Wykeham ;*" respecting which an old Latin historian* tells the following story :—"The courtiers represented to the king that the architect had arrogated to himself all the glory of the palace ; but when the king, greatly incensed, charged Wykeham with the crime, he, not with a sorrowful and affrighted countenance, but with great composure and good humour, replied, the man was either ignorant of grammar, or a malicious calumniator, who founded a criminal charge upon a mere inversion of grammatical cases. 'Neither, serene prince,' he added, 'did *I make this castle, but this castle made me all I am ;* that is, it has placed me in your majesty's favour, and raised me from a humble condition to the highest fortune :' which reply, so facetious and worthy of Wykeham (for it was a true specimen of learning, readiness, and wit), not only removed the displeasure of the king, but raised him greatly in his estimation."†

Of the general appearance of Edward III.'s castle, some idea may be formed from a consideration of the style of architecture which prevailed in the fourteenth century, combined with such historical statements regarding this noble edifice as antiquarian research has brought to light.

---

* "Historica Descriptio Vitæ Wicam," quoted by Bayle *in loco* "Wicam."

† Lowth, the biographer of Wykeham, discredits the whole story.

At that period a considerable change took place in the construction of baronial residences. While regard was had to
defence, more attention was paid to effect. The solidity of
the fortress was united with somewhat of the beauty and
grandeur of the palace. Buildings designed for the comfort of the lord and his family formed a more prominent
feature in the general plan. The solidity of the keep and
the strength of the outworks were no longer the sole consideration. The grouping of towers variously shaped, those
flanking the gateway being generally the most conspicuous for
lofty proportions, formed a characteristic distinction. The
loophole gave place to the glazed window, and even to the
elegant oriel; while the machicolation, at once defensive
and ornamental, crowned the gateways. The improved
character of the architecture of the period is not only a
sign of increasing taste, but an indication of the more
settled and peaceful state of society.

Before the time of Edward III., Windsor Castle did not
extend to the east much beyond the round tower; the
buildings forming the quadrangle were his additions. They
formed a third and upper ward. On the southern and
eastern sides they presented an aspect of defence. A ditch
ran along their base, guarded by curtain walls, blank and
unbroken save by the gateways and loopholes of the towers.
The north side, before Queen Elizabeth added the present
fine terrace, probably presented the same appearance. The
apartments were lighted from the inner courts; and hence
several smaller courts, known as the Brick Court, Kitchen
Court, and Horn Court, were introduced on the north side,
which had a double range of buildings.

The round tower crowning the middle moat was a striking
and characteristic feature of Edward's fortress. It is, no
doubt, the same as the "*Unus Turris vocat la Rose*," mentioned in the accounts of Adam de Hertyngdon; from

which it appears that this building was painted externally,
and gilded too.   White lead, verdigris, vermilion, and blue,
as well as leaves of gold, are enumerated for the use of
William Burdon, the painter, who for a hundred and thirty-
three days and a half was engaged on the work.*   The
tower must have looked gay, and even gorgeous, as it shone
in the sun, so brilliantly tinted ; and altogether—with
tapestry hangings, and standards, and armorial bearings,
and equestrian equipments, and royal array, and knights'
mantles, and suits of armour, and heralds' tabards, and the
costumes of squires, and the robes of ladies, and the picturesque dresses of the commonalty—Windsor Castle, on a
tilt-day or a tournament, must have been a brilliant scene
in an age of feudal festivity.

Of the external appearance of Edward's castle no remains
have been spared ; but the square outlines of the towers
in general seem to have been relieved by lofty and picturesque turrets, most of which disappeared under the moder-
nising ravages of the reign of Charles II.†

Two interesting relics of the interior of Edward's castle
may be still seen—in the groined vaulting which forms the
basement to the Devil's Tower, and that which runs for a
considerable distance along the north side of the quadrangle,
under the guard-chamber of St. George's Hall.   The hall

* "Annals of Windsor," vol. i. 179.

† A chair of great antiquity, belonging perhaps to the time of
the founder, remained till within a few years in St. George's Hall ;
when, through some strange neglect, it was suffered to be removed,
and is now, I am informed, in the possession of the Marquis of
Salisbury.   Chairs were at that period often richly painted and
gilded ; in illustration of which we find in the wardrobe book of
Edward I., an entry of £1 19s. 7d. to Walter the painter, for a step
to the foot of the new chair, in which the stone of Scotland was
placed, near the altar, before the shrine of St. Edward at Westminster ; and to the carpenters and painters, for painting the said
step, and for gold and colours to paint it with : also, a case for its
covering.

was restored by George IV., somewhat in its primitive style. The architect, Sir Jeffrey Wyatville, adopted the original form of the windows; but the roof at first was of open timbers, the main rib being a four-centred arch, springing from an embattled cornice, and the space between the arch and the rafters being richly ornamented with open foliated panelling. The wall at the upper end, above the springing of the arch, was also richly panelled, in a style which might have seemed at first to be of a later date; but the English perpendicular architecture was gaining ground before these buildings were completed.

While the castle was being rebuilt under Sir Jeffrey Wyatville a curious subterranean passage was discovered under the east terrace, close to what is now the Victoria Tower. It is walled and arched with stone work, and was originally, it appeared, a sally-port in the fortifications constructed in the time of Edward III. As an illustration of the curious changes produced by modern habits, it may be remarked, that this gloomy excavation, intended for defence or escape in warlike times, has been turned into a furnace chamber connected with the heating apparatus that now comfortably warms the long corridors and winding passages. Much more recently, while several new rooms were being made to the east of the York Tower, the clerk of the works, Mr. Turnbull, lighted on a stone which he found covered a short shaft, leading to an under-ground passage. This, too, the author has been permitted to examine. It is from six to eight feet high, by five broad, walled and arched, partly round and partly pointed. Several fragments of Norman architecture are inserted in the masonry. After running twenty feet, the stone work terminates, and the rest of the passage is cut out of the chalk. It ends in what was the castle ditch on the south side, and on the chalk there are still a few rude inscriptions of names. Here again, no doubt, we have a sally-port of the time of Edward III., built up with fragments of Henry's, or it may be of William the Conqueror's castle. Another hidden relic of the ancient building exists in a modern underground passage, near the equerry's entrance. It is a piece of wall which does not run flush with the building above it. There can be no doubt it belongs to Edward III.'s additions, the upper part having most likely been altered in the reign of Charles II.

Edward III. took down the old chapel, and erected another more spacious. Writs were issued, as in the case of the castle, empowering the master of the works to impress artificers, and convey them to Windsor, and to arrest and imprison them summarily in case of refusal. He also erected houses adjoining for the accommodation of the custos, or dean and canons. Geoffrey Chaucer, the great poet, was appointed clerk of the works to the chapel, in the year 1390, and empowered to imitate his predecessors in pressing workmen. He was allowed a payment of two shillings a day for his own services. At that time the chapel, which had been erected but forty years, was described to be in a ruinous condition, and its unsafe state was the cause of its being rebuilt by Edward IV.,—a fact which has led some architects to conjecture that there must have been some very great settlement in the foundation of the structure.

CHAPTER III.

ORDER OF THE GARTER.

HE reader's attention must now be directed to the institution of the Order of the Garter, an event intimately connected with the history of Windsor in the fourteenth century. Orders of knighthood are of ancient date, and the indefatigable Ashmole has given a laborious disquisition on the various kinds, both religious and military. He describes the Knights of the Holy Sepulchre, of St. John the Baptist, of the Order of St. Lazarus, and others to the number of forty-six, of the religious class, and also specifies their various insignia ; and then he adds a catalogue of the military class, beginning with the far-famed Knights of the Round Table, for which the worthy antiquary entertained the highest veneration, and enters upon minute particulars relative to forty-five other orders. No wonder he thus expatiates on the theme, for he observes that, " in the dignity, honour, and renown of knighthood is included somewhat of magnificence, more excellent than nobility itself, which, mounting the royal throne, becomes the assertor of civil nobility, and sits as judge at the tribunal therefore."

The institute of the Garter sprang from the spirit of chivalry, which appeared in its greatest splendour in the fourteenth century. Religion, whose genius was sadly mistaken, was made to impart her sanction to a life of violence and bloodshed, and the sword and the cross were strangely coupled ; while gallantry animated the bosom of the holy soldier, and " God and the ladies" was his favourite watchword.

In tracing the particular origin of the symbol of the order, Ashmole repudiates, as unworthy of so glorious a society of knights, the common tale of the Countess of Salisbury dropping her garter, or the equally silly one of the queen's meeting with the same misfortune. He also notices the story of Richard I. binding a leather thong round the legs of some of the knights at the siege of Cyprus and Acon, as an heroic badge, and then adds, with characteristic solemnity, " the true motive was neither the ladies' garters or King Richard's leather thong that it owes its original to ; but King Edward being a person of consummate virtue, gave himself to military affairs, and being engaged in war for recovering his right to France, made use of the best martialists of the age, and thereupon first designed (induced by its ancient fame) the restoration of King Arthur's Round Table, to invite hither the gallant spirits from abroad, and to endear them to himself, and adjudging no place more requisite than Windsor, upon new year's day, 1344, he issued letters of protection for the safe going and return of foreign knights, to try their valour at the solemn jousts to be held there on Monday after the feast of St. Hilary." Then he briefly describes the solemnity, and guesses that either the queen or the countess might have dropped her garter while dancing at the ball, thus giving rise to the story of the origin of the order.* The

* Respecting the origin of the symbol of the Garter, Mr. Beltz remarks : " Amidst such various speculations, and in the absence of positive evidence upon the point, we shall adopt an opinion which has been formed by other writers—that the garter may have been

celebrated round table at Windsor was made about 1356 ;
in that year £26 13s. 4d. was paid to the prior of Merton
for fifty-two oaks cut from his wood near Reading, for
making the round table at Windsor. But in 1344, " The
king," says Stow, in his " Chronicles," " caused to be called
together a great many artificers to the castle of Windsor,
and began to build a *house*, which was called the Round
Table, the floor whereof, from the centre or middle point
into the compass, was an hundred foot, and the whole
diameter two hundred foot, and the circumference thereof
six hundred foot three quarters."

When Edward had arranged the plan of the order, he
placed it, according to the custom of the age, under the
protection of the Holy Trinity, and of certain saints. The
Blessed Virgin, St. George of Cappadocia,* and St. Edward
the Confessor, were the patrons whose aid and benediction
were invoked by the monarch.

The laws and ordinances of the order are elaborate
affairs, and amusingly illustrate the punctilious character of
that chivalrous age. They fill two ponderous folios, edited
by Anstis. There, and in Ashmole, the reader will find the

intended as an emblem of the tie or union of warlike qualities, to be
employed in the assertion of the founder's claim to the French crown ;
and the motto as a retort of shame and defiance upon him who should
think ill of the enterprise, or of those whom the king had chosen to
be the instruments of its accomplishment. The taste of that age for
allegorical conceits, impresses, and devices, may reasonably warrant
such a conclusion."—" Order of the Garter," Introd. p. xlvii.

* " This blessed holy martyr saynt George, is patrone of this
roiaume of Englond, and the crye of men of warre, in the worshyp
of whome is founded the noble Ordre of the Garter, and also a noble
college in the Castle of Wyndsore, by kynges of England, in which
college is the herte of saynt George, whyche Sygismunde the
emperor of Almayne brought and gave for a grete and precious
relique to K. Harry the fythe ; and also the said Sygismunde was a
broder of the sayd Garter, and also here is a pyece of hys head.
Whyche college is nobly endowed to thonour and worship of almighty
God, and his blessed martyr saynt George."

most minute account of the habits and ensigns of the knights. "In describing the mantle," says Ashmole, "we shall first set down its various appellations it is mentioned by in the records of the order; secondly, the materials whereof it consists; thirdly, the colour; fourthly, the quantity; and last of all, the ornamental trimmings, that nothing may be omitted to satisfy any curious inquirer:" a pledge which the author fully redeems, for several closely-printed pages follow, treating upon these momentous topics.

In reference to the costume of the order, it may be stated that it consisted of a mantle of woollen cloth, the staple manufacture of this country, of a blue ground, lined with scarlet cloth, the garters of blue cloth, or silk, embroidered with gold, having on them the motto of the order in letters of gold, and the buckles, bars, and pendants of silver-gilt; of a surcoat, also of woollen cloth, narrower and shorter than the mantle, and fastened to the body by a girdle, the colour to be changed every year; and of a hood, made of the same materials as the surcoat.

The mystic meaning of the several badges is a favourite theme with Ashmole and other antiquaries. The garter itself betokened the golden bond of unity and internal society; its being bound on the leg was a caveat against the knight's running away in battle; and its well-known motto taught the members not to admit anything into the actions of their lives, or among their thoughts, unbeseeming to themselves. The image of St. George, hanging at the breast, is to put the knights in mind of that illustrious saint, and to excite them to imitate him as the soldiers of Christ. The purple robe is the mark of majesty. The collar of the order, in all cases of equal weight and of a like number of small links and knots, is a witness of the bond of faith, peace, and unity, strictly to be observed among them; and, to make the bond and tie of love and friendship more close and binding, the members of the order are to be called fellows, associates, colleagues, brethren, and knights-companions, and their habits and ornaments to be all alike as to fashion and material—"to no other end but to represent how they ought to be united in all chances of fortune, both in peace and war."

In connexion with the Order of the Garter and the Chapel of St. George, Edward appointed the foundation of the Military Knights, originally called *Milites Pauperes*, or "Poor Knights." The number at first was twenty-four, but shortly after, upon the institution of the Order of the Garter, which consists of twenty-six, there were added two more to the former number. To each alms-knight was appointed a red mantle, with a scutcheon of St. George, but without any garter around it. Their exhibition at first was twelve-pence a day, and forty shillings per annum besides. They had to attend divine service, and pray for the prosperity of the sovereign and knights-companions; but for every day's absence from chapel, they forfeited the allowance of twelve-pence; and whatsoever was raised in that way was set apart for the use of the rest of the alms-knights.

The exact date of the institution of the order is uncertain. As early as 1347, garters were worn at a tournament in Windsor. About the same time, the first mention of the well-known motto occurs. In 1348, on the feast of St. John the Baptist, there was a joust in honour of the queen's purification after the birth of her fourth son, William. A robe is mentioned as given to David of Scotland, then a prisoner in England. Vanquished at the battle of Neville's Cross, by the arms of the heroic Philippa, who, in her husband's absence, led his army against the Scots, the monarch was taken captive, and conducted in triumph to London. Eleven long years he spent in imprisonment, first at Nottingham, then at Windsor, his affectionate

Queen Joan, Edward's sister, following him in his fortunes, and alleviating his sorrows with exemplary devotion. In 1348, also, Edward, Prince of Wales, presented twenty-four garters to the knights. In 1350, Stow describes a feast of the order. " The knights, together with the king, were clothed in gowns of russet, powdered with garters blue, wearing the like garters also on the right leg, and mantles of blue, with scutcheons of St. George. In this sort of apparell they, being bareheaded, heard mass, which was celebrated by Simon Islip, Archbishop of Canterbury, and the Bishops of Winchester and Exeter."

The chronicler, after touching on the scene in the chapel, leads us to the banqueting hall, and tells us that the knights went to the feast, "setting themselves orderly at the table, for the honour of the feast, which they named to be of St. George the Martyr, and the choosing of the Knights of the Garter." In 1358, on the feast of St. George, a grand tournament was held at Windsor, indicative of the growing splendour of the institution of the Garter. John, King of France, taken captive at the battle of Poictiers by Edward the Black Prince, was at that time a prisoner at Windsor.*

* The following extracts from the royal accounts, inserted by Mr. Beltz in his work on the Order of the Garter (p. 5), show some of the expenses incurred on this memorable occasion:—

" A payment to Queen Philippa of £500, as a gift from the King for the preparation of her apparel against the feast of St. George, to be celebrated at Windsor.

" To divers messengers and runners sent into various parts of England with letters under the privy seal and signet directed to several lords and ladies, inviting them to the feast of St. George at Windsor, 47s. 11d.

" To Walter Norman and his twenty-three fellows, for the carrying of oats to Windsor, about the time of St. George's Feast, 13s. 4d.

" To William Volaunt, king of the heralds, in money issued to him of the king's gift for his good services at the said feast, 66s. 8d.

" To Hankin Fitz-Lebbin and his twenty-three fellows, the king's minstrels, for their services at the said feast, £16."

The feast for which the above services were rendered is mentioned

Beneath a golden canopy, splendidly arrayed, sat Queen Philippa, on whose dress £500, according to the wardrobe account, had been expended. Squires, pages, and yeomen, in rich liveries, were standing or moving in attendance about this royal spot ; and knights and nobles were amongst the spectators of the spirit-stirring scene. Heralds and pursuivants ran to and fro, their gorgeous coats sparkling in the sun. Cased in steel, reining in his steed, with a white swan conspicuous on his shield, rode the founder of the festival, King Edward ; and near him, clothed in sable armour, was Edward the Black Prince, the mirror of chivalry. On a horse richly caparisoned, sat John of France, and in his rear were several nobles of his court, who, though prisoners in England, were allowed by the courtesies of chivalry to enter the lists.*

Then came the banquet. St. George's Hall on one side was painted with quaint scenes and objects taken from chivalry and scripture, and on the other side enlivened by the richly-stained windows, while the oaken roof and rafters with sober grandeur spanned the apartment. At the upper end was the dais, with the chair placed for the monarch ; on either side ran a long table spread for the guests—rude ornaments, gaily painted, adorned the board, with here and there costly pieces of gold and silver plate,

by foreign, as well as domestic historians. A MS. in the Harleian Library records the royal feast, at which was present King John of France, " the which king said in scorn, that he never saw so royal a feast, and so costly, made with tallies of tree, without paying of gold and silver."

* The Earl of Salisbury met with a fatal accident at this tournament. His countess was a favourite with the king, and was the noble lady whose garter, according to common report, was picked up by the monarch, and suggested the badge for the knights' order. This lady must have possessed distinguished charms ; for it is said that John, King of France, on this occasion, was captivated by her beauty. She was, however, proof against both these royal suitors, and after the death of the earl lived in perfect seclusion.

saltcellars, cups, bowls with covers, chargers, spice-plates, large covered vessels, splendidly chased, and ornamented with eagles, herons, and leopards.

The next morning the tournament was renewed, and the pleasures of the tilt were succeeded by those of the chase. The knights, ladies, and dignified ecclesiastics, led on by Edward, followed the hounds in pursuit of the deer, or amused themselves with the sport of falconry.

Ten years afterwards the chroniclers show us, stretched on a bed in Windsor Castle, and watched by the monarch, the noble lady who graced the tournament. Her dying words are thus recorded :—" We have enjoyed our union in happiness, peace, and prosperity : I entreat therefore of you, that on our separation, you will grant me three requests. My lord, I beg you will acquit me of whatever engagements I may have entered into formerly with merchants for their wares, as well on this as on the other side of the sea. I beseech you also to fulfil whatever gifts or legacies I may have made or left to churches, here or on the continent, wherein I have paid my devotions, as well as what I may have left to those of both sexes who have been in my service. Thirdly, I entreat that when it shall please God to call you hence, you will not choose any other sepulchre than mine, and that you will lie by my side in the cloisters of Westminster." "Lady," replied the king, " I grant them."*

In connexion with the Order of the Garter, it appears that during the reign of Richard II. it was not uncommon for ladies to attend the feasts, and to wear the badge of the order.

In reference to the custom of that period, Mr. Beltz, in his " History of the Order of the Garter," introduces the following remarks :—

* Froissart, vol. ii. p. 14.

"To the chivalrous gallantry which characterizes the heroes of the middle ages, and which tempered in no unimportant degree the natural ferocity of their spirit and manners, can alone be ascribed the happy conception of imparting to the fair sex a portion of the honours of this illustrious order. The origin of the custom of decorating ladies with the robes and insignia may easily be traced to the natural wish of the victorious knight, in joust or tourney, to share the distinction which he had acquired with the beloved witness of his triumph.

"Whether an addition, at once so graceful and interesting, to the splendour of the ceremonies at Windsor, had been made during the time of the royal founder, cannot be learnt from the statutes or other public records. We have noticed the superb array of Queen Philippa and her numerous train of ladies at the first feast, and the large sum issued for her ladies on another occasion ; we find, also, that in 1362 she made an oblation during the celebration of high mass in St. George's chapel on the day of the feast ; and that in 1358 messengers were despatched to invite the attendance of ladies at the festival of the order ; but, admitting the inference from these facts, that they were usually present at such solemnities, it might be considered that they assisted as spectators only.

"In a wardrobe account, however, under a warrant of the 8th of April, 1376, towards the close of the preceding reign, there is a charge for the issue of a long robe, together with a hood of cloth, of the colour of sanguine in grain, made in the fashion of those of the Knights of the Garter, for the king's daughter, the Countess of Bedford, to be worn by her at the then approaching feast. But if this be the only memorial yet discovered of the custom in question, during the life of the founder, it is certain that the taste for pomp and magnificence which distinguished the court

of his successor, produced a more general participation in
the knightly decorations; and that ladies of high rank, as
well as others, who probably occupied stations of honour
near the person of the Queen, received robes and hoods,
ornamented with garters, and corresponding in other
respects, as to the colour, quality, and quantity of cloth
and furs, with those of the knights; and that they wore
around the left arm, a little above the elbow, a garter of
the same fashion and materials, with a motto of the order
embroidered thereon. It appears also that the ladies so
favoured were sometimes designated, "*Dominæ de Sectâ et
Liberaturâ Garterii*," and at others, "*Dames de la Fraternité
de Saint George;*" that the habits were delivered to them
annually, to be worn at the feast, by warrants from the
Crown, in the same course of delivery as to the knights;
and that the robes and hoods were differenced in the number of garters thereon, according to the superiority of the
titles and degrees of the ladies upon whom this singular
privilege had been conferred.

"By what system the admission to the distinction was
regulated,—whether the nominations were solely at the
pleasure of the sovereign, or by election in chapter,—
whether any ceremonies were observed at the investiture,
or ordinances prescribed for the governance of those invested,
are points upon which no light has hitherto been thrown.
It will be seen by the list of ladies so distinguished, that
the favour was not limited to the consorts and relicts of the
knights of the order, but extended to others of their families :
and where such connexion does not appear, there is room for
the conjecture that the distinction was an especial homage
to eminent personal or mental endowments, spontaneously
paid by the sovereign himself, or at the suggestion of a
knight, who, by some martial act, had acquired a claim to
the nomination."*

* Beltz, p. 244.

CHAPTER IV.

FROM RICHARD II. TO EDWARD IV.

WINDSOR CASTLE was the occasional residence of Richard II. It was here that he parted from his Queen Isabella, then but a girl. He had assisted at mass, chanted a collect (for he was musical) and made a rich offering at the altar; then leading his little consort to the door of the chapel, he took her in his arms and repeatedly kissed her, exclaiming, "Adieu, madam, adieu, till we meet again." But the unhappy pair saw each other no more. It was here, too, that the lively historian, Froissart, took leave for the last time of the ill-fated prince. After describing his munificence and hospitality, he adds, "And I, John Froissart, canon and treasurer of Chirnay, saw it and considered it ; and I lived in it a quarter of a year ; and good cheer did he give me, forasmuch as I, in my youth, had been clerk and familiar to the noble King Edward, his grandfather ; and when I departed from him (it was at Windsor), on my leavetaking, he gave me a silver goblet, and gilt, and having within one hundred nobles . . . . therefore am I much bound to pray God for him."

Froissart gives us a peep at a scene in Windsor, illustrative of the politics of the day. The Londoners, in 1386, were grumbling about the fire-tax. The Duke of Gloucester advised them to address the king at Windsor. So off they went in a body sixty strong, on horseback, accompanied by deputations from other places. They lodged in the town, and must have crowded the hostelries and excited no small stir amongst the quiet Windsor folk, as they went upon St. George's day to have an audience with his majesty in the town hall, "without the new building where the palace stood in former times." Simon de Sudbury was the opening orator on the occasion, followed by seven others, who said some startling things, dwelling upon grievances at large, and declaring, "It is not justice, sir king, to cut off heads, wrists, or feet, or any way to punish ; but justice consists in the maintaining the subject in his right, and in taking care he live in peace, without having any cause of complaint." The conference ended in what in modern parlance we should call the appointment of a committee of inquiry—really in putting off the evil day.

Other circumstances in Richard's history also occurred at Windsor. It was here, on a scaffold erected within the castle, that Richard heard the appeal of high treason brought by Henry of Lancaster, Duke of Hereford, against Thomas Mowbray, Duke of Norfolk. "In riding from Windsor to Brentford, in December, 1397, they conversed on the king's bad government. Mowbray observed, 'We are about to be ruined.' Henry asked, 'For what?' 'For the affair at Radcot Bridge,' answered Mowbray. 'How can that be, after a pardon?' replied Henry. 'As easily,' says Mowbray, 'as he has recalled the pardons granted to others.' The Duke of Norfolk at last said, that Richard had broken all his oaths." Lancaster complained to the king against Mowbray, who had charged him with having uttered these scandalous words. The parties were at length summoned to meet at Windsor. They did so ; King Richard was seated on a platform in the castle square, with his lords and prelates around him. The constable and marshal, by the king's desire, sought to make peace between the quarrellers, but in vain. So it was agreed that the matter should be determined by single combat. Coventry was the place appointed for the contest, and there occurred the scene, so important in its results to the sovereign and the nation, which Shakspere has so well portrayed in his tragedy of "Richard the Second."

Henry IV. ascended the throne in October, 1399. About Christmas time that year, a plot was formed to rush on him and his sons at a tournament at Kingston. The king, at the time, was at Windsor, little apprehending the contemplated violence, when the Earl of Rutland, one of the conspirators, revealed the plot. The disaffected lords set out with five hundred horse, intending to surprise the king at Windsor. But Henry had escaped before their arrival, and repaired to London, where he issued writs for their apprehension, and raised forces to quell their rebellion. Disappointed in their plans, they were suddenly surprised by the appearance of a royal army, and were glad to flee to their respective castles. Not long afterwards, the same monarch had another escape of a different kind, an instrument called a caltrappe having been concealed in his bed, it is reported by one of Queen Isabella's household.

Windsor Castle in the fifteenth century has some well-known historical associations. The first circumstance of interest here during the century, was the long imprisonment of James I. of Scotland. On his way to France, in 1405, to receive his education, being then eleven years of age, he was taken prisoner by an English corsair, contrary to the law of nations, for England and Scotland were then at peace : but knowing the importance of keeping such an hostage, the English king, Henry IV., resolved to detain him, exclaiming, " In fact, the Scots ought to have given me the education of this boy, for I am an excellent French scholar."* After two years' imprisonment in the Tower of London, he was removed to Windsor, where for sixteen years he was unjustly detained by the English monarch. It may seem strange that no vigorous efforts were made by the Scotch to recover their young prince from his captivity, but it should be remembered that the Duke of Albany, after the death of James's father, which took place in 1406, was Regent of Scotland, and it was to his interest to allow the royal boy to remain a prisoner, that he might himself exercise the dominion of a sovereign. Henry and the Regent seem to have understood each other, and poor young James was the victim of their crafty policy. During the period of James's imprisonment, however, his education appears to have been carefully conducted, as his literary taste and attainments amply proved. Nor were there wanting other influences to cheer the captive's sorrows. The tale of his love for Joanna Beaufort, the niece of Richard II., a tale to which the author of the " Sketch Book " has imparted additional charms, is familiar to every reader. The lovely countenance and form of Joanna made a tender impression on the heart of the royal youth, as he looked from his prison window, and saw her walking in the gardens below ; her image was engraven on his memory, her charms were the subject of his song ; and true to his early attachment, he afterwards sought and won her hand, when he had the prospect of returning to his country, and ascending his throne. The poem by James, entitled the " King's Quhair," in which his love for the Lady Jane forms the leading theme, contains a minute description of the garden at the

* Sir Walter Scott's " History of Scotland," vol. i. p. 240.

foot of the round tower ; and enable us, as we read it, to
transport ourselves to its green arbours and shaded alleys,
as they were in the days of the royal poet. " He had
risen, he says, at daybreak, according to custom, to escape
from the dreary meditations of a sleepless pillow."

> " Bewailing in his chamber thus alone,"

despairing of all joy and remedy—

> " Fortired of thought, and woe-begone,"

he had wandered to the window, to indulge the captive's
miserable solace of gazing wistfully upon the world from
which he is excluded. The window looked forth upon a
small garden, which lay at the foot of the tower. It was
a quiet, sheltered spot, adorned with arbours and green
alleys, and protected from the passing gaze by trees and
hawthorn hedges :—

> "Now was there made, fast by the tower's wall,
>   A garden faire, and in the corners set
> An arbour green, with wandis long and small
>   Railed about ; and so with leaves beset
> Was all the place, and hawthorn hedges knet,
>   That lyf* was none, walkyng there forbye,
>   That might within scarce any wight espye.
>
> " So thick the branches, and the leves grene,
>   Beshaded all the alleys that there were,
> And midst of every arbour might be seen
>   The sharpe, greene, sweet juniper,
> Growing so fair, with branches here and there
>   That, as it seemed to a lyf without,
>   The boughs did spread the arbour all about.
>
> " And on the small grene twistis† set
>   The lytel swete nightingales, and sung
> So loud and clear the hymnis consecrate
>   Of lovis use, now soft, now loud among,
> That all the garden and the wallis rung
>   Right of their song."

* Lyf, " person."   † Twistis, " small boughs or twigs."

The royal captive was liberated in the year 1424 by Henry VI., on the Scots agreeing to pay £40,000 ; not for the king's ransom,—that would have been an acknowledgment on the part of the English sovereign, that he had taken and held him as a prisoner, and would have reflected on his justice ;—but for the expenses of his board and education. A strange school, truly, was that old round tower ; and a rather heavy bill was this for the boy's schooling. So foolishly, sometimes, have kings and statesmen varnished over their wicked deeds with fine words and courteous phrases, as if posterity would never see through them. James proved the father of his country after his restoration ; and perhaps the mental and moral education he had received in his captivity, unjust as it was, tended to improve his character, and to fit him for his subsequent usefulness. But this monarch, unfortunate in his boyhood, met with a corresponding destiny at the close of life. The story of his death is a mournful episode in Scotch history. One night when he was in the Dominican monastery at Perth, with his faithful queen, a band of armed men rushed into the place, and made their way to the royal apartment. Catherine Douglas, a lady in waiting on the queen, thrust her arm through the staple of the door to supply the place of a bolt, but the frail fastening soon snapped in twain, and the conspirators entered. In the mean time the king had been let down by the queen and her ladies into a vault beneath, and might have escaped, but leaving the vault too soon, the assassins discovered their victim, rushed upon him, overpowered his valiant resistance, and plunged their weapons in his body. The leading person implicated in his murder was the furious Grahame, a Scottish chief of whom tradition reports that when asked, " How dare you slay your king ?" he replied, " I dare do anything ; I dare leap from the highest heaven to the pit of hell :" an exclamation highly characteristic of the spirit of many a chieftain of those days.

The early affection and the mournful fate of this ornament of the Scottish throne, have shed a soft but melancholy hue around the tower of Windsor ; and often as the beautiful composition of Washington Irving's is read, that rainbow hue of love and sadness will shine on the reader's soul.   I remember, long before I knew Windsor, revelling in the scenes which that little tale awakened, and longing for an opportunity, " on some soft sunny morning, when the weather is of that voluptuous kind which calls forth all the latent romance of a man's temperament," to visit the round tower ; pace the deserted chamber ; lean on the window where James looked out ; gaze on the suit of armour hanging up in the hall, and transport myself to days gone by.   What, then, was my mortification, when, as a stranger, I first went to see the round tower, and asked, with anxiety, to be shown the rooms where James was imprisoned, to find the workmen dismantling the walls, pulling up the floors, and sweeping away, with most unromantic diligence, all the romantic charms with which poetry had clothed the spot !   Such alterations do sad violence to the feeling which Irving thus expresses, when visiting the tower as it was :—"There is a charm about the spot that has been printed by the footsteps of departed beauty, and consecrated by the inspirations of the poet, which is heightened rather than impaired by the lapse of ages.   It is, indeed, the gift of poetry to hallow every place in which it moves ; to breathe round nature an odour more exquisite than the perfume of the rose ; and to shed over it a tint more magical than the blush of the morning."

A more elegant and imposing form given to a building— more convenience and comfort spread over an apartment— afford no compensation for the loss of that spell of antique beauty which once hallowed such places, and which, when broken, is broken for ever. The resources of wealth and art can easily rear an edifice fit for a monarch's abode, but no power can reproduce a single venerable relic which has perished under the hand of modern utilitarianism. We do not profess to belong to that class of double-dyed anti-quarians who regard as sacred all which is ancient,—who look with equal veneration on old buildings and old laws, old books and old prejudices, the rust which covers a coin, and the rust which corrodes the constitution ; we would let no veneration for the past stand in the way of social improvement, we by no means sympathize with those who crowd round the nodding ruins of cumbrous, useless, and perhaps pernicious institutions, and sigh over the ruthless devastations of reform : but we do plead for the preserva-tion of those antiquities which in no way cross the path of the progress of society, which are the rich remembrances of days gone by, and which assist in giving the past predomi-nance over the present,—thus raising us " in the scale of thinking beings."

In the reign of Henry V., the hero of Agincourt, and during the imprisonment of James of Scotland, mention is made in the Black Book of the Order of the Garter, of a splendid solemnization of the feast of St. George at Windsor. It was in the fourth year of the monarch's reign ; and to add to the splendour of the occasion, Sigismund the Em-peror of Germany was present, and was created a knight of the order. " The finery of the guests," says the above-mentioned record, " the order of the servants, the variety of the courses, the invention of the dishes, with the other things delightful to the sight and taste, whoever should en-deavour to describe would never do it justice." It is re-corded that two years later, when the English monarch was engaged in his wars with France, he took care to celebrate the feast of St. George at Caen in Normandy, where he was at the time ; and that on the same day a feast was held at Windsor with due solemnity, John, Duke of Bedford, presiding on the occasion as the king's representative ; and thus the patron saint of England this year was doubly honoured.   This Duke of Bedford filled the vice-regal office several times ; and there is preserved, in the annals of the Order of the Garter, a commission from Henry VI., which is dated " Leicester, in the fourth year of our reign," and in which he authorizes the duke to be present as his deputy at the next feast at Wyndesor."

The last-mentioned monarch was born at Windsor, and it seems, in the judgment of his father, under an evil destiny.   The great warrior appears to have had some skill in astrology, the favourite science of the middle ages ; and, in the anticipation of the birth of an heir, strictly forbade the Queen's residence at that time in Windsor ; over which he thought the stars would then shed no benign influence. Catherine, for some reason, disobeyed the order, and gave birth to her son within the walls of the forbidden fortress ; a circumstance which greatly grieved the king, who, on hearing it, is said to have repeated the following oracular but unpoetical stanza :—

> " I, Henry, born at Monmouth,
>   Shall small time reign, and much get ;
> But Henry of Windsor shall reign long, and lose all :
>   But as God will, so be it."

Both his predictions were verified.   He died within a few months after the birth of his boy ; and his queen, who seems to have had a great partiality for Windsor, retired to the castle after her husband's death, to cheer her widowhood by the nursing of her babe.

It comes not within the scope of this work to pursue the history of Catherine, or even to relate the bloody wars of the houses of York and Lancaster, with which the fate of her son was identified. That contest, rich in romantic incident, but deficient in political and moral interest, as it was no conflict of principles, but merely a war of parties, issued in the dethronement of Henry and the accession of the victorious Edward IV. Both these monarchs are associated with Windsor in their life and death. Henry probably often visited his birthplace, and pursued here those punctilious and superstitious observances which gained for him the reputation of extreme sanctity, in an age when religion was supposed to consist in habits of monkish devotion. Weak, but amiable, poor Henry stands on the roll of history as an object of pity. Altogether disqualified for swaying a sceptre, it had been well for him if, instead of being born to rule a kingdom, he had been the child of some humble peasant, and had spent his life in the lowly pursuits of the field, or the religious exercises of the cloister. Nor were his faculties, feeble in themselves, constantly retained; for he was subject to insanity, of which an instance is related as having occurred at Windsor. Some commissioners came to visit him, to ascertain his capacity for government; and, when admitted to his chamber, could obtain no reply to the questions they proposed. "The Bishop of Chester read to him part of his instructions. To this statement they could get no answer nor sign for none of their prayers or desires. After dinner they moved him again for an answer, but they could get none. From that place they willed the king to go into another chamber, and he was led between two men to the chamber where he lieth, and there they stirred him the third time; but they could have no answer, word nor sign, and therefore, with sorrowful hearts, came their way."*

* Mackintosh's "History of England," vol. ii. p. 18.

As it regards energy of mind, his heroic queen, Margaret, was far more fitted to rule than he; though as it respects the moral qualities for government, she did not possess such as were most likely to make a nation happy.

After a life of misfortune, the poor King met a death of violence in the Tower of London. Attempts have been made to discredit the story of his murder; but there is too much evidence of the fact to admit of its being doubted. On the day of Ascension, May the 22nd, he was borne barefaced on his bier to St. Paul's, when it is reported by ancient chroniclers that the blood streamed from his wounds, in testimony of his violent death—a circumstance which, they relate, occurred again at Blackfriars—whence he was afterwards removed at night, in a lighted barge, to Chertsey Abbey, where his body for a while reposed. As one reads the account in the old historians, that barge, with its royal corpse, gliding along "the silent highway" of the Thames, and shedding on the waters a melancholy light, passes before the imagination an emblem of fallen greatness, and rich in moral lessons of the vanity of this world.

Margaret, broken down by sorrow, was removed from the Tower, where she had been long imprisoned, and taken to Windsor, where she remained till she was removed to Wallingford under the charge of Alice Chaucer, Dowager Duchess of Suffolk, and granddaughter of the celebrated poet.

The body of Henry did not find its final resting-place at Chertsey, but was afterwards brought, in the time of Richard III., to St. George's Chapel. "The holy body," we are gravely told, "on this occasion was found very odoriferous, which was not owing to any spices employed about it when it was interred by his enemies and tormentors. It was in a great measure uncorrupted; the hair of the head and body perfect; the face as usual, but somewhat sunk, with a more meagre aspect than common. A number of miracles immediately proclaimed the king's sanctity, as sufficiently appears from the written account of them there."* " He was interred," says Sandford, " under a fair monument, of which there are now no remains. The arch on the south side of the chapel, between the choir and the altar, under which he was deposited, was gilt and painted with several devices of this king; on the keystone of which are carved his royal arms, ensigned with a crown, and supported by two antelopes collared and chained together; in the south window of which arch was pencilled the history of his life in coloured glass, which, with many more windows in the same chapel, was defaced in the late rebellion." †

Stow relates the removal of Henry's body to Windsor, and adds, " He was worshipped by the name of the Holy King Henry, whose red hat of velvet was thought to heal the headache of such as should put it on their heads. There he rested for a time; but now, his tomb being taken thence, it is not commonly known what is become of the body." Stow's supposition of the removal of the body probably arose from the fact that a bull was obtained from Julius II. to allow the removal of the monarch's remains, but the purpose of the bull was never carried into effect. An application was also made to Rome for the canonisation of Henry, a project which, like the other, remained unaccomplished. Though no altar was ever erected to this unfortunate prince, we find that prayers to him were inserted in service-books in the early part of the sixteenth century.

Gough gives the design of a splendid monument for Henry VI.; but whether it was intended for St. George's

* Gough's " Monumental Antiquities," p. 231.
† " Genealogical History of the Kings of England," p. 298.

Chapel or Westminster Abbey does not appear. In connexion with the history of Henry's burial, it may be here observed, that in the year 1789, when the workmen were preparing for the new pavement of the aisle in which he is interred, they found the entrance of the vault, but were directed not to open it.

Edward IV., whose white rose was drenched in blood while the red rose of his rival was pale in death, appears to have made Windsor Castle the scene of magnificent pageants. Stow gives an account of the celebration of St. George's Feast at Windsor, in the sixteenth year of Edward's reign.

And as we read the graphic pages of the old annalist, we see the knights entering the castle yard on Saturday afternoon with bands of retainers. There in the chapel sits the king in his stall, with a long line of knights arranged on either side ; while the priests at the altar and the esquires and heralds standing on the pavement of the choir present a display of glittering pomp, rendered somewhat sombre by the gathering shadows of the evening. We listen to the service chanted by the priests and minstrels. as the stern old warriors are melted into tender mood, till the last echoes of the evensong melt into silence. The plumed knights are seen returning to the castle, the vesper star shines softly over the grey towers, the shades of night thicken, and all is still. At Sunday morning mass, the prelate of the order, with his attendant priests, the pompous worship, the ascending incense, the uplifted host, the worshippers with bowed heads and bended knees, are all before us. The feast in St. George's Hall, and the offering in the royal chapel, with all their chivalrous associations, also pass before our imagination. But these exciting dreams of olden times, however they may interest us in the review, were marked by a state of society, of manners, and of reli-

E

gion, by no means to be desired, and which are now succeeded by times of purer, though less gorgeous brightness.

Mention is made in Stow's description of the perform-
ance of vespers in the royal chapel, and it may be interesting here to notice an account which is preserved of the
choral establishment of the monarch. It appears that it
included thirteen minstrels, whereof some were trumpets,
some shawms, some pipes. Their pay was fourpence a day,
beside clothing and other rewards. They were allowed
every evening four gallons of ale, three wax candles, six
of pitch, and four billets of wood. Two servants were
appointed to wait on them. Dinner was provided in a
common hall. Besides the minstrels, there were eight
choristers, placed under the direction of the dean, or "of
the master of the song assigned to teach them."* Though
this account does not refer to the Windsor establishment,
yet that in all probability was of a similar kind. Of the
banquets of the period we have also some full descriptions.
Most persons have read of the entertainment once given in
the fifteenth century by the Archbishop of York, when 104
oxen, 6 wild bulls, 1000 sheep, 304 calves, as many swine,
2000 pigs, 500 stags, bucks, and roes, and 204 kids, were
provided; besides 22,512 fowls, large and small, rare and
common; with mountains of fish, pasties, tarts, and jellies;
and rivers of ale and wine, to say nothing of twelve por-
poises and seals. At the end of a substantial course, it
was not unfrequent in those days to introduce a dish called
"Subtilty," consisting of curious figures made of jellies and
confectionary, to represent men and animals, or allegorical
characters illustrative of some event intended to be com-
memorated by the feast, with a label on them couched in
quaint enigmatic language.

* "Pictorial History of England," vol. ii. p. 235.

In the thirteenth year of his reign, Edward IV. appointed Richard Beauchamp, Bishop of Salisbury, to the office of surveyor of the chapel, and gave him full authority to remove whatever might be necessary to make room for the erection of the new edifice.* In consequence of this, three towers, and some other buildings on the east and north sides of the chapel were pulled down, and the materials employed in repairing the castle. The new chapel was soon commenced, and the work was speedily prosecuted; for within five years it was ready to receive the bells, and contracts were entered into for carving the stalls in the choir. Most of the stone was brought by water from Tainton in Oxfordshire, and some came from Caen in Normandy, whence, as every one knows, large supplies of stone were often obtained for ecclesiastical edifices in the middle ages. The timber was procured from places in the neighbourhood of Windsor. Many entries in the accounts of Bishop Beauchamp, which have been preserved, throw light upon the expenditure incurred in the undertaking. There is an entry in the eighteenth year of King Edward's reign, of 9755 feet of stone, at 2s. a foot; of £151 12s., for the conveyance of stone from Tainton to Windsor Bridge; of £29 10s. 3½d. for the carriage of timber; of £141 8s. 1d. for materials and stores necessary for the prosecution of the works; and £556 6s. 1½d. for workmen. Several entries of charges for carved work also appear. Six tabernacles for the choir, made by Robert Ellis and John Filles, cost £40; and St. George and the Dragon, with St. Edward and other saints, were paid for at the rate of 5s. the foot in length. Other years furnish other examples of sums paid for timber, stone, and workmen.

* Mr. Britton thinks it is more likely that Edward IV. enlarged, altered, and embellished the royal chapel, than that he built it anew. —"Architectural Antiquities," vol. iii. p. 28.

The funds for the erection of this noble structure were obtained from the estates of Lords Shrewsbury, Wiltshire, and Morley, who were minors at the time, and wards of his majesty; a fact illustrative of the unjust prerogatives of the crown at that period, and by no means calculated to reflect honour upon the royal builder, or to add pleasing associations to the origin of an edifice devoted to the service of religion.

At the time of Edward IV.'s death, the eastern portion of the church was roofed, and the choir nearly finished. The roof of Lincoln Chapel, with the adjoining compartment at the east end of the south aisle, the corresponding compartment on the north side, and the passage at the back of the altar, are the only portions which could have been executed by Beauchamp. After his death, the works were carried on by Sir Reginald Bray, who seems to have united the talents of a statesman with the genius of an architect. He was an important agent in the elevation of Henry VII. to the throne, and promoted the marriage between that prince and Elizabeth, the daughter of Edward IV., an union which happily terminated the long-continued animosity between the rival houses of York and Lancaster. His patriotism and integrity are celebrated by Polydor Vergil, but his talents and virtues do not seem to have ever been fully appreciated by posterity. So devoted was he to the erection of St. George's Chapel, that he liberally contributed to it while he lived, and devoted all his property to the same object after his death. He died in 1502, and in his will he directed that his executors should, after his decease, "cause a convenient tombe to be made in the said chapell upon his grave in all goodly haste;" and that thirteen poor men and women yearly should receive a pound each at "the dore of the said chapell." The directions respecting his tomb were most ungratefully disregarded, and no monument but the building itself, which he so zealously carried forward, remains to perpetuate his fame. Dr. Christopher Urswick was for some time associated with Sir Reginald Bray in superintending the works in St. George's Chapel. He was raised to the Deanery of Windsor in 1495, after having been one of the canons for a considerable period. Like his coadjutor, he possessed talents as a statesman, and was employed by Henry VII. on several important foreign embassies. In the year 1505 he resigned his preferments, and retired to the rectory of Hackney, where he spent the remainder of his days, and died in 1521. The little chapel containing the well-known cenotaph of the Princess Charlotte, still bears his name ; and the dean's residence, erected at his expense, is an instance of his liberality.*

* The following is an account of the yearly expenses of St. George's Chapel, in the latter part of the fifteenth century, extracted from the Sloane MSS. in the British Museum, No. 4817 :—

	£	s.	d.
"To yᵉ deane	100	0	0
Item, xii. chanons	210	0	0
Item, xv. vicars	150	0	0
Item, a gospeller	8	0	0
Item, yᵉ apisteler and organ player	2	13	0
Item, xiii. queresters	52	0	0
Item, xiii. clerkes	130	0	0
Item, yᵉ sacristaries	8	0	0
Item, yᵉ bellringers	6	13	4
Item, ii. chauntry priests for King Edward	26	13	4
Item, ii. for Dutchess Exetur	16	0	0
Item, i. for Bishop of Sarum	6	13	4
Item, Lords Ferrars and Hastings	16	0	0
Item, a verger	10	0	0
Item, yᵉ clerk of yᵉ counts	10	0	0
Brede, wine, wax, oyle	20	0	0
Item, officers outward and inward	20	0	0
For ryding officers, &c. the errauds necessarie	20	0	0
Fees to councell lerned	20	0	0

"£23 1s. 8d. to yᵉ 2 chaplins, by yᵉ king's letters patent; £20 by yᵉ grant which follows of yᵉ said letters."

Before the Reformation, several shrines adorned the chapels in this interesting edifice. In one of these, now called Lincoln Chapel, at the east end of the south aisle, there once stood the shrine of John Shorne, who was rector of Northmarston in Buckinghamshire in the year 1290. He was held in high reputation for the healing virtues he had imparted to a holy well in the neighbourhood where he lived, and for other miracles he had wrought; one of which, the feat of conjuring the devil into a boot, was so remarkable as to be represented on the east window of his church. Bishop Beauchamp obtained permission to remove the shrine of this wonderful man from Northmarston, where it formerly stood, to any place he pleased; and as a mark of his special regard for St. George's Chapel, Windsor, he caused the precious treasure to be placed there.

The beautiful fabric attached to the east end of the choir of the chapel, and covering the royal mausoleum, was erected during the reign of Henry VII., and was intended by that monarch as a burial-place for himself. In Rymer's "Fœdera" there is a papal bull granting Henry the right of preparing an edifice connected with the chapel of St. George, in which he might choose himself a sepulchre.* The king, however, altered his purpose, and prepared for himself a more noble resting-place in the chapel at Westminster. The former building, at least the interior, was left in an unfinished state; and in the reign of Henry VIII. was given by him to his favourite, Wolsey.

During the reign of Edward IV. a serious collision occurred between the dean and canons of Windsor and the alms-knights connected with the chapel. As early as the

---

* "Proponat unam capellam in Ecclesiâ S. Georgii, in quâ sepulturam suam eligere intendit, de propriis bonis suis fundare et construere."—Rymer, "Fœd." vol. xii. p. 565.

time of Henry VI. disputes had commenced respecting the allowances made to the latter, who complained of being deprived of their rights ; but in the tenth year of Henry's reign, the arrears were appointed to be forthwith paid ; and in case the treasurer of the college became negligent in future, he was to forfeit his own daily allowance until he settled the account with the alms-knights.   But the differences between the parties afterwards became so serious, that an act of Parliament was passed in the twenty-second year of the reign of Edward IV., containing this clause : " That the dean and canons, and their successors, should for evermore be utterly quit and discharged from all manner of exhibition or charge of or for any of the said knights." " This was, under cover," says Ashmole, " that the king had greatly augmented the number of the ministers of the chapel, and that the revenue was insufficient to maintain them and the alms-knights : but in the dean and canons' answer to the knights' petition to repeal this act, the cause is alleged for that some of these knights used their utmost endeavours before this act to incorporate themselves, and to be exempt from the obedience and rule of the dean and canons."*

Some of the accounts preserved of the complaints made by the alms-knights about this time are very amusing.   It seems that a last of red herrings, from the town of Yarmouth, was annually sent for the use of the college, and hence the alms-knights considered that they had a right to a share of the herrings : but they complained that while the canons yearly caused the said herrings to be received at Yarmouth, and brought to Windsor at the cost of the common revenues of the college, the canons residentiary take care to divide the fishes among themselves, excluding the knights from their portion ; yet they state that the dean

* " History of the Garter," p. 97.

and six of the canons did by no means approve of this arrangement, but thought that the herrings should be deemed part of the common revenues.*

The breach between the canons and alms-knights has never been healed, and the latter still complain that they do not enjoy the rights which should accrue to them according to the will of the founder of the college.

Of the furniture of the castle and the fashions of the court during the reign of Edward IV., there are some curious illustrations to be found in an account written by Louis of Bruges, Lord of Grauthuse, who paid a visit to the king and his queen, Elizabeth Woodville. "When the Lord of Grauthuse came to Windsor, my Lord Hastings received him, and led him to the far side of the quadrat (quadrangle), to three chambers where the king was then with his queen." These apartments were very richly hung with cloth of gold arras; and when he had spoken with the king, who presented him to the queen's grace, they then ordered the Lord Chamberlain, Hastings, to conduct him to his chamber, where supper was ready for him. After

---

* The following is an extract on the subject from the MSS. in the Ashmolean Museum at Oxford :—

"The said chanons embesille withdrawe yerely a last of rede herings which the towne of Yarmouth hath geven to the sustenance of the said collage generally and in speciall wordes as hit may appere more playnley by a copie of a dede therof made by the gevers whereof a copie to these presents is annexed.[1] Howe be it that the said chanons yerely make the said herings to be received at Yarmouth and brought to Wyndesore at the cost of the comon revenues of the said collage agens the injuncions and the wille of the said deane, notwithstanding that the said herings is yerely devyded among the chanons residencers of the said collage. And yit the deane vj of the said chanons have full drelinged and ther names by ther owne handes writen set therto that the said herings shuld be part of the revenues and help to bere the comon charge of the said collage as it hath been used of old tyme and as the said dede makith mencion."

[1] Temp. Henry IV.

supper, he went to the queen's withdrawing-room, where she and some of her ladies were playing at the *marteaux*,* and the rest at *closheys*† of ivory or other games. "In the morning," the writer proceeds, "when matins were done, the king heard in his own chapel (that of St. George, at Windsor Castle), Our Lady mass, which was most melodiously sung. Then the king came into the quadrant. My lord prince, also, borne by his chamberlain, called Master Vaughan, bade the Lord Grauthuse welcome. Then the king took his guest into the little park, where they had great sport : there the king made him ride on his own horse, a right fair hobby, the which the king gave him. The king's dinner was ordained in the lodge in Windsor Park. After dinner, the king showed his guest his garden and vineyard of pleasure. The king, queen, and divers ladies and gentlemen afterwards conducted their visitor to his apartments, which are described as being hung with white silk and linen cloth, and the floor covered with carpets. The bed was of down ; the sheets of Rennes cloth ; the counterpane, cloth of gold furred with ermine ; the tester and ceiler also of the same material ; the curtains of white sarcenet ; the head, suit, and pillows of the queen's own ordering. In the second chamber was another state bed, all white ; a couch covered like a tent, and a cupboard. In the third chamber was a bath, covered with white cloth. All this indicates not only splendour, but comfort ; and, indeed, every provision seems to have been made for the most luxurious entertainment of this great lord ; for just after he had been in the bath, and was preparing for bed, there was sent to him, by order of the queen, "green ginger, divers syrups, comfits, and hyppocras." In the morning he took his cup with the king, and returned

---

* A game with balls, like marbles.
† Nine-pins made of ivory.

to Westminster, highly delighted, no doubt, with his visit
to Windsor and the hospitable reception he had expe-
rienced there.*

But from all this splendour Edward was shortly after
snatched by the hand of death ; leaving behind him the
reputation of possessing more mental vigour than the rival
he had dethroned, but none of his gentleness and purity. He
lies in St. George's Chapel, in the aisle opposite to that in
which Henry is entombed ;—the grave, that mournful peace-
maker, having long since quelled those animosities which
for years rocked the kingdom with tempests and deluged it
with blood.   " The body was placed in a chariot drawn by
six horses, and so went to Charing Cross, where the chariot
was censed ; and from thence to Syon, where it was received that night with the usual ceremonies : from thence,
on the next morning they departed in good order to Eaton,
where they were received by the procession of Windsor ;
and at the castle gate the Archbishop of York and the
Bishop of Winchester censed the corpse : and from thence
they passed to the new church, where, in the choir, was
ordained a marvellous well-wrought hearse, being that
night watched with a good company of nobles and esquires
of the body, and was there buried with all solemnity."†

In the year 1789 the coffin of Edward IV. was discovered by some workmen.   It was of lead, seven feet
long, and was much compressed in some parts, and a little
decayed.   On opening it, the entire skeleton was found,
measuring six feet three inches and a half in length.   Some
brown hair was found lying near the skull and neck.   The
coffin also contained a liquid, which at the feet was three
inches deep, and which Dr. Lind, who examined it, pro-

---

* The document from which this description is taken is given in
Miss Strickland's " Lives of the Queens of England," vol. iii. p. 335.
† " Genealogical History of the Kings of England," p. 392.

nounced to be the result of the decomposition of the body.*

Elizabeth Woodville (or, as it is spelt on her tomb, Widville) survived her royal husband, and at the same time survived her peace and happiness; for, after his decease, troubles came, wave on wave, with overwhelming force. After a series of misfortunes, she died at Bermondsey, where she had spent her last days in monastic seclusion. In her will she said, "I bequeath my body to be buried with the body of my lord at Windsor, without pompous interring or costly expenses thereabout;" a direction observed to the letter, if we are to believe an account of her funeral written by an eye-witness. "On Whitsunday the Queen Dowager's corpse was conveyed by water to Windsor, and there privily through the little park conducted unto the castle, without any ringing of bells or receiving of the Dean, but only accompanied by the Prior of the Charterhouse and Dr. Brent, Mr. Haute, and Mistress Grace, a bastard daughter of King Edward IV., and no other gentlewomen; and as it was told to me, the priest of the college received her in the castle (Windsor), and so, privily, about eleven of the clock, she was buried, without any solemn dirge done for her obit." The hearse was such as was used for common people, with wooden candlesticks round it. "Neither at the dirge were the twelve poor men clad in black, but a dozen divers† old men, and they held old torches and torches' ends." "The ladies came not to the mass of requiem, and the lords sat about in the quire."

* Gough's "Monumental Antiquities," vol. ii. p. 278.
† That is, dressed in the many-coloured garments of poverty.

CHAPTER V.

THE TUDORS.

HE opening of the sixteenth century found Henry VII. occupying the throne of England, occasionally residing at Windsor, and maintaining the pomp and pageantry of the Order of the Garter. It was there that, in the year 1556 he received Philip the Fair, the husband of the imbecile Joanna, Queen of Castile, and bestowed on him the honour of knighthood. Numerous allusions are made by Ashmole to the ceremonial of his installation, which seems to have been conducted with unusual splendour. The herald, with due solemnity, relates the affair, and introduces, in black letter, the following quaint quotation, containing an account of the furniture of the castle :—" To wit, of the gret rich cobbord, which continually stode in the gret hall, which was all gilt plate, or of the gret and rich beds of estate, hangings of rich cloth of gold, or of the rich and sumptuous clothes of arras, with divers clothes of estate, both in the king's loggings, and in the King of Castile's loggings, so many chambers, haulls, chappels, closettes, galleries, with odir loggings, so richly and very well appointed, with divers odir things, that I suffice or cannot discern, and as I suppose few or none that there were, that ever saw castell or odir loggings in all things so well and richly appointed, and the gret continual

fare open household, so many noble men so well appareilled and with so short warnyng, heretofore as I think hath not been seen." A full account of the arrival of the king has been dug out of the Cotton MSS. by the indefatigable authors of the "Annals of Windsor;"* whence it appears that the reception was conducted with wonderful state and ceremony; the king riding a mule out of Windsor to receive his Spanish guest, and welcoming him with a politeness that must have charmed the Castilian. "As the king perceived that the King of Castile's hat was off, he took off his hat, and would not do it on till the King of Castile was almost ready to do on his. And so went up the stairs, and so passed through the upper gallery to the king's great chamber, which was richly hanged with cloth of arras, &c."

It was during this visit at Windsor that the following conversation occurred, which may be taken as illustrative of the crafty disposition which characterized Henry VII. Philip had been driven by storms on the coast of England, and contrary to his own wishes had visited Windsor. "'Sir,' said Henry to Philip, 'you have been saved upon my coast, I hope you will not suffer me to be wrecked on yours.' The latter asked what he meant. 'I mean,' said the king, 'that hair-brained wild fellow, the Earl of Suffolk,† who is protected in your dominions.' 'I thought,' replied Philip, 'your felicity had been above such thoughts; but if it trouble you, I will banish him.' 'These hornets,' said the king, 'are best in their nests, and worst when they

---

* Vol. i. 434.

† "The persecution of a Yorkist," says Mackintosh, who gives the conversation from Bacon, "was still the favourite pursuit of the English monarch. He chose a moment of courteous and kind intercourse to sound Philip on the means of removing the jealousy, or satisfying the revenge, of which one of the most unhappy of these exiles was the object."—"History of England," vol. ii. p. 95.

fly abroad. Let him be delivered to me.' 'That,' said
Philip, 'can I not do with my honour, and less with yours ;
for you will be thought to have used me as a prisoner.'
'Then,' said the king with ready shrewdness and craft, 'the
matter is at an end ; for I will take that dishonour upon
me, and so your honour is saved.' Philip closed the conversation with equal quickness, and more honourable
address : ' Sir, you give law to me, so will I to you. You
shall have him ; but upon your honour you shall not take
his life.' The very ill-fated man in question was Edmund
de la Pole, the nephew of Edward IV. He was committed to
the Tower on his arrival in England. The king kept the
word of promise during the short sequel of his own reign,
but left directions for perpetrating the perfidious murder
among the dying injunctions to his son."*

From the period of the accession of Richard III. to the
reign of Henry VII., nothing of interest occurred in connexion with the castle works. The latter monarch erected
that part which now appears between the Star Buildings and
the Elizabeth Gallery. " Of two lofty oriels, on the complicated plan in fashion at that period, which originally
decorated the north front, one has disappeared, and the
other has suffered great wrong. The interior front has
been also materially altered by Sir Jeffrey Wyatville, but
with a judgment that has left its character unimpaired."†

The works in St. George's Chapel proceeded during the
early part of the sixteenth century. The fan-tracery of
the roof, at the intersection of the cross of the chapel, was
no doubt executed at that time ; and it occupies the place
where, according to the original design for the chapel, a
lantern was to have been erected. This contemplated

---

* Mackintosh's "History of England," vol. ii. p. 96.
† Introduction to "Illustrations of Windsor Castle."

addition to the beautiful structure does not, however, seem to have been altogether abandoned even after the completion of the groined roof, as allusion is made to it in records of a later date; the lantern, consequently, must have been intended merely for external decoration. The groining of the side aisles of the choir, which are extremely fine, and have an imposing effect, was not executed till some years later. The occurrence in that part of the church of the royal arms, bearing a label, seems to indicate that the building was not completed till some period posterior to the birth of Edward VI., which happened in 1537—an assumption confirmed by the fact of an entry in the records of the Garter of that year, alluding to the finishing of the fabric of the church, and to its being paid for without delay.

In connexion with the chapel, there was a building erected in the year 1519 which requires at least a passing notice.* Until very lately there were some finely carved canopied niches, an embattled wall, and an old doorway

---

* "This house, called the 'New Commons,' has for many years been converted into one of the canons' houses, and during the time that Lord Francis Seymour was possessed of it in his right as canon, he caused to be removed several figures in old stained glass, which were in an east window in a long inner room at the top of the house, intended most probably for a library for the chantry priests and choristers: the figures were half-lengths of Aristotle, Plato, and Socrates, as the inscription under them showed. The faces were very fine, and in high preservation, but the drapery was broken and very much damaged.

"In the window of the buttery, looking into the hall, were the remains of two round panes of stained glass, which exhibited a barrel or tun, *or*, charged with a scallop shell, *argent;* having these letters, D E N, in the middle of it, which, according to the fashion of those times, is clearly a rebus for Denton—the name of the founder.

"He assisted in the erection of a similar building at Lichfield."— MS. note in a copy of the "History of Windsor," in the Dean and Chapter's Library.

built up in front of one of the houses opposite the north
door of the chapel.   This interesting architectural relic
bore the following inscription : *"Ædes pro sacellanorum et
choristarum conviviis extructæ,* A.D. 1519 *;"* and formed a
part of a building erected for " the lodging and dieting of
such of the chantry priests, choristers, and stipendiary
priests as had no certain place within the college where to
hold commons in, but were constrained to eat their meals
in sundry houses of the town."   So runs the expression of
the founder's design, who was a certain John Denton, Canon
of Windsor and Dean of Lichfield ; at the latter of which
places he erected a building of a similar kind.   The house
was provided originally with all needful furniture, and set
apart for the use of the persons specified.   It cost
£489 7s. 1d.; and the following items of expense are still
preserved in the Ashmolean MSS.   The cost of furnishing
the house was £22 10s.; the hall, £2 14s.; the pantry,
£2 5s. 5d.; the kitchen, £6 11s. 7½d.; the cook's chamber,
11s. 4½d.; the storehouse, £7 6s. 8d.; and sundries, £2.
Honest John Denton no doubt thought that the hospitable
roof he had reared would be preserved, *in perpetuo,* as a
friendly shelter for the poor priests and choristers who had
no settled home ; that the hall would ever witness the well-
spread table ; and the kitchen smile with roasting fires for
the use of his beneficiaries ; but long since all disappeared,
except the doorway, which trifling fragment was incorporated with one of the prebendal houses.   But the whole
building now has shared the fate of the prayers for his
soul which he requested that the choristers should offer
as they entered the chapel ; and even the old arch with
its quaint-looking inscription no longer remains.   This last
memento of the kind-hearted canon was swept away
about a year ago.

    During the reign of Henry VIII. the chief addition made

to the castle was the gateway which still bears his name.* Though considerably repaired and renewed, it still retains much of its original character. The rose, portcullis, and *fleur de lis*, the badges of the monarch, continue to ornament the exterior front of the building; and on the other side of the gateway, facing the chapel, there is a specimen of those wide windows which characterized the Tudor style of domestic architecture. Another relic of the same period, of a different character, yet illustrative of the state of the arts at that time, is a beautifully wrought shield, preserved in the guard-room of the castle. This was presented to Henry VIII. by Francis I., at the memorable interview of those sovereigns on the Field of the Cloth of Gold. It was executed, it is said, by the famous artist, Benvenuto Cellini, whose strangely romantic history, written by himself, presents a lively picture of the state of the arts and of the habits of society on the continent of Europe at the time in which he lived. Hence the shield, besides the interest attached to it as a work of art, connects with it historical associations almost as numerous as the groups of figures which it elaborately represents.

A curious peep into the domestic economy of the castle at this time is opened in an inventory made in the thirtieth year of Henry VIII. "of such wardrobe stuff of the beds as remain within the standing wardrobe in Windsor Castle." It contains the particulars of eight beds, some of which are described as sore worn and needing to be amended. They were of satin, Tartar hanging, crape, tawney silk, and silk of baudekyn.† We find Henry VIII. repeatedly at Windsor, enjoying

* He also enlarged the Home Park by the addition of certain lands in Windsor and Datchet, the property of Sir John Norris, for which he gave in exchange certain estates at Wallingford, Swincome, and Ewelm.

† "Domestic Architecture," vol. iii. p. 100.

F

himself there with his "out-of-door" amusements—shooting, hunting, hawking, fishing, horse-racing, and playing at tennis; and in-doors, busy with backgammon, shovel-board, dice, and cards, witnessing dogs' tricks, and laying wagers and rewarding feats for eating bucks, and riding two hours at a time. In the midst of these unkingly recreations occurred the bestowment of the title of "Duke of Shoreditch" upon Barlow, the famous London archer, who performed before him at Windsor. Rusticating at the castle, Henry wished to have his letters conveyed as speedily as possible. It was complained that as to posts between London and the court there were none but two; that sometimes there were more than a couple of despatches in a day, and the post had to ride northward and southward—"too moche," it is said, "for one horse or one man."

Edward, Duke of Buckingham, a distinguished favourite of Henry VIII., excited his displeasure, and was condemned for treason in the year 1521. Being a Knight of the Garter, he was therefore degraded from the noble order, treason being one of the chief offences for which the penalty of degradation is inflicted. The ceremony connected with the removal of his arms and ensigns from the stall he occupied in St. George's Chapel is thus described by Ashmole, and in illustration of the ancient forms connected with such a proceeding, it is here introduced. Garter was sent to demand the badges of his knighthood. He then took down his achievements in the royal chapel. First, he "read aloud the instrument of degradation; after which one of the heralds, who was placed ready on a ladder set to the back of the convict knight's stall, at the words 'expelled and put from among the arms,' took his crest, and violently cast it down into the choir, after that his banner and sword; and, when the publication was read out, all the officers of arms spurned the achievements out of the choir into the body of the church—first the sword, then the banner, and last of all the crest—so out of the west door, thence to the bridge, and over the ditch."

During the reign of Henry VIII. the Order of the Garter seems to have flourished in all its splendour. The taste of the monarch could not fail to delight in its gorgeous pageants. He directed his attention to the statutes of the order, and in the fourteenth year of his reign introduced some alterations, which are described and discussed by Ashmole and Anstis with as much profound attention as if they were laws of the empire upon which the fortunes and lives of millions depended. In connexion with this very important reformation, an account is preserved of a magnificent cavalcade of the sovereign and knights to Windsor on the eve of the grand feast.

"The king entered Windsor with his great horses—that is to say, nine coursers—with nine children of honour upon them, and the master of the king's horses upon another great courser's back following them, having and leading the king's horse of estate in his hand—that is to say, a rich courser with a rich saddle, and trapped and garnished—following the king, and so entered the castle.

"At the castle gate the ministers of the college received the king with procession; and the king and knights of the order, at the church door, took their mantles and entered the choir, and stood before their stalls till the sovereign had offered and returned to his stall; then every knight offered according to his degree, as by statute is ordained, and entered their stalls; which was a long ceremony, or ever they had all offered, because of the great number of knights that were then present, which were nineteen in number beside the sovereign. The offering done—putting off their mantles at the church door—all rode before the king from the college unto the quadrate of the castle, and so conveyed his highness to his lodgings. The king had attendant on him all the officers at arms, wearing their coats of arms, and all his trumpeters which blew the entry of the king all the time of the said entry."

Leaving this flourish of trumpets, which may serve as no inappropriate introduction of the distinguished character now to be noticed, we will call attention for a moment to Cardinal Wolsey, in connexion with that elegant chapel which was given him by Henry, and which has ever since been designated by his name. At the time of which we have just been speaking, Wolsey was enjoying the zenith of his master's favour : rising from an obscure origin, he had mounted above the rank of nobles to be second in the kingdom ; and only on the throne was Henry greater than he. Having received from the monarch the princely dona-tion of the tomb-house attached to the royal chapel, Wolsey intended that it should be a fit mausoleum for his remains. We should expect that the man who raised the splendid palace of Hampton, and who lived in a state of pomp which crowned heads might envy, would prepare for him-self some proud memorial to cover his ashes when removed from the scenes of his ambitious life. History testifies that this was the case. Lord Bacon states that the monu-ment of Wolsey was far to exceed that of Henry VII. at Westminster. It was of white and black marble, with eight brazen columns around it, and four others in the shape of candlesticks. It was the work of Benedetto, a Florentine artist, who began it in 1524, and in the course of five years received 4250 ducats for his labours, beside £380 13s. expended upon the gilding, which by that time was only half completed. The work was never finished. The fall of the cardinal interrupted its progress, and it long stood a splendid ruin, emblematical of its founder. On Wolsey's removal to York, he sent instructions to

Cromwell to procure for him his image, with such part of the tomb as it might please the king to grant him, in order that he might dispose of it in the chapel for his burial, which, he adds, "is likely, by reason of my heaviness, to be shortly." * Some portion of the tomb remained in the chapel till the year 1646, when it was sold by order of parliament, under the description of defaced brass, for £600, and the money given to Colonel Venn, at that time governor of Windsor Castle ; but the sarcophagus of black marble, under which the cardinal intended to slumber, was preserved ; and after lying neglected for many years, was at length appropriated as a covering for Nelson's tomb in St. Paul's Cathedral; so that one of England's greatest heroes now rests under the identical slab intended for England's proudest churchman.

This interesting story of Wolsey's Chapel connects Windsor both with his prosperity and fall—his pride and humiliation. As we stand and look upon the hoary edifice, visions of the past flit before us, and we seem to see the cardinal in gold and velvet, seated on his mule, richly caparisoned, slowly riding up to the castle from the new gateway of his master, followed by an endless train of attendants, and pausing to look at his own chapel, and to inspect the works ; dreaming, no doubt, that the sun of his glory would never set, and that the splendours of his life would linger around his tomb :—and then, anon the scene changes, and we see him at Leicester broken down with misfortune and despair,—

"Lodged in the abbey ; where the reverend abbot,
With all his convent, honourably received him :
To whom he gave these words :—' O father abbot,
An old man, broken with the storms of state,
Is come to lay his weary bones among ye :
Give him a little earth for charity.' "

* Fiddes' " Life of Wolsey."

The fall of Wolsey is connected with the rise of one whose name has excited the interest, and whose ultimate fate has commanded the pity, of successive generations— we allude to Anna Boleyn. There, under that old gateway which bears his name, 'tis said that Henry came to meet her when she entered the castle under the sunshine of his favour and his love ; and there, too, in the old presence-chamber, attired, as we are told, in velvet and ermine, she was created a peeress of the realm, and had the coronet of a marchioness placed on her brow as a prelude to her elevation to the queenly throne whence Catherine, the faithful wife of the tyrant, had been hurled.

Another of Henry's victims is connected with Windsor. The gallant Earl of Surrey spent many of his early days at the castle, with its " large green court," as he tells us in a poem written in the round tower when a prisoner there for eating meat in Lent. This touching lament over bygone joys, composed on the spot, and the verses in celebration of his love of the fair Geraldine, one of the beauties of the court, have shed over Windsor Castle a gleam of poetic beauty, mingling with the light which the name and poetry of James of Scotland have left shining there, but, as it must be acknowledged, far less pure. For this love of his for Geraldine was either purely fictitious, or, what was worse, a passion for a girl of thirteen (the age of Lady Elizabeth Fitzgerald at the time he wrote his poem), cherished, too, several years after his own marriage. Still it is but just to speak of Surrey as a poet in terms of praise. He was one of the first to gather flowers from the soil of Italian literature, and transplant them into England—to mould the English language into the form of blank verse— and to impart to it something of modern elegance.* The

* " Introduction to Literature of Europe," vol. i. p. 588.

following verses, in which he gives an animated description
of Windsor Castle and its associations, afford a specimen of
his poetical talents :—

"So cruel prison, how coulde betyde, alas!
  As pronde Windsor; where I, in lust and joy,
With a kinge's sonne my childishe yeres did passe,
  In greater feast than Priam's sonnes of Troye.

"Where eche swete place returnes a taste full sower,
  The large grene courtes where we were wont to hove;*
With eyes cast up into the mayden's tower,
  And easie sighs, such as men draw in love.

"The statelie seates, the ladies bright of hewe,
  The daunces short, long tales of great delight;
With wordes and lookes, that tygers could but rewe,
  Where eche of us did pleade the other's right.

"The palme-play,† where, dispoyled for the game,‡
  With dazed yies, oft we by gleams of love
Have mist the ball, and got sight of our dame,
  To bate her eyes which kept the leads above.

"The gravel ground, with sleves tied on the helme,
  On fomyng horse, with swordes and frendly hartes;
With cheare§ as though one should another whelme,
  Where we have fought and chased oft with dartes.

"The secret groves, which oft we made resounde,
  Of pleasant playnt, and of our ladies' praise;
Recording ofte what grace eche one had founde,
  What hope of speede, what drede of long delayes.

"The wilde forest, the clothed holtes‖ with grene,
  With raynes avayled,¶ and swift ybreathed horse;
With crie of houndes, and merry blasts betwene,
  Where we did chase the fearful harte of force.

"The wide vales** eke, that harbourd us eche night,
  Wherewith, alas, reviveth in my breast
The swete accord! Such slepes as yet delight,—
  The pleasant dreames, the quiet bed of rest.

---

* To loiter.   † Game at balls.
      ‡ Rendered unfit or unable to play.
§ Looks.   ‖ Thick woods.   ¶ Loosened reins.   ** Walls.

" The secret thoughts imparted with such trust,
    The wanton talke, the divers change of play ;
The friendship sworne, eche promise kept so just,
    Wherewith we past the winter night away.

" And with this thought the bloud forsakes the face,
    The tears berayne my cheeks of deadly hewe ;
The which as sone as sobbing sighs, alas,
    Upsupped have, thus I my plaint renewe.

" Oh ! place of blisse, renewer of my woes !
    Give me accompt, where is my noble fere,*
Whom in thy walles thou dost eche night enclose
    To others leefe, but unto me most dere ?

" Eccho, alas, that doth my sorrow rew,
    Returnes thereto a hollow sound of playnte ;
Thus I alone, where all my freedom grew,
    In prison pine with bondage and restrainte :

" And with remembrance of the greater griefe,
    To banish th' lesse, I find my chief reliefe."†

The days of Henry were now numbered. He left the world to appear before a more equitable tribunal than his own, about a week after the execution of the accomplished and ill-fated Surrey.

The magnificent funeral of the departed monarch, and the splendid tomb he intended to have had erected over his remains, require some notice. The most minute details relative to both of them have been preserved. " After lying in state at Whitehall, the king's body," says an old historian, " set forwards towards Windsor in a stately chariot, his effigies lying upon the coffin, with the true imperial crown on the head, and under it a night-cap of black satin, set full of precious stones ; and apparelled with robes of crimson velvet, furred with minever, powdered with ermine, the collar of the Garter, with the order of St.

* Companion.
† " Songs and Sonnettes of Henry, Earle of Surrey," 1557.

George, about the neck ; a crimson satin doublet embroidered with gold, two bracelets of gold about the wrists, set with stones and pearls, a fair armoury sword by his side, the sceptre in the right hand, the ball in the left, a pair of scarlet hose, crimson velvet shoes, gloves on the hands, and several diamond rings on the fingers ; drawn by eight great horses, trapped with black, adorned with escutcheons, and a shatfedon on their heads, on each of which rode a child of honour carrying a bannerol of the king's arms." They reached Sion that night, and there, according to a MS. in the Sloane Collection, quoted by Miss Strickland, the leaden coffin being shaken by the carriage, the pavement of the place was wetted by the monarch's blood, and in the morning a dog was seen licking it up, in fulfilment, some thought, of a certain friar's prediction, who compared Henry to Ahab, and threatened him with a similar fate to that of the king of Israel.*   However that might be, it is certain that the convent at Sion, where the corpse was lodged, had been the prison-house of Catherine Howard ; and that the day of the funeral tarrying there was the day following the fifth anniversary of her execution. After reposing there, " the next morning about six o'clock, after the third sound of the trumpets, the whole company (the Marquis of Dorset

* Fuller, in his own quaint style, thus notices the above rumour, in connexion with others which prevailed after Henry's death :—" As for the report of Sanders, that King Henry, perceiving the pangs of approaching death, called for a great bowl of white wine, and drinking it off, should say to the company, ' We have lost all ;' it is enough to say, it is the report of Sanders. As loud a lie is it which he affirmeth, that the last words heard from his mouth, were ' the monks, the monks,' and so gave up the ghost. This may go hand in hand with what another Catholic relates, that a black dog (he might as truly have said a blue one) licked up his blood ; whilst the stench of his corpse could be charmed with no embalming, though indeed there was no other noisomeness than what necessarily attendeth on any dead body of equal corpulency."—Fuller's " Church History," vol. ii. p. 132.

being chief mourner) proceeded for Windsor, and brought the corpse to the Castle College gate, about one of the clock; from which place to the west door of the church a large way was railed on both sides, and hung round with black cloth and escutcheons; the church and choir being likewise hung round with black. The Bishops of Winchester, London, and Ely, in their pontificals, with the subdean of the king's chapel, and the singing men of the same, and the Dean of Windsor, with the canons and the whole choir, received the corpse at the aforesaid place; whence, "after censing and such like ceremonies, it was carried into the church, the singing men of the King's Chapel on the right hand, and they of Windsor on the left, preceding it. Thus the effigy was first conveyed into the choir by divers knights and gentlemen; and then the coffin by sixteen yeomen with black staves in their hands, was brought into a hearse, made in the midst of the choir, under which was provided a goodly vault to bury the corpse in, over which was laid a grate, whereon stood the said hearse with the coffin and picture." The hearse consisted of thirteen pillars, and weighed 4000 lbs., having about it twelve banners of descent.

After remaining in the chapel all night, on the next day, about four o'clock, began the communion of the Trinity; when "after an offering of gold by the chief mourner, of the Knights of the Garter to St. George, and of the king's hatchments, bannerols and banners, and other trophies, as also of the king's horse richly trapped, came four gentlemen ushers, and took away the pall of cloth of tissue (the picture being conveyed away before by six knights into the vestry); after which, sixteen strong yeomen of the guard took the coffin, and with five strong linen towels, which they had for their fees, let it into the vault (near unto the body of Queen Jane Seymour, his third wife), the grate being first taken away ; then the Lord Chamberlain, the Lord Great Master, Mr. Treasurer, Mr. Comptroller, and the Sergeant Porter breaking their white staves upon their heads in three parts, as did likewise all the gentlemen ushers, threw them into the grave, when Garter, assisted by the Bishops of Canterbury and Durham, declared the state and the name of the most godly prince their master, King Edward VI. Thus the funeral ending, the trumpet sounded in the rood-loft, and the company departed."*

In Henry's will he commanded that his body should be interred in the choir of Windsor, midway between the state and the high altar, and that there should be made as soon as convenient—if it were not done in his lifetime—an honourable tomb for his bones to rest in, which he describes as "well onward and almost made therefor already," with a fair grate about it. This tomb Speed describes in his history, with a minuteness of detail that occupies a closely printed folio page. It was to be twenty feet broad and twenty-eight feet high, with pillars of oriental stone ; the capitals and bases copper gilt. Figures of the king and the queen were to be placed on black marble slabs ; images of the prophets, the apostles and evangelists, John the Baptist, and St. George, were to be erected five feet in height ; and numbers of angels and children, none of them less than two feet and a half high, were to adorn this transcendant piece of monumental architecture. The mystery of the " Life of Christ " was to be sculptured ; epitaphs for the king and the queen were to be introduced ; and ornaments of various kinds, enamelled and gilt, were to be scattered around. The number of statues was to be six hundred and thirty-four, with forty-four " histories," or bas-reliefs ; the whole to be surmounted by a statue of the king on horse-

* " Genealogical History of the Kings of England," p. 464.

back. This costly plan was never executed, and its details remain on the pages of the old historian, a monument of the monarch's pride.

The remains of Henry VIII. were deposited in the same vault which contained the body of his queen, Jane Seymour; she died a few days after the birth of Prince Edward, at Hampton Court, on the 13th of October, 1537, and was thence removed to Windsor, and interred in St. George's Chapel. In the same chapel there rest the remains of another distinguished individual connected with Henry, and related to him by marriage : we refer to Charles Brandon, Duke of Suffolk. He was remarkable for that personal gracefulness, and that skill in the tilt and tournay, which were likely to commend him to the notice of Henry. Brandon had been brought up with the prince, had been favoured with his friendship,—and in consequence was raised from a private station to the honours of the dukedom of Suffolk. He gained the affections of Henry's sister, the Princess Mary, one of the most beautiful women of her age. This lady, however, was first married to Louis XII. of France, but after his death, which happened about three months after the marriage, Charles Brandon sought her hand, and she became his wife, a distinction to which no other subject would have dared to aspire. Henry settled the succession of the crown in remainder upon the house of Suffolk ; and hence, upon the death of Edward VI., Lady Jane Grey, grand-daughter of the duke by the Queen Dowager of France, was exalted, for a few brief days, to the English throne. The Duke of Suffolk died in the year 1545, and was buried at the royal expense ; but nothing of grandeur remains at the present time to mark his tomb.

The reign of Edward has little connexion with Windsor, except that Ashmole, the historian of the Garter, deeply laments the gloomy period in its annals which his reign presents, as one of the common calamities of his age, "wherein most ceremonies," he says, "solemn or splendid, came under the suspicion of being superstitious, if not idolatrous." It appears that the youthful monarch or his advisers wished greatly to abridge the ceremonials of the institution, and to reform what he considered preposterous ecclesiastical rites ; "whereby," says Ashmole, "the solemnity, state, and magnificence of the grand festival was very much eclipsed."*

We read of one transient visit paid by Edward to the halls of his fathers. The Protector Somerset, entangled with difficulties and on the eve of his fall, fled with him, in the dead of night, from Hampton Court to Windsor,

---

* The following extract from the Hugget MSS. shows that some of the property belonging to St. George's College was, during this reign, appropriated by the dean and canons to their own private uses :—

"An. Reg. vi. Ed. VI.

"The answer of Owen Oglethorpe, canon, to the commissioners appointed by the king for inquiring after the sale of college plate, copes, &c.

"That, in passing backwards and forwards through Windsor, he did often sign acts of chapter, which the dean and canons told him were just and right; that he had for his share as much as sold for £25, but that he lost most of the money, and that because he did imagine it to have been unjustly gotten."

An account follows showing that property had been sold to the amount of £1529 4s.

It is added—"They sold the palls of the herses of Kings Henry VII. and VIII., and Edward IV., the organ and pipes, the plates of copper upon the graves, King Edward III.'s cap of maintenance, the sword and girdle of pearl and stone, the Duke of Suffolk's sword, &c."

The parties who thus sequestered the property alleged that they were put to certain expenses for repairs, &c.; but Mr. Hugget treats this as a mere excuse, and adds, "Henry VII. left by his will to the college, a great image of St. George, of gold, poising two hundred and sixty ounces, garnished with rubies, pearls, sapphires, and other stones; perhaps this was sold also."—Hugget MSS., Sloane Collection, vol. ii. p. 122.

when the young monarch was suffering from a cough. "There was haste and scurry, armour clanking, servants rushing to and fro, the flashing of lights, and the tramp of horses." The court reached Windsor Castle before day dawn on an autumn morning. The king's chest suffered from the wild, caseless ride. The castle was unprovided, but the council sent "waggons with supplies of food and furniture." Hence the Protector sent his letters to the council, from whom he had separated himself, " full of erasures, corrections, and after-thoughts," indicative of the distraction of his mind, but stating that if any two of them would come to Windsor, he should submit to any terms which, after discussion, should be agreed upon. It was here that he removed the Yeomen of the Guard, and manned the castle with his own servants in royal uniform. Hither, after further communication and the replacement of the yeomen, the lords of the council came down, and were received by Edward, after which the Protector Somerset was sent to the Tower.[*]

Mary and her husband Philip, immediately after their marriage, came to Windsor, where Philip was made a Knight of the Garter. On entering the town at the lower end of Pescod-street, they were met by the mayor of Windsor and his brethren. They then proceeded to the chapel, and Philip received his investiture within the west door ; where was prepared a form adorned with carpet and cushions. " The queen having received the mantle of the order, with a reverential kiss from the Earls of Derby and Pembroke (to whom it had been presented by the registrar of the order), put it upon the king, assisted by the said earls ; the Earls of Arundel and Pembroke, receiving the collar of the order from Garter, presented it to the queen (with

---

[*] Froude's " History of England," vol. v. p. 235.

the like ceremony as was the mantle), who put it about the king's neck.

"Then all the knights-companions put on their mantles within the chapel door, and proceeded into the choir, and stood before their stalls, according to ancient order. Then the queen went into her stall, taking the king by the hand, and setting him in the same stall with her, and after a little space, they both descended and proceeded up to the high altar, the queen keeping the right hand, and there offered. After which they returned to their stall, where they reposed themselves while all the knights-companions present did offer according to their degree, and had taken their stalls according to their ancient custom. Then was ' Te Deum' and 'De Profundis' sung, which being finished, they came all down from their stalls, and proceeded to the chapter-house door, where the king and all the knights-companions put off their mantles : and immediately going out of the chapel, they took their horses at the chapel-door, and proceeded in order up to the castle, where they reposed themselves that night."

It is worth noticing that when the flames of the Marian persecution were about to be kindled, three of the illustrious martyrs which it sacrificed—Cranmer, Ridley, and Latimer —were conveyed from the Tower of London to the Castle of Windsor, on their way to Oxford.

In the reign of Mary, the houses of the military knights, in the south side of the lower ward, assumed their present form, being completed in three years at a cost of £2747 7s. 6d. ; the square tower, and some portions of the structure to the east, were previously standing. The alterations were made with materials brought from other buildings ; some of the stone came from Reading Abbey, and lead and "old apparails for chimnies" from Suffolk-place. At the same time, a reservoir was formed in the

upper court of the castle, where water was brought from a
great distance, and thence conveyed by pipes over all the
building. It was surmounted by a magnificent fountain,
consisting of a canopy on columns in the Gothic style,
decorated with heraldic ornaments, and a dragon discharging
water into a basin beneath. A considerable sum was
expended on this, of which a minute account is preserved
among the Ashmolean MSS.

It was mentioned that in the reign of Edward VI.
certain alterations were made in the laws of the order,
tending somewhat to abridge its splendour: these new
regulations, however, were annulled in the reign of Mary,
who ordered them " to be speedily expunged out of the
book of statutes, and forthwith defaced, lest any memory
of them should remain to posterity."

But we must leave the times of Mary, and pass on to
notice Windsor during the reign of her sister. One of the
first acts of Elizabeth was to re-establish the foundation of the alms-knights, agreeably to the wishes of her
father, as specified in his will. The number was reduced
to thirteen; the sum of £600 was set apart for their
maintenance; and certain rules and orders were drawn up,
which were to be enforced by the dean and canons. " The
annual allowance," observes Pote, " to each of these alms-
knights, upon the establishment of Queen Elizabeth, is
£18 5s., to be paid by the Dean of Windsor, beside
£3 6s. 8d. to every one of them for a gown or surcoat of
red cloth, and a mantle of blue or purple cloth, on the left
sleeve whereof is embroidered the arms of St. George, in a
plain scutcheon."*

The queen made several alterations and improvements in

* " History of Windsor," p. 97.—The costume was altered in the
reign of his late majesty William IV.; the knights now wear a
military uniform.

and about the castle. The north terrace was raised by her command, and we certainly must feel that she laid posterity under some obligations to her munificence and taste, for the construction of this fine walk, commanding one of the most striking and beautiful views which the country affords. It would appear that a terrace of some sort, though not to the same extent, existed previously, as we find it mentioned as being out of repair in the year 1572, which could scarcely have been the case if it had been constructed subsequently to Elizabeth's accession in 1558. Be this as it may, it is quite certain that about the year 1576, works were in progress for the construction of the present terrace. It was carried out beyond the castle wall, facing the scarp of the hill, upon cantalivers of timber, protected by a wooden rail.* It further appears, from an account written some time afterwards, and which will be introduced in the next chapter, that the terrace was made with arches and buttresses of stone, with timber laid, for a fence, breast-high.

Paul Hentzner, who visited the castle in the end of the sixteenth century, describes it as "a walk of incredible beauty, three hundred and eighty paces in length, set round on every side with supporters of wood, which sustain a balcony, from which the nobility and persons of distinction can take the place of seeing hunting and hawking, in a lawn of sufficient space. For the fields and meadows, clad with a variety of plants and flowers, swell gradually into hills of perpetual verdure up to the castle, and at the bottom stretch out in an extended plain that strikes the beholder with delight."†

A little before the time that the terrace was made, the building adjoining the Norman gateway was altered to its

* Introduction to "Illustrations of Windsor Castle."
† "Journey into England, in 1598."

present appearance, and a few years later (in the year 1576), a new banqueting house was commenced in the eastern part of the terrace, described as an octagon building, with a cupola, and surrounded with windows, twenty-two feet in diameter. At the same period,. the new gallery (now the library), was erected, connecting the north tower of the Norman gateway with Henry VII.'s building. It was lighted by three fine windows on the south side, and there was a descent from it to the north terrace. The noble carved stone chimney-piece and the moulded work on the ceiling still remain.

Here we may as well avail ourselves of the opportunity of glancing at some of the curiosities which were shown to visitors in the days of Elizabeth. Let Paul Hentzner, the foreigner, who was at Windsor in 1598, be our guide through the apartments :—

"There are worthy of notice here, two bathing-rooms, ceiled and wainscoted with looking-glass ; the chamber in which Henry VI. was born ; Queen Elizabeth's bed-chamber, where is a table of red marble with white streaks ; a gallery, everywhere ornamented with emblems and figures ; a chamber in which are the royal beds of Henry VII. and his queen ; of Henry VIII., and of Anna Bullen ; and of Edward VI. ; all of them eleven feet square, and covered with quilts shining with gold and silver ; Queen Elizabeth's bed, with curious coverings of embroidery, but not quite so long or large as the others ; a piece of tapestry, in which is represented Clovis, King of France, with an angel presenting to him the *fleur de lis*, to be borne in his arms ; for before this time the kings of France bore three toads in their shield, instead of which they afterwards placed three *fleurs de lis* on a blue shield. This antique tapestry is said to have been taken from a king of France, while the English were masters there. We were shown here, among other things, the horn of a unicorn, of above eight spans and a half in length, valued at above £10,000 ; the bird of paradise, three spans long, three fingers broad, having a blue bill of the length of half an inch, the upper part of its head yellow, the nether part of a * * * colour ; a little lower, from either side of its throat, stick out some reddish feathers, as well as from its back and the rest of its body ; its wings, of a yellow colour, are twice as long as the bird itself ; from its back grow out, lengthways, two fibres, or nerves, bigger at their ends, but like a pretty strong thread, of a leaden colour, inclining to black, with which, as it has no feet, it is said to fasten itself to trees when it wants to rest. A cushion most curiously wrought by Queen Elizabeth's own hands."

People at that period, it appears, believed in unicorns and birds without feet ; absurdities, it is true, not quite so great as some which were received in an earlier age, when, for instance, a cocoa-nut was kept among the curiosities of a monastery, and shown by the brethren as a veritable griffin's egg. But whatever might be the curiosities preserved in the castle, little attention seems to have been paid to domestic convenience and comfort. Repeated complaints are made of the castle being out of repair ; the Garter Tower, Winchester Tower, the Keep, and Tennis court, were all reported to be in bad condition. Nearly £700 was spent "to keep out the choughes and piggins that do much hurt the castle." There is, in the report of the works for the year 1580, a statement, " that the maids of honour desired to have their chambers ceiled, and the partition that is of boards to be made higher, for that the servants looked over." And about the same time, it is said that certain young noblemen and gentlemen were guilty of similar indecorous behaviour, being fond of peeping over these boards, to the great annoyance of the ladies when at their toilet, whereat her majesty was highly displeased, and severely reproved them. From other parts of the report, it seems that the chamber for the squires of the body was "ruinous and cold," and required to be "ceiled overhead and boarded underfoot;" and that some part of the castle roof was so much out of repair, that the rain beat in. Even the royal bed-chamber was "evil favoured, and in great decay." Her majesty, too, complained of the dinner being cold when brought on the table; in explanation of which, it was stated that the bakehouse was so far from the castle* that it was impossible the provision could be placed hot on the royal board. What a change in all such matters since then! How would the ancient cooks have been astonished and entranced at the sight of the present magnificent kitchen in the castle, and all the various conveniences for culinary preparations!

But it will be expected that something should be said respecting the illustrious maiden queen, in connexion with the castle which she so often honoured with her presence. "About the middle of September," says Nichols, in his "History of the Progresses of Queen Elizabeth," "she came to Windsor, and was there every hour in expectation of the King of Sweden coming, being very shortly looked for at Westminster, where certain works were in hand, and the workmen wrought day and night to finish them against his reception. His business was to court the queen for his wife; but he came not himself, being advised to the contrary; yet his brother the duke did, and was a passionate advocate for his brother with the queen."† This Swedish king who sued for the hand of Elizabeth was Eric, a sanguinary tyrant, and the degenerate offspring of the brave and noble Gustavus Vasa. It was a happy thing for her and the country that she escaped this alliance; but there

* The bakehouse was in Pescod-street.
† Nichols, vol. i. p. 56.

was a very strong and natural feeling on the part of her subjects in favour of her entering on some matrimonial union, as the means of preventing the evils of an unsettled succession, which at that time were peculiarly formidable. The imperious temper of the queen, and her love of exclusive authority, no doubt influenced her in her repeated refusals of marriage. "I will have here but one mistress," exclaimed the haughty dame, "and no master." "Madam," said Melville, "you need not tell me that—I know your stately stomach; you cannot suffer a commander; you think if you were married, you would be but Queen of England, and now you are king and queen both."

From the numerous details we have of the habits and pursuits of Elizabeth, her court and people, we can easily fill up in our minds the picture of Windsor Castle in the sixteenth century. We are told that she was fond of the chase, often coursing through the Forest in pursuit of the deer; and that when she came in at the death, and the dogs were whipped off their prey, the huntsman would hand her majesty the knife, to cut the animal's throat. Nor were the amusements of the bear-garden wanting, and Elizabeth and her ladies might be seen watching from the windows the writhing of the hoodwinked bear while whipped by six or seven men in a circle. Bull-baiting and cock-fighting, and horses performing with apes on their backs, were also considered spectacles of interest. But it is just to exhibit her under another aspect. Elizabeth was a student, and is said to have diligently pursued her classical studies in the castle. We are told that she understood Greek better than the canons of Windsor, and was certainly a much greater pedant than her successor James I. In her cabinet she often dictated verses to her private secretary, or engaged in literary conversation, and received the brilliant flattery of her accomplished favourite, the Earl of Leicester.

The terrace was a favourite walk with her majesty, and there she might be seen most days, sometimes accompanied by a bevy of ladies and courtiers—ruffs, hoops, and embroidered petticoats, intermixed with satin doublets, bright-coloured hose, velvet cloaks, and gracefully plumed caps; at other times with a select few—Cecil, Leicester, Walsingham, Essex, engaged in earnest conversation on state affairs, or indulging in courtly wit—and not unfrequently alone, with her golden-bound prayer-book suspended to her girdle, her thoughts absorbed in the cares of empire, or engrossed with other and softer subjects which, notwithstanding all her maidenly resolves, often agitated her bosom.

CHAPTER VI.

THE STUARTS.

HERE are preserved in the British Museum two interesting MSS. illustrative of Windsor in the early part of the seventeenth century. One of these is a short paper in a volume of the Harleian MSS., and described in the Catalogue as written by John Stowe. But it would seem improbable that he wrote the paper, from the circumstance that in another MS. in the same volume, apparently in the same handwriting, a reference is made to him in the third person. But be the writer who he may, the paper contains a quaint and amusing description of the castle and the park.

He observes, that the ascent to the castle "upon the north side is by a hundred and twenty steps, as is to be seen by the canons' stairs, from their orchard, and the stairs in their walk upon the hill side," while the entrance on the south side is by "a stately gate and bridge." After describing the lower wards in the castle, in which description there is nothing remarkable, the writer relates the anecdote respecting the kings of Scotland and France, which was introduced in an early part of this work, and he then proceeds to give the following account of the upper wards, the terrace, and the park :—" The keep in the second ward and two mighty towers, with other buildings and walls,

were named to be at the expense of the Scottish king
(Winchester Tower excepted, which is in the same ward,
being made no doubt by the Bishop of Winchester as prelate
of the Garter), which keep being of . . . . steps in height,
and standing upon a round hill formed by hand, is notwithstanding so slope and easy to ascend, that a man may easily
ride up to the top thereof, like St. Mark's steeple in Venice,
and the compass thereof is one hundred and ninety paces.

"And the higher ward was made by the French king's
ransom, which ward indeed is the beauty and majesty of
the whole castle, as wherein all the prince's lodgings and
other offices, with the houses of officers, are contained, being
almost four-square—that is, one hundred and forty-six paces
in length, and one hundred and ninety-seven in breadth; in
the midst whereof, lest so large a space should be without
ornament, is a goodly great conduit, brought thither by
pipes under the earth above four miles; on the east and
south parts whereof are the noblemen's lodgings and houses
of office, and on the west part the tennis-court and keep
aforesaid, overlooking all the castle as the chief fort thereof;
from which also, when the weather is clear, may easily be
descried Paul's steeple; on the north part are the prince's
halls, chambers, wardrobes, and galleries, with his shower-
baths and banqueting-houses, and mainly that great hall
where St. George's feast is kept and celebrated, being in
length seventy-eight paces and in breadth twenty, with his
private chapel, which is of no less beauty than fine workmanship; upon the north side and outer part of which
lodgings also, between the same and the brow or fall of the
hill, which is very steep and pitchy, is an excellent walk (or
baye) running all along the said buildings on the side of the
castle, borne up and sustained by arches and buttresses of
stone and timber laid breast-high, which is in length three
hundred and sixty paces, and in breadth seven, of such an

excellent grace to the beholders and passers-by, being open to the sight even afar off, that the pleasure, stateliness, beauty, and use thereof seemeth to contend one with the other which shall have the superiority. In the goodly bottom under the which walk lieth a parcel of the park plain, as equal as it is possible, and continually green, with certain ponds therein, where the prince useth to see out of his windows the deer hunted with hounds, and in the end forced to take the said ponds, hunting as it were at one time both on land and water, and yet not stirring out of his chamber. At the end of this walk is a bridge, and dry ditch under the same as parcel of the castle ditch, whereby the said park is severed from the aforesaid walk and castle, which park containeth all the rest of the hill that the castle standeth upon, more than half a mile in length, shoring down very slope on the east and south parts, but steep and abrupt on the north side, with certain walks and downfalls, whereunto joineth the lawn or coursing-place, running all the length of the park, and all the hill serving as a continual standing to behold and judge of the course with ease; which lawn or pleasant bottom being a most delicate grass and fair meadow, lying along the side of the hill (like man and wife together) of a marvellous plain, direct, and equal level, seemeth no less praiseworthy in respect of the lowliness, than the stately hill in its elevation and haughty rising.

"The prospect east, west, north, and south is singular, but from the castle every way it is (sur)passing. The name whereof (not without cause) is called Windsor; whether it came, as some affirm, of the ferry over the river, the passengers using (in calling for a boat) to bid them wind to shore, because the boat then, as now, went with a rope and a pole, though not in the same place where it is now, but where the bridge is; or whether it took its name of the quality of the place, which, standing high and open to the

weather, is called Windsor, because the wind is sore and
the air very subtle and piercing there, as the inhabitants
find it, which etymology, divining with myself of the nature
of the place itself, I added another also thereto, at my first
coming thither, of this effect :—

> "'The wind is sore in High Windsor, whereof it may take name,
> And wind, for winding, may import ascending to the same;
> As e'en the hawk is said to sore that lieth on high above :
> All which etymologies one the truth I guess doth prove.'"

The other MS. relating to Windsor in the early part of
the seventeenth century, is Norden's survey.*

The bird's-eye view which he gives of the castle is the
earliest complete pictorial representation which we possess
of the royal edifice. It is an odd, quaint-looking affair,
but in extent and outline very much resembles the building
and precincts as we see them now. There is "the keepe."
The "pryvie lodgings" correspond with the present State
apartments. "The lodgings for the household" are on the
south side. "The tennys courte" is within the wall round
the keep, near to where the fountain now stands. Queen
Mary's fountain is seen in the midst of the quadrangle.
There are several little red-roofed houses hard by "the
lieutenant's lodging," now the Ivy or Store Tower, from
which to the Dean's house there runs a wall, with a gateway separating the keep from the lower ward. The
"chappell of the Garter" is fully portrayed, with "the

---

* It bears date 1604, and commences with the following dedica-
tion :—
   "To the Most Mighty and Magnificent Prince James, by Divine
Grace, Kinge of Great Britain, France, and Ireland, and of all the
Isles and Seas adjacent ; sole Emperor ; principal maintainer of the
most true Christian religion ; your Majesties loyal poor subject, John
Norden, most humbli exhibiteth this his imposed labours of the
description of your Majesties Castle and Honor of Windesore, and the
principal particulars belonging to the same."

poor knights' lodgings" opposite. "The petite canons' lodgings" are to the west—now the horse-shoe cloisters. The three old towers crown the west wall; and Henry VIII.'s gateway is named "the gate coming out of the towne." Around them is field, garden plot, orchard, and park, with strange, hideous-looking animals dotted about, intended to represent deer. Along the north side the terrace is distinct enough, terminating at the east end in a projection over two arches marked underneath "The Tarras bridge."

In Norden's survey we have a minute account of the number of parks included in the royal demesnes,—their respective extent, the length of the paling, the names of the keepers, and the number of the deer. He describes the Little Park as measuring three miles and three-eighths, and containing about two hundred and eighty acres of good ground. It was stocked with fallow deer, to the amount of two hundred and forty, and with sixty-eight antlers and thirty bucks. The Great Park, he states, measured ten miles and a quarter, and contained three thousand six hundred and fifty acres. The walks, he observes, "not having separation, the deer so interchase, that the particular number in each walk can never hardly be distinguished; but the whole number within the park are by the woodman supposed to be one thousand eight hundred deer, whereof about five hundred are bucks."

Thus the diligent surveyor goes through all the parks, which, according to his calculation, covered the country round to a great extent, embracing a circumference of seventy-seven miles, and reaching on one side as far as Guildford, and as far as Henley on the other. Some notes are inserted in the survey, illustrative of the aspect of the country at that time. Of Wokingham Park, he says some part "is barren and full of bogs," and the other part is "fat and fertile." In reference to Byfleete, Surrey, he remarks, that the "hooping bird, vulgarlie held ominous, much frequenteth this park." " Langley Park is divided into two parts by a new paling. The upper ground is full of bogs, unprofitable and impassable—the lower ground reduced to a better use for the game, and more delightful to hunt in, by reason of the fair artificial lawns, lately made and levelled, with many convenient and pleasant standings." With regard to all the parks, the surveyor complains, " that there is contention between every neighbour and keeper for the most part, for usurpation and intruding into another's walks, for not one of them truly knoweth his own bounds ; which controversy will hardly be justly determined until the verderers of the forest, and the regarders of every walk, aided by the ancient inhabitants, do perambulate, view, and enter the same."

These are trifling matters, but their antiquity gives them a certain interest. In looking over that old MS., one cannot but think how changed is the appearance of Windsor and its environs since Norden made his survey. Not a house, perhaps, remains in the town that then was standing. The castle has completely changed its aspect, and much of the wide forest has since been brought into cultivation, and peaceful farms and villages are smiling where then were sheep and deer walks, or wastes, " barren and full of bogs." Still, however, there are objects in those parks that connect us with the times when Norden paced and measured them. Oaks still thrive there which flourished in their beauty in his day, and perhaps formed a shade to cover him while accomplishing his survey. A few of these trees, it may be, have flourished from a period anterior to the Conquest, and fell into their soft receptacle when some skipping deer, hunted by Saxon princes, with " pointed hoof dibbled the glebe."

James I. occasionally resided at Windsor, and no doubt often amused himself with his favourite diversion of hunting in the noble forests described by Norden. Sir Dudley Carlton, in 1603, describes the arrival of the new king at Windsor. He brought a "mervilous great court," and adds, " there was some squaring at first between our English and Scotch lords for lodging, and such other petty quarrels." Lords Southampton and Grey, too, had a terrible quarrel, when the queen bade them remember where they were, and soon after sent them to their lodgings under guard. Little worth noticing occurred during James' reign, in reference to Windsor. A stray incident which time has left us, relating to that period, is a curious piece of litigation between the monarch and the Dean and canons. In December, 1603, a part of the castle wall near the royal chapel was blown down, and a dispute arose as to who should repair it. The crown contended that since the part of the castle where the breach had been made was given by Edward III. to the college of St. George—since they possessed revenues to maintain it in repair, and had opened windows in the walls, and made drains, which occasioned the breach, they were bound to bear the expense of repairing it. On the part of the Dean and Canons it was contended, that the wall was much more ancient than the foundation of the college ; that it was higher than the houses adjoining ; that it was built for the defence of the castle ; that they had no property in it ; that the charter of Edward had freed them from the charges of repairing the castle ; that the wall had fallen in, not through any fault of theirs, but through the lapse of years ; and that if they were now forced to repair it, a precedent would be set which would involve them in expenses for repairs at a future time, beyond their power to defray. The cause being heard, at their request, before the Barons of the Exchequer, on the

21st of February, 1606, more than two years after the wall
had been broken down, it was decided in favour of the
college.   The king was to repair the breach, and the lights
and casements in the walls, which had been there before,
were still to be retained by the Dean and Canons, but they
were to repair them at their own expense.

James I. seems to have emulated his predecessors on the
English throne in the zeal he evinced for the interests of
the Order of the Garter.   Commissioners were appointed
by the monarch to revise the laws of the institution, and to
bring them, as nearly as possible, to what they were in the
times of the founder.   The persons commissioned seem,
however, to have paid little attention to the affair, for a
few years afterwards another commission was issued for the
same purpose, with more extended powers ; and at length,
according to Ashmole, who gives a minute account of the
whole business, "they presented to the sovereign certain
articles subscribed with their hands, which, for the honour
of the order, they thought requisite to be duly observed."
In the reign of earlier sovereigns it had been the custom
for the knights elect to proceed from London to Windsor
in grand procession, in order to be installed.   They took
up their lodging in the Strand, in Salisbury-court, in
Holborn, or within the City ; and thence rode on horseback
to Windsor, accompanied by a large party of friends and
attendants.   It was a dazzling sight, in those days, to see
the cavalcade starting from the City residence of a knight ;
and vast were the throngs which gathered in the streets, to
see the train of horsemen, with their gorgeous apparel and
plumes of feathers, passing along on their way to Windsor.
But to such excesses of grandeur were the knights elect
sometimes carried by their ambition, that James I. put
limits to the extent of the processions, and enacted, " that
every of the knights-companions should have fifty persons

to attend him unto the annual solemnities of the order, and no more."

A full account of the installation of Prince Henry, in 1603, is preserved, as well as the visit of the King of Denmark in 1606, who, on receiving the order, was introduced to the goodly gentlemen that had served under Queen Elizabeth, "being in the robes of purple and scarlet, with the Garter and St. George's Cross upon them." With this at the beginning of the reign, it is interesting to couple what occurred at the close. The king kept the feast of St. George at Windsor in 1623, "when there was no great show. The knights and procession went not out their ordinary circuit, by reason the King was fain to be carried in a chair, not for any grief or infirmity more than the weakness of his legs, for otherwise they say he looks as well and as fresh as he did many a day."

One glance more at King Jamie. Matthew Day, an antiquary of Windsor, tells us that, in 1624, his majesty was hunting in Mote Park, when the mayor presented him with a petition on the behalf of the vicar, that, on account of the smallness of the living and the size of the cure, there being a hundred communicants under the vicar's charge, the king would annex a canonry to the vicarage. James would do nothing of the kind, but only took occasion to vent his spleen against the town, complaining of the poor, who, he said, stole wood out of the parks and forests. The words which the king spake, says Mr. Day, were as followeth : "Am I any ill neighbour unto you ? Do I do you any hurt ? Doth my coming be any hindrance to you ? Why, then, do you vex me by permitting and suffering your poor to cut down and carry away my wood out of my parks and grounds, and to sell the same." This does not bear much on the question of the poor vicar's need and desert of assistance, but it certainly reminds us of the admirable delineation of James's character by Sir Walter Scott in the "Fortunes of Nigel." All the mayor could get was an order to whip the wood-stealers, and those who bought the stolen property.

During the reign of James there were two persons who held the deanery of Windsor, and were therefore connected with the Order of the Garter, who ought not to be passed over in silence. The first of these was Giles Tomson, one of the parties employed upon the authorised version of the Bible. He was connected with the Oxford company, to whom was entrusted the translation of the Gospels, the Acts of the Apostles, and the Revelation. Anthony à Wood speaks of his high reputation, both as a scholar and a preacher; and his epitaph, in Bray's Chapel, where he lies interred, bears ample testimony to his learning, prudence, and piety. He was ten years dean of Windsor, and was then elevated to the see of Gloucester, a dignity which he enjoyed but a very short time, for he died within a year after his elevation. The other individual who claims our notice, was Marc Antonio de Dominis, a far different character. He had been archbishop of Spalatro; but on coming over to England, he published a famous book, entitled "De Republicâ Ecclesiasticâ," in which he appeared as a decided enemy of the Church of Rome, and concluded that the Pope had no superiority over other bishops. James rewarded him with the deanery of Windsor, and the mastership of the Savoy, to which was added the living of West Ilsley, in Berkshire. "Though the publication of his book was a crime never to be forgiven, he was weak enough to give credit to a letter, sent him by the procurement of Gondomar, which not only promised him pardon, but preferment, if he would renounce his new religion. He returned to Italy, relapsed to the Church of Rome, and was presently after imprisoned by the Inquisition. Grief and hard treatment soon put an end to his life, in the year 1625, and the sixty-fourth of his age. He was the first that accounted for the phenomenon of the rainbow, in his book, 'De Radiis Visûs et Lucis.' We are much indebted to him for Father Paul's excellent History of the Council of Trent, the manuscript of which he procured for Archbishop Abbot."* Mr. Hallam doubts whether he strictly belonged to the Church of England, remarking, that preferments were bestowed irregularly in that age. He further observes, that after the death of Antonio de Dominis, the "imputations of heresy against him so much increased, that his body was dug up and burned. Neither party has been ambitious to claim this vain and insincere, though clever prelate."†

Pursuing our history, we arrive at the melancholy reign of Charles I. In the year 1635, he effected some considerable alterations in the castle. Elizabeth's banqueting house was pulled down, the east end of the terrace was enclosed by a wall and gate, and the magnificent fountain, erected by Queen Mary, was demolished. Another banqueting house was planned, and another fountain designed, whereon were to be placed "the statues of Hercules worrying Antæus, as if by squeezing of him the water came out of his mouth;" but neither of these projects seem to have been carried into effect. Two years later a pyramid, or lantern, was placed on the front of the castle, and a clock was provided by David Ramsey, that illustrious clockmaker whom Scott has immortalised in his "Fortunes of Nigel." The clock was removed from the old tower in the late improvements: the bell bore the date of 1636, with the inscription—"God save our King Charles, God save my Lord the King," and the royal arms, decorated with the rose and thistle. About the same time, it appears,

* Granger's "Biographical History," vol. i. p. 359.
† Hallam's "Introduction," vol. iii. p. 71.

the royal chapel was far from being kept in good order ;
for complaints were made by the dean, of persons using the
royal closet as a thoroughfare to the leads, between the
chapel and the tomb house, and picking out the stained glass
from the east window, and also of the intrusion of improper
visitors into the knights' stalls : to remedy which his majesty
commanded that doors and locks should be provided, both
for the entrance to the leads, and the stalls in the choir.

Charles I. spent much of his time at Windsor Castle, and,
in the early part of his reign, frequently held his court
within its walls. His attention seems to have been early
directed to the affairs of the Order of the Garter. "He
designed and endeavoured," says Ashmole, "the most complete and absolute reformation of any of his predecessors ;"
and after relating the steps taken to effect his purpose, in
the appointment of certain commissioners, the enthusiastic
herald breaks out into the following lamentation :—"Now,
who would suppose that, after so noble an intention of the
sovereign, and his earnest solicitude to issue forth a second
commission, his hearty recommending and exciting their
diligence for a speedy dispatch, and, lastly, his expecting
an account of their transactions the next feast, these
honourable persons, companions of the order, should need
a spur to accomplish so laudable a design : but it was so."
Nothing seems to have been done in the affair ; indeed, all
parties, then, had more important matters to attend to ; and
the monarch's care for his favourite order was soon absorbed
in the deeper anxiety which he felt for the security of his
crown, and the safety of his life.

We now reach a crisis in English history, in the passing
effects of which Windsor sustained an ample share. That
mighty struggle between the supporters of two opposing
systems of political principles,—a struggle which convulsed
the empire for so many years,—appears with such pro-

minence in our history, and is fraught with incidents and lessons so interesting, though awful,—so instructive, though terrific,—that, to the end of time, it will attract the attention of political philosophers, aiding their speculations, and especially teaching them practical lessons.

It has been the fashion, with almost all writers on the antiquities of Windsor, to allude, in terms of strong indignation, to the character of the Puritans, who took the Parliamentary side in that unhappy contention. They are represented as base, hypocritical, factious, and contemptible. It would be out of place to treat of their politics in a work like this ; but it is not improper to say, that if they were enthusiasts, there was a sublimity in their enthusiasm, such as rarely characterizes the deeds of mortals ; and Macaulay, who certainly was not prejudiced in favour of Puritanism, discriminatingly observes—" We perceive the absurdities of their manners, we dislike the gloom of their habits ; we acknowledge that the tone of their minds was often injured, by straining after things too high for mortal reach ; and we know that, in spite of their hatred of popery, they too often fell into the vices of that bad system—intolerance and extravagant austerity ; that they had their anchorites and their crusaders, their Dunstans and their De Montforts, their Dominics and their Escobars ;—yet, when all circumstances are taken into consideration, we do not hesitate to pronounce them a brave and honest body." *

We are willing also to do justice to the Cavaliers. We admit that they were not heartless, dangling courtiers ; not mere machines for destruction, dressed up in uniforms, defending without love, and destroying without hatred ; that they felt a strong sentiment of individual independence ; that they were misled by no merely selfish or sordid motives ; that

* " Edinburgh Review," vol. xlii. Article on Milton, by Lord Macaulay.

compassion and romantic honour, the prejudices of child-
hood, and the venerable names of history, threw over them
a potent spell ; that they fought for the old banner which
had waved in so many battles over the heads of their
fathers, and for the altars at which they had received their
brides ; that, with the vices of the Round Table, they had
many of its virtues ; that they had more of polite learning
than the Puritans ; and that their manners were more en-
gaging, their tastes more elegant, often their tempers more
amiable, and sometimes their households more cheerful. It
may be added, both Puritan and Cavalier were *Englishmen*
—Englishmen to their heart's core : they, for the most part,
loved their country, though one party must have been mistaken in the means employed for its welfare ; and they
exhibited, the former in its severer, the latter in its gayer
mood, that character of deep, enduring, disinterested patriotism, which has for ages past been nursed in the bosoms
of the sons of Britain. To the history of the mighty
struggle of the seventeenth century, Englishmen of every
political creed may turn with national pride, to mark the
superiority of character displayed by both parties over our
Gallic neighbours in their revolution at the close of the
last century. Indeed, the civil wars of England present
perfectly sunny scenes, compared with the "red flame
picture" of the Reign of Terror.

A curious pamphlet, bearing date October 20th, 1642,
presenting the following title, " Exceeding true and joyful
News from Windsor Castle, declaring how several Troops
of Dragoons have taken Possession of the said Castle for
the King and Parliament," introduces us at once to some
historical recollections connected with Windsor during the
Civil Wars. The pamphlet exhibits a specimen of the
kind of publication which then occupied the place of
modern newspapers, in the communication of political

intelligence. It evidently proceeded from the Parliamentary party. The king and the Cavaliers, it tells us, "intended to draw to Windsor, and to take possession of the castle—that being a place of greatest strength in this part of the kingdom, by reason of the height and strength, the country lying under it so that the castle can command it round about. Could they have obtained this castle, they would there have fortified themselves till such time as they could gather strength ; which having obtained, they then intended (as is generally thought) to have marched against London, that being their only aim ; but God, which sees the secrets of all hearts, hath brought their practices to light, and made them apparent to the eyes of the world : their intentions were discovered to the High Court of Parliament, who, by God's assistance and direction, have taken the most speedy and effectual course to prevent so great a mischief. For, by the appointment of the Parliament, several well-affected gentlemen, and valiant, religious commanders, are gone into Essex, Middlesex, Bucks, Berks, Surrey, Hampshire, and other adjoining counties, to raise several troops of dragooners and volunteers ; some of which are arrived already at Windsor, and have taken possession of the castle for the use of his Majesty and Parliament ; others are in march towards Windsor, where, being arrived, they intend to fortify themselves, and to make outworks ; so that the Cavaliers have lost their labour. The counties are very ready to go on this service, and stand generally for the Parliament, because they see that the Cavaliers plunder all the places they come at, taking and seizing horses and all things which are portable ; and if any one resist, they presently burn their houses, to the utter ruin and destruction of all those who have dependence thereon."

The castle was taken by the Parliamentary army on the

20th of October. Three days afterwards, Captain Fogg, with a Parliamentary warrant, took possession of the royal chapel. The beautiful edifice is said to have sustained considerable injury from the violence of the soldiers; a circumstance resulting partly, no doubt, from that misguided zeal and want of taste which too generally distinguished the Parliamentary army, and for which no other excuse can be pleaded than the very slender one, that such excesses are but too commonly the result of victorious war.

Christopher Wren, the father of the famous architect, was at that time Dean of Windsor, and exerted himself in recovering as many of the records of the chapel as he could procure. "He had the good fortune," says Granger, "to redeem the three registers distinguished by the names of the Black, Blue, and Red, which were carefully preserved by him till his death. They were afterwards committed to the custody of his son, who, soon after the Restoration, delivered them to Dr. Bruno Ryves, Dean of Windsor." *

The castle remained in the hands of the Parliament; and on the 13th of May, 1643, an order was issued by the House of Commons for the payment of the Windsor garrison, consisting of a regiment of foot and a troop of horse, under the command of Colonel Venn; the payments to be made out of the moneys which should be levied "in the county of Berks, upon the ordinances for the weekly assessments." †

---

* "Biographical History," vol. ii. p. 166.

† The following passage occurs in the Huggett MSS. relative to the ejection of the dean and canons from their residence at Windsor:—"Anno 1643, May 24. The lords in parliament's answer to the dean, canons, petty cannons, &c. (upon their petition to them to continue their places in the college),—they have not thought it meet that they should enjoy their dwelling-houses; but that they may take away their books and utensils, and enjoy the same at their several habitations elsewhere."—Huggett MS. vol. ii. p. 163.

Among the domestics who were devotedly attached to the unhappy Charles was a person named Dowcett, an inhabitant of Windsor. He was intrusted with the conveyance of various communications to his master's friends; and the following notes, which relate to this circumstance, and which were written by Charles during his imprisonment, will introduce the reader to the monarch's privacy, and show the ingenious modes which he adopted for obtaining information. With regard to these notes Dowcett states—"This is all the letters which I could save of his late majestie, for I was forced to burn a matter of twenty when I was prisonner att Carisbrooke Castle."*

"A TRUE COPY OF HIS LATE MAJESTY'S LETTERS TO DOWCETT.

I.

" I thanke you for your causions, and be confident that I will be as carefull as you cane be; for your discouery will preiudice me as much as you; nor will I needlesly employ you in this kynde : as now, this is most necessary that you send it soon awaye to him who sent you that which you gave me this morning. Keepe your wafers untill I call for them, for yet I doe not want."—January 13th, 1647.

II.

" This is chiefly to show you how I cane keepe corespondency with you : and withal I desyre to know when you cane send a letter of myne to London: but especially when your wife goes. Also I desire you to deliuer this enclosed to Mary with your owne hands, and you may safely send

---

* The MS. from which these letters are printed is in the handwriting of James Jennings, of Windsor, a friend of Dowcett, who allowed him to copy them. He was carpenter to Charles II., and died in 1739, at the advanced age of one hundred and four years.

me an answer the same way that this comes to you. Hereafter know me by M——, your selfe by F——, and Mary by B——."

III.

"That which you gaue me with this paper informed me that the same party sent you a former letter for me by one of my owne messengers; his name, as I take it, is Greeg. Werfore, if you haue it not allready, inquire after it, for I know by this last that I have not yet gott it; this way I meant to F—— A——. I shall not trouble you a good whyle; but I would fain haue you once a week conuey a letter for me to my wife; therefore expect one from me on Munday morning. You must not take it ill that I looke sowerly upon you in publick; but, by the grace of God, you will neuer repent the seruices you daily doe me."

IV.

"I thanke you for your cautions, and doubt not of my carefullness. I shall obserue your days, and not trouble you oftener, except upon very urgent occasion. I hope the tyme will come that you shall thanke me for more than looking well upon you; but who was she that brought me the first letter att Homby? That which you last giue, was it that I looked for? In a word, lett not cautiousness begett feare, and be confident of me.—Wednesday, January 19th, 1647."

V.

"F——,—Deliuer the biger of thease two unto your wyfe; it is for France. I neede say no more; you knowe to whome: and giue the other to young Worsley, and desyre him to send it to him from whom hee had that packett which hee sent to me by you. Lett your wyfe assure all my friends that, by the grace of God, I will neither be cheated nor frighted from my grounds."

VI.

[To Dowcett's Wife.]

" I know not your hand, but I finde by your sence that you are one of my good friends, and that you judge rightly of these people in whose power I now am, who yet haue made noe adresses to me ; but be confident that now I knowe them to well to be any more deceaued by them. However, I hartily thanke you for your aduerticement. Desiring to know who you are, for, seriously, I cannot guese . . . . and I hope you neither will mistrust my discretion nor secresie : wherefore I expect that you will not lett me be long ignorant to whom I owe the thankes of this tymely warning and good aduyce. Besides, I would by this safe way aske you some questions, if I knew by which of my friends ye were trusted. M.—I haue burnt your letter. February 27th, 1647."

VII.

[To F———.]

" F———, I haue spared you as long as I could, for that from B———, which I had from you upon Munday last, most necessarily requyring an answer ; and now I absolutely promise you not to trouble you any more in this kynde, unles your selfe, giuing me the occasion, shall thinke it fitt, untill D——— shall come ; nor doe I urge an answere to this, but by sygnes :—that is to say, your right hand bare, for the receipt of this ; then, if the last packett you had from me (which, indeed, was of importance and haste) went a waye upon Munday, lett fall your hankercher ; if since (for I am confident it is gone), let fall one of your gloues : besides, when you haue giuen this packett to B———, tell me newes of fresh sparagos from London ; and if shee tells you that shee belieues shee will be able to obserue my directions, then tell me newes of artichockes. And now know that I am not ignorant neither of the paynes nor hazard that you daily undergoe for my seruice, and particularly in receiuing of thiese papers; assuring you that, by the grace of God, I shall soe think of you for them, as, if I prosper, you shall esteeme all thiese paynes and hazards well bestowed."

VIII.

"I could haue despatched this soe soone yesterday as to have giuen you the sygne yesternight att supper; but I would not presse upon you too soone, because of the good seruice you did me on Munday last, by the quick receiuing of my important dispach; but now I shall not blame you, though you hazard not to fetche this, until I be gone to Bowles : which is at that howre, euery day as I conceaue you may come in hiether without much danger : I say this only to assist you with my obseruations, and not to impose any command upon you."

IX.

"Seruant,—You now by experience that my condition is much wors than you thought it would haue been, but yet it is not so ill as I expect it will be. However, all that I desyre of you for the present is, that ye will seek to setle some way of intelligence betweene you and me, and that ye would send me a chifer, to the end I might write freely to you. So farewell.—Saterday, February 28th."

Whatever we may think of Charles, there is something in these little notes which strikes a chord of sympathy in the heart, and calls forth a sigh over the unhappy captive. The ingenious contrivances adopted to convey and obtain intelligence were very natural; and his looking sourly upon his servant in public should receive a lenient judgment. Confidential letters of this kind bring us very near the parties between whom they passed, and one feels as if at the monarch's elbow, while reading these documents. There he is with his peaked beard, and his pensive countenance, looking with a sly, suspicious air about him as he holds his pen, fearful of detection. As to Dowcett, one admires the fidelity of the old servant, and his love of his master, his value for his smile, his exposure to danger for his sake, his careful preservation of those few letters, when he was forced to burn so many in Carisbroke Castle. There is true nobility in the conduct of such a man cleaving close to fallen sovereignty, instead of yielding to the tide of popular feeling, and leaving his master to shift for himself. He was worth a thousand silken courtiers, who sport and flutter before the radiance of the throne. He was no hireling, no parasite, but, under the habit of a servant, carried the heart of a friend, a character rather rare in this world, and, when found, worthy of all love and reverence. In the calendar of documents in the State Paper Office we find the following, which evidently refers to this trusty royalist.

"Abraham Dowcett.—For confirmation of the grant of paddock walk, Windsor, made him by the late king, whom he served abroad under the Earl of Holland, and on his return as page of the bed-chamber. Waited on his majesty at Newcastle and in Holdenby; there, at hazard of his life, supplied him with pen and ink, when the Commissioners debarred him from them, and conveyed letters between him and the queen, and other secret intelligence. In May, 1648, did his utmost, by bribing the soldiers, to promote his majesty's escape from the Isle of Wight, but was discovered, imprisoned, his estate forfeited, and he accused of high treason, but he escaped to Holland." The grant of Charles I. is annexed, and order is given for its confirmation, and for the place of page of the bed-chamber which

he held under the late king.* In connexion with this is
"a petition from Thomas Symonds, page of the presence
to Queen Anne and the queen-mother, for the keepership
of the great park of Windsor, as granted him by the
late king, who used to come to his lodge while squirrel
hunting."

Another document connected with Windsor at this period,
is a tract bearing the following awful title, " Terrible and
bloody news from Windsor, since the bringing in of the
King's Majesty by the army, and a dangerous fight on
Saturday last, between the Parliamentary forces and the
Royalists ; who, by a strange design and unheard of strata-
gem, would have rescued the king from the power of the
army." It illustrates the violence of parties at that unhappy
period, and is a curious specimen of the sort of newspapers
then in circulation. The date is Windsor, December 24,
1648, and we are informed that—On Thursday night
last, his majesty arrived, being guarded by Colonel
Harrison and ten troops of horse. Upon their coming, a
great concourse of people greeted the king, crying " God
bless your majesty, and send you long to reign." He was
conducted to the castle, and the royalists began to drink
and carouse in honour of their prince, but—to use some of
the absurd language of the paper—with an eagle's eye being
discerned, they were soon taken off from that ceremonial
and court-like action, for notice thereof being given to
the captain of the guard, musqueteers were sent to disperse
them ;—the royalists stood in a posture of defence, whereupon the soldiery forced a passage, wounded some, killed
three, and secured the rest, who were committed to safe
custody.

In connexion with the account of the arrival of Charles

* Calendar (Domestic), 1660, 1661, p. 241.

from the Isle of Wight, given in this tract (the contents of which, by the way, do not exactly harmonise with the fearful title which it bears), we may relate the subjoined interesting anecdote of the monarch and Colonel Harrison. On their way, the party slept at Farnham, and started the next day for Windsor. They were to pass Bagshot, where lived Lord Newburgh, a friend of Charles. The royalist, aware that he would come that road, had arranged that the king should stop and take refreshment, and, under the pretence of his horse being lame, should be provided with a fleet steed from Lord Newburgh's stud, on which he might escape through the intricacies of the forest, where in happier days he had followed the chase. When Charles came to Bagshot, he complained that his horse did not carry him easily, and expressed a wish to stop and dine at Bagshot Lodge ; Harrison at first was unwilling to consent, knowing that Newburgh was a royalist, but at length yielded to the monarch's wishes. But poor Charles was not to escape out of the hands of his enemies. The horse provided for him by Lord Newburgh had received a violent injury ; the plan was thus defeated ; and, in the meantime, Charles having complained so much of his horse, Harrison provided him with a better one. Thus the king was brought a prisoner to his own castle, and while immured within its walls, he was treated with little of the respect due to his rank. That monarch in captivity, within his own beautiful castle, once the scene of domestic enjoyment, guarded by sentinels pacing under the very gateway at the end of the terrace which he had himself built, is a truly mournful and touching spectacle ; and even those who may feel disposed to condemn him as a mistaken and despotic monarch, may surely spare him their pity as a suffering man. Sad, but few, were the days that passed over him while a prisoner in the castle. On the 19th of

January, he was removed to St. James's Palace, whence, on
the memorable morning of the 30th, he was conducted to
Whitehall, there to close on the scaffold his melancholy
career.* Conducted from Windsor a prisoner, he was
brought back a dishonoured corpse. Amongst accounts of
his interment, a copy of an old MS., given in the forty-
second volume of the "Gentleman's Magazine," relates
some incidents not generally known. "Wednesday, the 7th
of February, 1648, the corpse being brought to Windsor Castle
in a hearse, by Mr. Murray, the king's coachman, accompanied with the Dukes of Richmond and Lennox, the Marquis
of Hartford, the Earl of Lindsay, the Earl of Southampton,
and Bishop Juxon, and being placed in the dean's hall, the
aforesaid lords sent for a plumber to open the coffin [and
lead]. Thus being fully satisfied it was the king, his head
was sewed to his body. They gave orders to the plumber
to cast a piece of lead some two feet long, with this inscription—' This is King Charles I., 1648,' and solder the lead
across the roof of the coffin. This being done, the coffin
was nailed up, and remained two days in the hall, being
darkened with a velvet pall, and two lighted tapers upon
the coffin. After which time the corpse was carried by two
soldiers of the garrison into the chapel, the lords above-
named bearing the pall ; Bishop Juxon and the governor
of the castle, whose name was Whitcot, and the officers of

---

* Particular mention is made by Ashmole of the garter which
Charles wore on the day of his execution.—" It had the letters of the
motto composed likewise of diamonds, which amounted to the number
of four hundred and twelve. It came to the hands of Captain Preston
(one of the usurper's captains), from whom the trustees for the sale
of the king's goods received it, and sold it to Ireton (sometime Lord
Mayor of London), for £205. But after the Restoration, the king's
attorney-general proceeding upon an action of trover and conversion,
verdict was given for the king against him for £205, and £10 costs
of suit."—" History of the Order of the Garter," 8vo. p. 157.

the garrison, with others, following the corpse ; which corpse, with the velvet pall, was placed upon two trussels, in a vault in the middle of the choir, by King Henry VIII. and Queen Jane. The governor commanded some of his officers to see the workmen close up the vault. The governor would not suffer the bishop to bury the king after the Church of England manner, neither would the lords allow of his way. There was, therefore, nothing read at his grave, though the bishop's lips were observed to move. They were all full of tears and sorrow. The soldiers had twelvepence a-piece for carrying the corpse to the grave."

Fuller, in his " Church History," gives a long account of the circumstances connected with the selection of a grave for the royal corpse. He says that a grave was dug on the south side of the communion table, in St. George's chapel ; but that the Duke of Richmond, who was commissioned by the Parliament to superintend the funeral, with a charge that it should not exceed £500 in expense, and the other lords already mentioned, on coming to Windsor, resolved that he should not be interred there, but in a vault, as became his dignity, if the chapel afforded one. After seeking one in Wolsey's chapel, then used as a magazine, where they found all was solid earth, they tried the choir, to see whether a hollow sound would be produced, indicative of the existence of a vault, and were at last directed, by one of the aged poor knights, to a vault which was situated in the middle of the choir. On entering it, they found it not more than five feet high, and very dark ; in the midst of which they dimly discerned a large coffin, and a far less one on the left side of it. These, for various reasons stated, they concluded to belong to Henry VIII. and Jane Seymour. The lead coffin which enclosed the body of Henry VIII. being very thin, was casually broken, and some yellow matter, like powder of gold, taken out : this was quite scentless, and was probably the gum employed in embalming; it was put back again, and the coffin closed up. Herbert, in the interesting description of the royal funeral, as given by Wood, in his "Athenæ Oxonienses," is less circumstantial on these points, but adds a touching incident, not elsewhere recorded. "When the hour of interment arrived, the king's body, having been brought from his bed-chamber,* was conveyed, with a slow and solemn pace, to the chapel; when first brought out, the sky was serene and clear, but presently it began to snow, and the snow fell so fast, that by the time the corpse had reached the west end of the chapel, the black pall was all white;"—a circumstance which this honest royalist interprets as an emblem of his sovereign's innocence, and which, apart from such interpretation, forms an affecting incident at the close of the fatal tragedy. That humble procession, so different from the pompous one which conveyed Henry VIII. to his grave, pacing along the courts of the castle in the snow-storm till the pall was whitened, would form a subject not unworthy of the artist's pencil; nor, one would think, could the republican, any more than the royalist, suppress a sigh, on looking at that melancholy spectacle of fallen and dishonoured majesty.

After such minute accounts of Charles's funeral, it seems strange indeed that any doubt should have been entertained respecting his being actually interred in St. George's Chapel; yet such doubts were entertained. Some idle tale was told after the Restoration, to the effect that the body had been disinterred by the republicans, and buried at Tyburn; but the chief authority on which any doubt could rest, was the statement of Lord Clarendon, that search was

---

* This differs from the account in the MS. before quoted, where the body is said to have been placed in the dean's hall. Most likely Herbert is correct.

made for the royal remains, in order to their being re-
interred with honour ; but, after much fruitless examination in the choir of the chapel to find the vault, the
task was given up as impracticable. This is certainly
one of the most extraordinary accounts ever heard. If
the distinguished persons employed by Charles II.
to discover the place of his father's sepulchre found any
difficulty in doing so, they were the only persons who ever
did. Fuller published his " Church History" in 1655,
many years before the search was made, and gave
a particular account of Charles's grave. Herbert's narrative could easily have been consulted ; and no doubt
there were persons about the castle fully aware of the spot
where the king was interred. Ashmole, in his " History
of the Order of the Garter," published 1672, accurately
describes it ; Evelyn, in his " Diary," does the same ;* and,
from a MS. in the dean and canons' library, it appears,
that in 1686 the coffin of King Charles I. was found, lying
on wooden tressels on the south side of Henry VIII.'s
vault, in a fresh and sound state, covered with a velvet
pall, and with a plate on the coffin, inscribed " King
Charles." A mystery rests over the transaction, unless
it be supposed that the alleged impossibility of discovering
the grave was merely a pretext to enable the son to spend,
in a way more to his own satisfaction, the money voted

---

* " 1654, 8th June.—My wife and I set out in a coach and four
horses, in our way to visit relations of hers in Wiltshire and other
parts. We dined at Windsor, and saw the castle and the chapel of
St. George, where they have laid our blessed martyr, King Charles,
in *the vault just before the altar.* The church and workmanship in
stone is admirable. The castle itself is large in circumference, but
the rooms melancholy and of ancient magnificence. The keep or
mount has, besides its incomparable prospect, a profound well ; and
the terrace towards Eton, with the park, meandering Thames, and
sweet meadows, yield one of the most delightful prospects."—
Evelyn's " Memoirs," vol. i. p. 267.

by the Parliament for funeral rites in honour of his father.

But though so complete were the proofs that Charles was buried in St. George's Chapel, doubts still lingered in some minds : these were finally dissipated by the discovery of the coffin in 1813, and the examination of the remains by Sir Henry Halford.   He published, as is well known, an interesting account of the appearance of the corpse, of which we have received confirmation from an aged relative, who saw it immediately after the examination had taken place.   The oval face, the pointed beard, and the remains of the features, were sufficient to identify them as the original of Vandyke's fine pictures of the monarch ; and the evident severance of the vertebræ of the neck by some sharp instrument, completed the evidence of its being the corpse of the unhappy Charles.*

During the Commonwealth, some of Charles's faithful cavaliers were imprisoned in the castle, and occupied the rooms over the Norman gateway ; and, perhaps, from their prison window saw the mournful procession of the monarch's funeral in that memorable snow-storm.   One of them, Sir Edmund Fortescue, has left an inscription on the wall, dated so early as 1642, and therefore must have been taken prisoner in one of the first battles between Charles and the Parliament ; and some others, who seem to have been taken prisoners in South Wales, after the victorious battle of St.

---

* I find that in the journals of the House of Lords there is the following entry.   "Monday, July 23rd :—Mr. Rushworth was called in, and the Speaker, by directions of the House, asked him what he knew of a meeting at the ' Bear,' on the bridge foot, Windsor, or any other place, concerning the contrivance of the king's death. Mr. Rushworth said that scout-master Watson told him that some officers of the Army at Windsor did speak about trying of the king, and were of opinion that if the Army did desire the same of Parliament, that the Parliament would not deny it."

Fagons, and who forfeited their estates, and probably lingered here in captivity till released by death or the restoration of Charles II., have also left the memorials of their imprisonment carved on the walls, and dated 1648.

Among the distinguished persons who suffered in the service of Charles was the Marquis of Worcester, who is buried in St. George's Chapel. At the time of his valorous defence of his royal master's cause he was eighty years of age, but displayed all the ardour of a youthful volunteer. He is described as being equally distinguished by courage and wit, and is said to have retained both to the close of life. It appears, too, that his eccentricity was as great as either, for Granger relates,* that he was remarkable for the singularity of wearing a frieze coat, in which he was always dressed when he went to court. He died in custody of the officers of the black rod, being a prisoner of the Parliament, in December, 1647, in the eighty-fourth year of his age.

We have glimpses of Cromwell at Windsor. "We did meet at Windsor Castle," says Adjutant-General Allen, "about the beginning of 1648. There we spent one day together in prayer, inquiring into the causes of that sad dispensation (the advancing of the Scotch army), coming to no further result that day but that it was still our duty to seek. And on the morrow we met again in the morning, when many spake from the Word, and prayed ; and the then Lieut.-General Cromwell did press earnestly on those present a thorough consideration of our actions as an army, and of our ways particularly as private Christians."

During the Commonwealth, Windsor Castle was in the possession of Oliver Cromwell. The Parliament determined upon selling it, to replenish the resources for national pur-

* "Biographical History of England," vol. ii. p. 126.

poses,* but the measure was never carried into effect, and the protector often made the venerable structure the place of his residence. We connect it with his name, and remember that here did his vigorous mind often revolve those plans of policy which, whatever may be thought of the Commonwealth, raised England to a point of greatness in the estimation of foreign nations, which commanded their respect; and here did he display, as a husband, a father, and a man, those domestic virtues which his bitterest enemies cannot deny that he possessed, and which fully placed him on a level, as to private character, with the monarch whose throne he occupied. Perhaps, too, here sometimes occurred the circumstance of his visiting twice a-day the apartments of his venerable mother, who lived with him, to give her ocular demonstration that her son "Noll," whom she loved and was proud of, was still alive; for the old lady was in constant fear for him, and thought every pistol that was discharged was aimed at him.

Though he made no improvements nor additions to the castle, it is but justice, says Mr. Poynter, to believe that he prevented all spoliation of the royal property after it came into his possession. "He certainly kept together the endowments of the college, and the landed estates were improved in value during his administration. He instituted a regular establishment for the service of the chapel, and attached it to the foundation of the poor knights, which he maintained, and issued an ordinance of twelve articles for its regulation." †

* "Saturday, November 27.—The house sat again, and concluded that sale be made of Hampton Court House and Park, Greenwich House and Park, Windsor and Hyde Park, for supply of the navy." —Proceedings in Parliament from Thursday the 25th of November, to Thursday the 2nd of December, 1652,—"King's Pamphlets," vol. 549; British Museum.

† Introduction to "Illustrations of Windsor Castle."

It may be observed that the houses of the military
knights, called Crane's Buildings, were erected during the
Commonwealth, by Sir Francis Crane, to whom Sir Peter
le Maire, his brother-in-law, had bequeathed the sum of
£1700, in trust, to be disposed of in a charitable manner,
according to his discretion.

By an ordinance, dated the 5th of April, 1655, Lord
Commissioner Whitelock, and many others, including the
mayor and aldermen of Windsor, were appointed trustees
and governors of the almshouses of Windsor Castle, to rule
and govern them, according to the statutes found among
the statutes of the late dean and canons of Windsor. They
were to appoint the knights, with the recommendation,
approbation, or consent of the Lord Protector. Sir Francis
Crane's establishment was subjected to the same regulations.*

The restoration opens a new era in the history of the
castle. The following extract from a MS. by Matthew
Day, an inhabitant of Windsor, gives a lively idea of the
ceremony of the proclamation :—" King Charles II. was
proclaimed King of England, Scotland, France, and Ireland,
upon the 12th of May, 1660, at the round market house
in New Windsor ; at which time the troop of the county
horse was in the town ; and Mr. Gallant, an innkeeper,

* The following were the orders appointed by Oliver Cromwell
for St. George's Chapel :—" To the preacher, yearly, £100 ; to the
weekly lecturer, £10 ; to four poor scholars, £80 ; to the poor of
Windsor, £100 ; to the poor knights, £40 a-piece per annum, out of
which they were to buy a gown every two years, of four yards of
cloth, at 13s. 4d. per yard, with boys of the same colour, at 24d. per
yard."—Huggett MSS. in the Sloane Collection. The collector of these
papers, who was a minor canon of Windsor, compares the value of
the college property in the reign of Elizabeth with its value in the
time of Cromwell. He shows that what was valued at £661 6s. 8d.
per annum, in the former period, was worth £4430 0s. 11d. in the
latter.—MSS. vol. ii. p. 164.

being Major, was there attended with his company in their gowns, who had a trumpeter sounding a trumpet before them ; and from thence went to Windsor Bridge, and from thence went to the Castle Gate, and there with the troop of horse and trumpet did likewise proclaim the king ; and was desired by the officers that were in the castle to come into the castle, and there proclaim King Charles II. in the castle, which was also there also proclaimed with great joy."* This joy, however, must have been dashed in the case of certain poor people, who, during the Commonwealth, had lived in various parts of the castle, for they were of course now dismissed. The ejected tenants were thrown on the town, whereupon the mayor and corporation presented a petition to the House of Commons, who " referred to the Justices of the Peace to take care of the poor women and children who are commanded out of the castle of New Windsor, to dispose of the said women and children according to law."†

There were others removed from comfortable berths, with very much more difficulty. Viscount Mordaunt, who was appointed Constable of the Castle, in a letter preserved among the State papers, complains that Cromwell's poor knights are insolent, that they refuse commands, will not remove, and have been tampering with the soldiers. He wonders that any should interpose in their behalf, and begs one of the vacant places for Colonel Hastings, his kinsman. Other petitions for admission as poor knights at that time are preserved. For example, from one John Whitton, who was in arms for the late king, and his father, as Comptroller of Woodstock, and had laid out on the park money which should have been kept for his children : and from a Captain

---

E. Leyton, who had served in the late wars, and was old and sickly. Among the State papers there are documents relating to the Windsor poor knights, which afford interesting illustrations of the period. Under date, March, 1661, is a " Petition of Thomas Freebody, to the king, for licence to follow his business at London and elsewhere, on attendance as a poor knight of Windsor of Sir Francis Crane's foundation, at Christmas, Easter, and Whitsuntide. Is scarcely able to walk out of the castle, so that his affairs are neglected, and his place rather a loss than a benefit." Of about the same date also is a " Petition of George Barbor, Thomas Freebody, and William Cwome, to the king, for continuance of the places bestowed on them as poor knights of Windsor, for which they have purchased robes, recovered the profits, &c., but from which the Dean threatens to dismiss them, as being unduly elected, and married men, though his majesty has granted them a dispensation, and they are on Sir Francis Crane's foundation, which has no injunction against marriage." Along with these we find a " Petition of the poor knights of Windsor, to the king, for confirmation of their places at the chapter of the Garter to be next held. These are installed by the dean and chapter, and have been at great expense in furnishing their houses since their admission."

To go beyond these struggles for getting or keeping the place of poor knights, we find in the same valuable collection of papers, that one George Drake, an inhabitant of Windsor, applied for office of secretary to the intended council for trade, on the ground of his sufferings in the royal cause, having been imprisoned in London, and kept on " pump water and pottage," till April, 1647, when he was turned out half dead and naked into Lambeth fields. He states that he returned to Windsor, and engaged in a design, which was long continued, to surprise the castle for the king, had spies in Cromwell's council, and spent large sums on intelligence, and holding correspondence with his majesty and his friends.

But we must conclude these extracts, which might easily be multiplied, with "a petition," dated November 15, 1660, of thirty-eight innholders, victuallers, &c., of New Windsor, to Parliament, for redress. They state that they have paid their taxes for the disbanding of the army, expecting to be freed from the quartering of soldiers, but three hundred lately enlisted for Windsor Castle are quartered upon them, even a dozen in a house, to whom they have to lend sixpence a day, and allow fire, candle, dressing of food, and lodging, so that they have few or no spare rooms, and the incumbrance will be their ruin. In connexion with this we may remark that the resumption of crown rights after the Commonwealth must have entailed much individual hardship, of which we have here an example:— "Edward Scotton and three others apply for relief, inasmuch as being purchasers of land in Windsor Great Park, upon the improvement of which they have spent large sums, the corn, hay, grass, and wood now growing on the same land are claimed for his majesty."

Viscount Mordaunt, on taking possession of his new office as constable, must have found the building in a state of strange confusion, for there still exists amongst the State papers, under date of March 25, 1662, a warrant to Lord Chamberlain Manchester, that so long as the apartments belonging rightfully to John Viscount Mordaunt, as Constable of Windsor Castle, are taken up for preservation of the magazines, a kitchen, buttery cellar, dining-room, and four chambers, at the east end of the castle, be repaired, and set apart for him, his attendance being absolutely necessary as often as the king repairs there.*

* These illustrations are gleaned from the " Calendar of Domestic

The Order of the Garter was restored upon Charles' accession to the throne. Chapters indeed had been held abroad during the Commonwealth, and knights had been elected ; and the day after the royal landing at Dover, there was a chapter at Canterbury, when General Monk and Admiral Montague were declared companions. A grand feast was celebrated at Windsor in 1662, when, according to Ashmole, " the knights-elect were constrained to receive their investiture below in the choir, yet directly under their proper stalls, because of the great concourse of people which at that time had flocked to Windsor (greedy to behold the glory of that solemnity which for many years had been intermitted), and rudely forced not only into and filled the lower row of stalls, but taken up almost the whole choir." He also adds the interesting information that for this occasion there was an anthem then composed and sung to the music of an organ placed in an organ loft, and "this was the first time that instrumental music was introduced into the said chapel."

In the " Diary " of Pepys, the celebrated secretary of the Admiralty in the reigns of Charles II. and James II., and president of the Royal Society, there are numerous allusions to Windsor. This singular person, who with such exquisite *naïveté*, relates the current rumours of the court, and the most trifling incidents in his own personal and domestic history, down to the wearing of a new coat, and the proceedings of his maid-servants, dwells at considerable length upon his visits to Windsor and the neighbourhood. The following extract, relating to an early part of the reign of Charles II., details in a characteristic and amusing style the incidents of one of Pepys' journeys to Windsor,

State Papers, 1660—1661, and 1661—1662 ;" edited by Mrs. Green.

and a minute account of a visit he paid to St. George's Chapel and Eton College. The reader will excuse the characteristic diffuseness of the worthy gossip, and allow him to tell his stories in his own way :—

"February 26th, 1666.—Called up about five in the morning, and my Lord up, and took leave, a little after six, very kindly of me and the whole company. So took coach and to Windsor, to the Garter, and thither sent for Dr. Childe, who come to us, and carried us to St. George's Chapel, and there placed us among the knights' stalls (and pretty the observation, that no man, but a woman, may sit in a knight's place, where any brass-plates are set) ; and hither come cushions to us, and a young singing-boy, to bring us a copy of the anthem to be sung. And here, for our sakes, had this anthem and the great service sung extraordinary, only to entertain us. It is a noble place, indeed, and a good quire of voices. Great bowing by all the people, the poor knights in particular, to the altar. After prayers, we to see the plate of the chapel, and the robes of knights, and a man to show us the banners of the several knights in being, which hang up over the stalls. And so to other discourse, very pretty, about the order. Was shown where the late king is buried, and King Henry VIII., and my Lady Seymour. This being done, to the king's house, and to observe the neatness and contrivance of the house and gates ; it is the most romantique castle that is in the world. But, Lord ! the prospect that is in the balcone in the queene's lodgings, and the terrace and walk, are strange things to consider, being the best in the world, sure ; and so, giving a great deal of money to this and that man and woman, we to our tavern, and there dined, the doctor with us ; and so took coach and away to Eton, the doctor with me. At Eton I left my wife in the coach, and he and I to the college, and there find all

mighty fine. The school good, and the custom pretty of
boys cutting their names in the shuts of the window when
they go to Cambridge, by which many a one hath lived to
see himself a provost and fellowe, that hath his name in the
window standing. To the hall, and there find the boys'
verses, 'De Peste,' it being their custom to make verses
at Shrove-tide. I read several, and very good they were;
better, I think, than ever I made when I was a boy, and
in rolls, as long, and longer than the whole hall, by much.
Here is a picture of Venice hung up, and a monument
made of Sir H. Wotton's giving it to the College. Thence
to the porter's, in the absence of the butler, and did drink
of the college beer, which is very good; and went into
the back fields to see the scholars play. And so to
the chapel, and there saw, among other things, Sir H.
Wotton's stone, with this epitaph :—

> 'Hic jacet primus hujus sententiæ Author:
> Disputandi pruritus fit ecclesiæ scabies.'

But, unfortunately, the word 'Author' was wrong writ,
and now so basely altered that it disgraces the stone."

Upon the restoration of Charles II., Windsor Castle
became his summer residence. He effected those extensive alterations which totally changed the character of the
building, and gave it the appearance it retained till the
reign of George IV. The precise period when these alterations were made cannot now be ascertained, as the papers
relating to them are missing; but from the following passage,
in the "Diary" of Evelyn, it would appear to have been
about the year 1670 :—

"August 28th, 1670.—Windsor was now going to be
repaired, being exceeding ragged and ruinous. Prince
Rupert, the constable, had begun to trim up the keep, or
high round tower, and handsomely adorned his hall with

furniture of arms, which was very singular, by so disposing the pikes, muskets, pistols, bandoliers, holsters, drums, back, breast, and head pieces, as was very extraordinary. Thus those huge steep stairs, ascending to it, had the walls invested with this martial furniture, all new and bright, so disposing the bandoliers, holsters, and drums, as to represent festoons, and that without any confusion, trophy-like. From the hall we went into his bedchamber, and ample rooms hung with tapestry, curious and effeminate pictures, extremely different from the other, which presented nothing but war and horror." He adds :—"The king passed most of his time in hunting the stag, and walking in the park, which he was now planting with rows of trees." *

Charles II., having been entertained for some time, during his exile, at the splendid court of Louis XIV., had imbibed a thorough taste for that gorgeous magnificence in building and decoration, which distinguished the palace of the *Grand Monarque;* and, therefore, on his return to the castle of his fathers, he determined to re-fashion and adorn it according to the models which had inspired his admiration. Sir Christopher Wren was appointed to superintend the alterations, and, under the hand of that famous architect, the fine old Gothic structure of Edward III. was transmuted into an incongruous imitation of the palatial architecture of the Continent. As regarded the exterior of the edifice, its appearance was rendered exceedingly mean and untasteful. A new building was added in the middle of the north side, called the Star Building, from its exhibiting a large star in front ; and this, together with the whole of the external walls, extending from it to the Devil's Tower, on the south side, was made to present a mere flat surface of

* "Memoirs," vol. i. p. 409.

stone-work, with towers pared down to an insipid outline, and mean circular-headed windows, some of which exhibited a strange attempt at composition, being divided across the middle by a balustrade. It has been well remarked, that because the architect could not *Italianise* the whole castle, and would not *Gothicise* his own building, he devised the unhappy expedient of obliterating all architectural style whatever. The interior, it must be acknowledged, was far different, though out of all keeping with that indelible character of a fortress which belonged to the castle. A suite of seventeen rooms on the principal floor, with a grand staircase of dimensions and proportions truly palatial, extended round the north wing, from the building erected by Henry VII. to the tower at the corner of the quadrangle, called King John's Tower.* The ceilings, by Verrio, of which a few remain, were among their characteristic ornaments.†

Among the alterations made in the reign of Charles II. we may particularly notice the new facing of the north terrace with stone, the extension of the walk round the

---

* Introduction to "Illustrations of Windsor Castle."

† "Antonio Verrio, a Neapolitan, was an artist of more invention than taste, and of greater expedition than correctness. His pompous staircases and his ceilings are popularly esteemed the greatest ornaments of our villas and palaces. He excelled in painting marble steps and columns, which he took care to introduce on every occasion."—Granger's "Biographical History," vol. iv. p. 114.

"There is a curious anecdote of this artist related by Lord Orford, namely, that while Verrio was employed at Windsor, he quarrelled with Mrs. Marriott, the housekeeper (whose portrait is now at Hampton Court), and borrowed her ugly face for one of the furies, in order to gratify his personal pique. To flatter the court, he represented Lord Shaftesbury among the demons of faction, distributing libels. There is a study for a proposed ceiling by Verrio, in which he introduced Sir Godfrey Kneller, Mr. May, surveyor of the works, and himself, in long periwigs, as spectators of our Saviour healing the sick. The sketch is at Hampton Court." —Mr. Jesse's "Summer's Day at Windsor," p. 120.

east and south sides of the castle, and the construction of
an engine for supplying the royal establishment with water.
The following curious account of the latter is found in
the "London Gazette," of the 4th of August, 1681 :—
" Windsor, July 30th.—This evening the King, Queen,
and Prince of Orange, being attended by divers foreign
ambassadors, and other persons of eminent quality, and not
a few of the English nobility, together with a numerous
train of near one thousand persons, returning from the
park, Sir Samuel Morland, with the strength of eight men,
forced the water (mingled with a vessel of red wine, to
make it more visible), in a continual stream, at the rate of
above sixty barrels an hour, from the engine below at the
park-pale, up to the top of the castle, and from thence into
the air, above sixty foot high, to the great admiration of
their majesties, and all the beholders, as well foreigners
as others ; who unanimously concluded, that this was the
boldest and most extraordinary experiment that has ever
been performed by water in any part of the world. On
Monday morning the King and the Prince of Orange saw
the said engine (wrought only by two men), force the water
from below, through the leaden pipe, in a full stream,
above the top of the castle."

Evelyn's " Diary" gives glimpses of Windsor at different
periods of Charles' reign, just before and after these alterations took place. He was at Windsor in 1670, when he
tells us that the castle was "ragged and ruinous," but
"going to be repaired." Rupert had begun to trim up the
keep, and handsomely adorn the hall with "furniture of
arms, which was very singular, by so disposing the pikes,
muskets, pistols, bandoleers, holsters, drums, back, breast,
and head pieces, as was very extraordinary." " From the
halls," adds the visitor, " we went into his bedchamber, and
ample rooms hung with tapestry, curious and effeminate

pictures, so extremely different from the other, which presented nothing but war and horror." The same worthy chronicler of passing events tells us in August, 1674, that in one of the meadows at the foot of the long terrace below the castle, works were thrown up to show the king a representation of the city of Maestricht, newly taken from the French. There was a mimic siege performed for the entertainment of his majesty, approaches made, trenches opened, batteries raised, counterscarp and ravelin taken after a stout defence. " In short," says Evelyn, " all the circumstances of a formal siege to appearance, and what is most strange, all without disorder or ill accident, to the great satisfaction of a thousand spectators." Part of the exhibition was at night. And he " went with Mr. Pepys back to London, where they arrived about three in the morning."

He paid Windsor a visit soon after the alterations and improvements had been made, and he shows the high admiration in which Verrio's productions were held by the connoisseurs of the day :—" May 16th, 1683. —I went to Windsor, dining by the way at Chiswick. That which was new at Windsor since I was last there, and was surprising to me, was that incomparable fresco painting in St. George's Hall, representing the legend of St. George, and triumph of the Black Prince, and his reception by Edward III., the roof not totally finished ; then the Resurrection, in the chapel, where the figure of the Ascension is, in my opinion, comparable to any paintings of the Roman masters : the Last Supper, over the altar. I liked the contrivance of the unseen organ, behind the altar ; nor less, the stupendous, and beyond all description, the incomparable carving of our Gibbons, who is, without controversy, the greatest master, both for invention and rareness of work, that the world ever had in any age, nor

doubt I at all that he will prove as great a master in the
statuary art.   Verrio's invention is admirable, his ordnance
full and flowing, antique and heroical ; his figures move ;
and, if the walls hold (which is the only doubt, by reason
of the salts, which in time, and in this moist climate, prejudice), the work will preserve his name to ages.   There
was now the terrace brought almost round the old castle ;
the grass made clean, even, and curiously turfed ; the
avenues to the new park, and other walks, planted with
elms and limes ; and a pretty canal, and receptacle for
fowl : not less observable and famous is the throwing so
huge a quantity of excellent water to the enormous height
of the castle, for the use of the whole house, being an extraordinary invention, by Sir Samuel Morland."

The castle, completely transformed by the gay monarch,
and furnished with the luxurious grandeur of French and
Italian taste, was the favourite residence of Charles, and
the scene of many a revel.   A theatre was fitted up within
its walls, and accommodated to the use of the French come-
dians ; and there, and in the ball-rooms, and other apartments, the dissolute monarch, surrounded by his courtiers
and courtezans, exhibited those spectacles of licentiousness
and dissipation, which every virtuous historian has condemned, and over which we must, in the present volume,
draw a veil.

There is an anecdote told of Charles, in connection with
Windsor, which shows, that though he was so depraved,
there were those around him who were disposed to go to
lengths of wickedness, from the thought of which even he
recoiled.   The queen of Charles is well known to have
been neglected and despised by her husband.   He longed
for her death or removal, and the infamous Buckingham
proposed a plan for gratifying his master.   The king and
his consort were accustomed to divert themselves by run-

ning about the streets of Windsor, disguised in masks, and entering the houses of the inhabitants, whom they disturbed by their wild and unprincely extravagances. Buckingham suggested that, on one of these occasions, her majesty should be seized and sent off to some colonial plantation, and that a report should be spread to the effect that she had deserted her husband, on which ground a divorce might be obtained. Charles was not, after all, so heartless as to assent to this barbarous plan, and declared that it would be a wicked thing to make a poor lady so miserable, only because she was his wife, and had no family.

A man, however, who could run masked about the streets, and play tricks with his subjects, was utterly unfitted for the throne ; and just was the reproof once conveyed to him by Killigrew, who, dressing himself in a pilgrim's habit, accosted the monarch, telling him that he hated himself and the world, and asking his royal permission for a visit to the lower regions. " For what are you going ?" asked Charles. " May it please your majesty," said he, " I am going to speak to the devil to send Oliver Cromwell to take care of the English government, as I have observed with regret, that his successor is always employed on other business."* The admonition was pertinent, while the terms in which it was conveyed, present a specimen of

---

* Sir Thomas Killigrew was page of honour to Charles I., and gentleman of the bed-chamber to Charles II. Granger refers to a portrait of him dressed like a pilgrim, with these verses inscribed :—

" You see my face, and if you'd know my mind,
'Tis this, I hate myself and all mankind."

The portrait seems to allude to the anecdote given above. There is a picture of Killigrew in the Vandyke Gallery, in Windsor Castle, painted by that admirable master.

K

that habit of profane allusion to the most awful subjects
which so generally prevailed among the wits of Charles's
court.

The name of the beautiful Eleanor Gwyn, one of
the chief favourites of Charles II., is especially associated with Windsor. The licentious monarch provided
her a residence near the castle, situated on the spot now
called the Queen's Mews. The house was styled Burford
House, and the only letter she is known to have written is
dated from it ; there, accompanied by some of the
kindred spirits whom he cherished in his court, Charles
spent many an hour in the society of this ex-orange girl
and actress, charmed by her beauty, and captivated by her
vivacity and wit.

During the reign of Charles II., the royal chapel had
remained in a neglected state, but early in the reign of his
successor, it was repaired and restored by Dr. Childe,
the organist. The following extract relative to this reparation is taken from a MS. in the dean and chapter's
library :—

" February 7th, A.D. 1686 and 1687.—This day the
area of the choir of St. George's Chapel began to be paved
with black and white marble, at the sole cost and charges
of William Childe, doctor in musick, and organist of the
chapel. At the breaking-up of the old pavement, we had
the curiosity to look into the vault in which King Henry
VIII. and his queen, the Lady Jane Seymour, are interred.
This vault lyeth in the middle of the choir ; and if you
stand on the lower *haut pas*, going up to the high altar,
and account three of the stalls of the Knights of the Garter,
and then place yourself in the middle of the choir, opposite to that stall, you shall stand exactly on the head of the
vault, which is about eight or nine feet square, encompassed
on all sides with brick-work, and a brick arch turned over

the top of it ; it is about seven or eight feet deep, neither is there any passage by steps or otherwise, as some do conjecture. On the north side lieth the body of the Lady Jane Seymour, and next to her the body of King Henry VIII., both of them lying in coffins of lead, and standing on wooden tressels ; these coffins, especially the queen's, are much broken and decayed, the lead being turned of a yellowish colour.* On the south side of the vault lieth the body of King Charles I., in a coffin of lead, and on wooden tressels, as the others : this coffin is very fresh and sound, it is covered with a purple coloured velvet pall, and on the middle of his coffin, over his breast, is fixed a plate, on which, in capital letters, embossed, are written, KING CHARLES."

Upon the death of King Charles II., his brother and successor on the throne carried on and completed the alterations in the castle, which were already so far advanced. Indeed little remained to be done beyond finishing the decorations of the ceilings, which was soon accomplished by the pencil of Verrio. He was also employed by James to paint the roof of Wolsey's Chapel in his usual allegorical style. It exhibited James in the robes of the Garter, seated on an arch, treading down a hydra; while Mars was introduced crushing Faction, Fury, and Rebellion. Juno and Peace were represented placing a crown on the monarch's head, attended by Plenty, who unfolded a scroll inscribed *"Concordia fratrum."* Jupiter was placed on the right hand with a group of figures, one of which held a crosier to represent the church; and Mercury was placed on the left, in the act of relating the glory of the monarch. Fame, too, was there, holding in one hand a medallion of Charles I.,

---

* The statements here with regard to the height of the vault and the appearance of the coffin are not correct.

and in the other a medallion of Charles II., a scroll being
exhibited over the head of the former, bearing the motto
"*Calamitas publica.*" To say nothing of the miserable taste
that is displayed in the introduction of this style of painting into a Gothic edifice, and in the monstrous combination
of mythological and Christian emblems in such a place, we
cannot but characterize as exceedingly contemptible the ingenuity with which the fawning artist endeavoured to glorify
his royal masters.

The object of the monarch in thus adorning the chapel
was that it might be employed for the purposes of Popish
worship, to which he was so notoriously attached.* Mass
was celebrated there, but the proceeding was so unpopular
that the Protestant inhabitants assembled around the place,
and expressed their intolerant indignation by demolishing
the windows and otherwise injuring the edifice. The circumstance reminds us of a similar incident in the life of
James's ancestress, Queen Mary of Scotland, who, when she
attempted to celebrate mass in her chapel of Holyrood House,
was assailed by a mob, which the lords were unable to
appease without great difficulty.†

Another circumstance occurred at Windsor in July, 1687,

* Evelyn repeatedly mentions the celebration of mass at
Windsor :—

"Sept. 6th, 1685.—Went to hear a Frenchman who preached
before the king and queen in that splendid chapel next St. George's
Hall. Their majesties going to mass, I withdrew to consider the
stupendous painting of the hall.

"July 11th, 1686.—Doctor Megot, Dean of Winchester, preached
before the household in St. George's Chapel at Windsor, the late
king's glorious chapel now seized on by the mass priests."—
"Memoirs," vol. ii. p. 569.

† Randolph wrote to Cecil, September 12th, 1561 :—"Her mass
is terrible in all men's eyes. The Erle of Cassilis said unto myself
that he wolde never here any moe. I know not yet what mischief
it may worke."

in connexion with the attempts of James II. to restore the dominion of the Papal Church in England. This was the public reception of the Pope's nuncio. D'Adda, who sustained that office, had hitherto been recognised simply as a private nobleman and layman of the Court of Rome. But now the king resolved that he should be publicly received in his papal character, and prepared for such public reception by first securing his consecration by three Romish bishops in the Chapel Royal at St. James's, as Archbishop of Amasia. On the same evening the king and the queen received him, habited in his archiepiscopal vestments, when they humbly sought and accepted on their knees his sacerdotal benediction. The Spanish ambassador, who has then present, warned James of the consequences that were likely to ensue from his thus allowing himself to be priest-ridden, when the infatuated monarch asked, "Is it not the usage in Spain that kings consult their confessors?" "Yes, sire," he replied; "and hence it is that our affairs go so badly."

The public reception of D'Adda, as papal nuncio, was fixed to take place at Windsor on the 3rd of July; and the Duke of Somerset received orders to be in attendance on the occasion to introduce the dignitary. He begged to be excused on the ground that compliance would bring him within the statute of treason. "Do you not know," said James, "that I am above the law?" "Your majesty may be," replied the duke, "but I am not." For this he was dismissed from court.

On the day appointed the nuncio publicly entered Windsor in great pomp and state, and was received at the castle by the Popish monarch with all marks of reverence—a scene altogether such as had not been witnessed in England for a hundred and fifty years. "Great multitudes," says Macaulay, "flocked to the little town. The visitors were so numerous that there was neither food nor lodging for them, and many persons of quality sat the whole day in their carriages waiting for the exhibition. At length, late in the afternoon, the knight-marshal's men appeared on horseback; then came a long train of running footmen, and then in a royal coach was seen Adda, robed in purple, with a brilliant cross on his breast. He was followed by the equipages of the principal courtiers and ministers of state. In his train the crowd recognised with disgust the arms and liveries of Crewe, Bishop of Durham, and of Cartwright, Bishop of Chester."

Windsor soon afterwards became the scene of far different movements. The unconstitutional proceedings of James having led to the invitation of William, Prince of Orange, to come over to England preparatory to the crisis of the Revolution, the latter, after having remained for a short time at Henley, removed with his court to Windsor, where those councils were held which terminated in his accession to the English throne.

Whitehall, where the lords in the confidence of James assembled, and Windsor, which was the head-quarters of William and his council, became now the great central points around which were clustered the sympathies, the hopes, and the interests of the two parties into which the nation was divided. Were the old walls of the castle endowed with memory and speech, what revelations could they make respecting the anxious hours of debate which were spent there at that memorable period ! We fancy that we can see the council sitting round the board in deep deliberation; that we can witness the stir occasioned throughout the place by the arrival of messengers bearing tidings respecting the movements of James, or conveying despatches of importance to the prince; and that we can detect the alternating feelings of hope and fear depicted in the countenances of the whole party, as the various intelligence is announced in relation to the stirring affairs of the time.

It was at Windsor Castle that the blow was struck which removed the king. The following message was there prepared, and immediately despatched to Whitehall, to be delivered to the foolish monarch :—

" We desire you, the Lord Marquis of Halifax, the Earl of Shrewsbury, and the Lord Delamere, to tell the King, that it is thought convenient, for the greater quiet of the city, and for the greater safety of his person, that he do remove to Ham ; where he shall be attended by his guards, who shall be ready to preserve him from any disturbance.

"W., PRINCE OF ORANGE.

" Given at Windsor, the 17th of December, 1688."

On receiving this, James quitted Whitehall and repaired to Rochester, whence he soon after removed to France. The issue is familiar to every reader. James lost the throne—William ascended it.

Though the male Stuarts were driven for ever from the British throne, there are abundant mementoes of the family in their ancient abode. One of these—an equestrian statue of Charles II., placed on the west side of the quadrangle—is too conspicuous to be unobserved. The statue itself has been severely criticised, but the pedestal on which it stands has justly called forth the deepest admiration. It is of white marble, and, under the skilful hand of Grinling Gibbons, has been wrought into the most exquisite imitations of fruits, fish, and implements of shipping. This fine monument of art was raised, as the following inscription upon it testifies, at the expense of Tobias Rustat, a faithful servant of Charles II.:*—

> CAROLO SECUNDO.
> REGUM OPTIMO.
> DOMINO SUO CLEMENTISSIMO
> TOBIAS RUSTAT
> HANC EFFIGIEM HUMILIME,
> DEDIT ET DEDICAVIT,
> ANNO DOMINI MDCLXXX.

Tobias Rustat, who has thus identified his name with Windsor Castle, belonged to that estimable class of characters who, by the frugality of their personal habits, are enabled to perform acts of princely generosity. Though he held no higher situation than that of keeper of the palace of Hampton Court and yeoman of the robes, and possessed by no means a large fortune, it is stated that he gave away no less than £10,735 in benefactions before his death.† He contributed largely toward the erection of public edifices, particularly Saint Paul's Cathedral. Taking a deep interest in the prosperity of the Universities, he gave £1000 to the augmentation of thirteen fellowships at St. John's College at Oxford, and founded eight scholarships at Jesus College in Cambridge, for the orphans of poor clergymen. The blessing of Providence seems to have rested on this generous-hearted man, thus marking him out as a worthy example, for it is said in his epitaph that "he found the more he bestowed upon churches, hospitals, universities, and colleges,

---

* The bronze statue of Charles II. in the middle of the court of Chelsea Hospital was also raised at his expense.

† Granger's "Biographical History," vol. iii. p. 416. It is a mystery how he could come by so much money, for his salary during forty years was only £40 per annum: it was afterwards doubled. His epitaph says—"the greatest part of his estate he gathered by God's blessing, the king's favour, and his industry."

and upon poor widows of orthodox ministers, the more he had at the year's end; neither was he unmindful of his kindred and relations, in making them provisions out of what remained."* Evelyn speaks of him as a "very simple, ignorant, honest, and loyal creature;" but surely a man who had so large a heart, and whose life was distinguished by such munificent deeds deserves a higher eulogium.

* "Collectanea Cantabrigiensia," p. 145.

CHAPTER VII.

WILLIAM AND ANNE.

ILLIAM III. was only an occasional resident at Windsor. During his reign he was too much occupied in the pursuits of war and in the affairs of state to allow of his enjoying the tranquil retreats of the castle and its parks; yet he made some improvements in both, and projected others. He planted the Long Walk in the Home Park, by the path to Datchet, and built the boundary wall which formerly encompassed that part of the park; and in the introduction to the "Illustrations of Windsor Castle," there is an account of certain plans, which were at that time drawn by Sir Christopher Wren, for an alteration of the palace and the gardens. Among the few existing relics which belong to Windsor Castle in connexion with William III. is a paper, found among the records of that period, granting permission to a poor woman named Elizabeth Edwards to erect a shed in the gateway of the lower ward, that she might there pursue her avocation as a sempstress, since, as it is stated in the Earl Marshal's warrant, "by reason of great debt her husband had withdrawn, and herself had been deprived of her dwelling in Windsor, and having many children, she was willing, by her trade as sempstress and otherwise, to get maintenance for herself and children, that they might not be chargeable to the parish." The royal permission granted for this purpose is a trifling yet pleasing incident; and amidst the wars and intrigues of William's reign, we gratefully turn to look at this honest sempstress, plying her avocation beneath the arch of the old gateway, under the special protection of the stern and warlike monarch. The record of such little acts of kindness possesses a charm in the estimation of benevolent minds, the beauty of which will not be lost, even amidst the most splendid and imposing array of historical associations.

Queen Anne resided in a house on the Castle-hill during the reign of William III., and was often at Windsor Castle after her accession to the throne, and in her reign the great staircase was painted by Sir James Thornhill, and the double steps made in the centre of the east terrace. She laid out £40,000 in repairs, and planned a garden shown in Collier's map, but never completed. In 1707, she planted " the Queen's Walk." In 1710, the carriage-road was made through the Long Walk.

No reader of English history can fail to associate with the reign of Anne the name of Sarah, Duchess of Marlborough, whose history is also linked to the locality of Windsor by several interesting incidents. There, in her palmy days, she gave examples of the marvellous influence which she had acquired over her royal mistress, an influence which it has been well remarked, was the same as the sorcery which Leonora Galligai avowed to her judges over Mary de Medicis— " the power of a strong upon a weak mind." She was appointed by the queen ranger of Windsor Park, an appointment which she greatly valued, and had a residence there appropriated for her use, to which she was much attached. The lodge of the park, she remarks, was a very agreeable residence; and " Anne had remembered, in the days of their friendship, that the duchess, in riding by it, had often wished for such a place." The castle was the scene of many a visit from " Queen Sarah," as she was popularly called, till her influence was undermined by the intrigues of the famous Mrs. Masham, that singular personage in English history. Tradition reports, that it was while the duchess was sitting at tea with the queen, in a little room, now part of the library, whose windows overlook the north terrace, the tidings of the victory of Blenheim were brought to the castle. The note containing the intelligence, written by the duke upon a leaf torn from his memorandum-book, and addressed to his lady, is preserved among the archives of Blenheim. " I have not time," says the great general, " to say more, but to beg you will give my duty to the queen, and let her know that her army has had a glorious victory. M. Tallard and two other generals are in my coach, and I am following the rest. The bearer, my aide-de-camp, will give her an account of what has passed. I shall do it, in a day or two, by another, more at large." A memorial of the victory of Blenheim is still preserved in the guard chamber of the castle, where the attention of the visitor is particularly directed to the ancient standard of France, suspended over the bust of the hero ;—the standard is annually presented to the sovereign by the heir of his titles and domains, as the tenure on which he holds the magnificent estate at Woodstock.

After the retirement of the Duchess of Marlborough from court, and especially after the death of her husband, she spent a considerable portion of her time at the lodge in Windsor Park. Though she resigned the rest of her offices, she retained that of ranger, and therefore continued possessor of her favourite residence. It was while she was residing at Windsor that the hand of the illustrious duchess was solicited by Charles, Duke of Somerset. He was generally called the proud duke, being a man of most arrogant pretensions, and carrying his pride so far as to punish one of his daughters, by cutting off £20,000 from her fortune, for daring to sit down in his presence, a liberty which he never allowed his children to take. But great as might be his pretensions, they had no weight with the lady whose alliance he sought, and who gave him that memorable answer : " I deem a second marriage unsuitable to my age ; but were I addressed by the emperor of the world, I would not permit him to succeed to that heart which has been devoted to John, Duke of Marlborough." This un- dying attachment to her departed lord was a fine trait in her character, and shines with beautiful lustre amidst the assemblage of talents and eccentricities which distinguished her famous name. Of all affections, the love which sur- vives the tomb, and only lives on memory, is the purest and the brightest that can exist in the human bosom.

Other anecdotes of the Duchess of Marlborough, in con- nexion with Windsor, present her under a less amiable aspect, and illustrate the love of power and the imperious temper, which were so characteristic of this noble dame. She had a great dislike to Walpole, whom she continually annoyed by applications relating to repairs in the park ; but to the Duke of St. Albans, who was governor of Windsor Castle, and warden of the forest, she had a still greater aversion. " The duchess was outrageous when she saw the Duke of St. Albans coming into the park with coaches and chaises whenever he pleased, under pretence of supervising the fortifications, a term which she thought very ridiculous, unless he meant by it the ditch around the castle. No one, except the royal family or the ranger, had ever been allowed, during her experience of fifty years, such a liberty before. But that was not all the offence. The duchess in addressing her complaints to Pelham Holles, Duke of Newcastle, who had married her grand-daughter, Lady Harriet Godolphin, assured his grace that the Duke of St. Albans had, to use a military phrase, 'besieged her in both parks, and been willing to forage in them at pleasure.' Having got the better of him in some points, he had pursued her to the little park, and her only resource was to address her relative, then secretary of state, to intercede with the queen, that the intrusive warden might not be permitted to have a key. Which of the belligerent powers prevailed does not appear."*

Some little time after this, she was greatly annoyed at a matrimonial alliance formed by her grandson Charles, who succeeded to the dukedom of Marlborough. He married Lady Trevor, whom the duchess greatly disliked. She therefore banished them both from Windsor Lodge, and, to vent her spleen upon the unfortunate young lady, who, she said, had stripped the house and garden of all she could take, set up eight figures on the premises, to personate the eight Misses Trevor, cousins of the new duchess, representing them in a puppet-show, tearing up the shrubs, while the latter was portrayed carrying away a hencoop under her arm.†

Energetic and ambitious to the last, she contrived to arrange, not long before her death, a matrimonial alliance between her relative, Lady Diana Spencer, and Frederic, Prince of Wales, who were to be married at her lodge in Windsor Park ; but the match was broken off through the interference of Walpole, who felt a pleasure in thwarting her plans. The mighty Sarah's spirit was often chafed, in her latter days, by such annoyances, and by the repeated contentions in which she was engaged in relation

* Mrs. Thomson's " Life of the Duchess of Marlborough," vol. ii. p. 395.

† Mrs. Thomson relates this story on the authority of Walpole, but deems its truth somewhat questionable.—" Memoirs," vol. ii. p. 404.

to her office and claims as ranger of Windsor Park.
The peacefulness of the surrounding scene, with all its
beauty, could not tranquillize her tempestuous soul; nor
could her abundant wealth remove the infirmities of age
and disease which oppressed her frame. Her biographer
describes her at Windsor, as—"Wrapped up in flannels, and
carried about like a child, or wheeled up and down her
rooms in a chair."

CHAPTER VIII.

HOUSE OF HANOVER.

HE first two sovereigns of the House of Hanover resided at Hampton Court and Kensington; and we have scanty notice of their even visiting Windsor. The constables who resided at the castle in succession were the Duke of Kent, Lord Cobham, the Earl of Carlisle, the Duke of St. Albans, and the Earl of Cardigan. Strange to say, "Apartments to let" might have been written over the royal gates, for we are told by Pote, in his "History of Windsor," that many gentlemen and families of estate constantly resided either in the town or *in the lodgings* in the castle during the absence of the royal family.

Marshal Belleisle was the last state prisoner confined in the Round Tower, which seems to have been in a very dilapidated condition. In 1730, the roof was in danger of falling in; the next year the stairs were so ruinous as to be almost entirely useless. Matters continued getting worse, and in 1752 the great stones were falling from the curtain of the Round Tower, threatening to undermine the parapet wall. The sylvan beauties, however, of the royal domain continued as attractive as ever; and the little park is described by Pote, in 1749, "as most delightful for the many shady walks, especially that Queen Elizabeth's Walk, which on the summer evenings is chiefly frequented by the best company." Nor is there an entire absence of chivalric splendour in the Chapel of St. George during the dull reigns of that Saint's namesakes ; for in 1730 there was an installation, the king being present—the sword of state carried before him— procession formed in the aisle—trumpets sounding all the way to the stair foot that led to the royal presence chamber. It may be mentioned in contrast with this relic of an old age, that an odd difficulty occurred in connexion with certain circumstances indicative of a new era. America was grow- ing in prosperity, and certain tribute was paid to the Crown by the Penns of Pennsylvania. It consisted of two Indian arrows and two bearskins. The former had been sent every Easter, but the skins were a new expression of homage which puzzled John Olivier at Windsor Castle, who wrote to know of the Governor, Lord Cardigan, what he was to do with them, because they were *undressed*.

George III. was attached to Windsor, and made it his abode ; but as the castle was unsuited for his family, he determined to erect a detached building in the precincts, in which he might live with them in retirement, as a country gentleman, rather than as King of England. Accordingly, the Lodge, which stood opposite the south terrace, was completed in 1782, at a cost of £44,000. The history of George III. at Windsor was one of domestic quietude, until it was disturbed by quarrels with his son, and finally broken up by his own sad affliction. Often were the king and queen, the princes and princesses, seen walking in procession up and down the terraces, the people making way for them as they passed. The urbanity and condescen- sion of the monarch endeared him to the inhabitants of Windsor, and the younger branches of his family, imitating him in this respect, gained no small popularity. They would notice the children, even stop to kiss some pretty

L

baby, and on grand festivals at Frogmore, entertain the respectable tradespeople with an illumination, a banquet, and a dance. The king was familiar and kind towards his workpeople and servants, and would occasionally treat them to a little humour. We have heard several instances of this, but especially one. There was a porter or messenger who was apt to be very loud in repeating the responses at family worship in the chapel, which the king punctually attended. One day, after having made himself heard, this worthy missed his hat. Seeing him disconcerted, the king asked, "Eh, eh! what's the matter? what's the matter?" "I have lost my hat, please your majesty." "Eh, eh! you prayed well, but you didn't watch, you didn't watch," was the witty rejoinder. The well-known pages of Madame D'Arblay give graphic pictures of royal life at Windsor, in George III.'s reign; and it is very touching to read the account of his removal after his first attack in 1788; when, as he walked to his carriage, the passage was lined by the royal household, eager to see him once more; and all Windsor collected round the rails to witness his departure. All was joy on his return in 1789, when he entered the castle on horseback, attended by a large party of gentlemen. Everybody came out to meet him. The next day being Sunday, the king "renewed his public service at church, by taking the sacrament at eight o'clock." Then came renewed aberration, and scenes reminding one of his royal predecessor at Windsor, Henry VI. Blindness ensued; and, shut out from the world, he was carefully watched and tended in the Queen's Lodge, which now gathered round it a melancholy interest, as the retreat of a king who had endured so sad a dethronement.

The College for Naval Knights, connected with the castle, and situated at the foot of the terrace, near the South-Western Railway, was erected in the reign of George III.

The founder was Samuel Travers, Surveyor-General under William III., who, by his will dated the 16th July, 1724, bequeathed property for the support of some gentlemen, lieutenants of the English navy, "to be added to the eighteen poor knights of Windsor." The estates of Mr. Travers were thrown into Chancery, and it was not till the beginning of the present century that his benevolent project was accomplished ; when, by letters patent, the college was incorporated, soon after which the present structure was erected. The knights are forbidden to marry ; they have a common hall, with separate apartments ; and are required to attend divine service in St. George's Chapel. Lieutenant Holman, the celebrated blind traveller, who died a few years since, was a member of the College, and was enabled to indulge his spirit of enterprise by special permission of the trustees.

The reign of George IV. will ever be celebrated in connection with Windsor, for the rebuilding of the castle. Extensive repairs and restorations had been executed during the reign of his father in St. George's Chapel ; and the design of Charles I. to construct a royal sepulchre under the tomb house at the east end, had also been carried out, the superstructure being appropriated as a chapter house for the Knights of the Garter. But the grand work of rebuilding the *domus regis* did not begin till 1824 when a royal commission was appointed to execute the magnificent designs of Sir Jeffry Wyatville. The first stone was laid by George IV., on the 12th of August, 1824. The principal part of the works was completed in six years ; but the entire execution of the plan, including the erection of the royal stables, was not finished till 1838, after the accession of our present gracious sovereign. The entire cost has amounted to between £800,000 and £900,000.

TOWN.

CHAPTER I.

MEDIÆVAL WINDSOR.

HE first glimpse we have of the history of Windsor apart from the castle, is in the notice of a church, dedicated to John the Baptist, which was granted in 1189 to the Abbey of Waltham; originally it was a chapelry of Clewer.

By a charter of Edward I., granted in 1276, Windsor was constituted a borough, and appointed the county town of Berkshire. But so many inconveniences arose from its situation at one corner of the county, that the removal of the assizes to Reading was soon felt to be desirable. A petition to this effect was presented to the king in the year 1314, but Edward II., then occupying the throne, in the first instance gave a decided negative to the request, declaring that he would have the county gaol in no other castle than his own; an indication of the lingering spirit of feudalism in the royal breast. The original charter conceded, for the monarch and his heirs, that New Windsor should be a free borough; and that the worthy men of the town, and their heirs and successors, should be free

burgesses, should have a merchants' guild, and enjoy all
the liberties and customs granted to other boroughs. The
original burgesses were evidently the inhabitants of the
town, those who had settled dwellings and paid scot and
lot. Strangers—occasional residents—were not burgesses;
and since birth, apprenticeship, and marriage, were modes
of ascertaining stated residence, they generally constituted
a title to borough freedom.

All the stated inhabitants formed the community, corporation, or guild of merchants. No notice of a corporation,
consisting of mayor, bailiffs, and burgesses, distinct from
the bulk of the town, is to be found in any charter of
Windsor, prior to the reign of James I. Then we find the
appointment of the separate body. The original mayor, or
bailiff, was, no doubt, like other mayors of that time,
chosen by the whole body of the burgesses, or inhabitants.
The old Anglo-Saxon boroughs appear to have been free
institutions; but on the Norman invasion they lost their
primitive character, and the Norman bailiff, appointed by
the king, succeeded the Saxon boroughreeve elected by the
people. But the towns at length, impatient under the
yoke, panted for municipal liberty, and sighed after their
old institutions, offering to transmit to the royal exchequer
larger sums than the bailiff could obtain, if they made the
collection themselves, thus purchasing by a bribe the
privilege of self-regulation. The primary aim of the first
monarchs who granted charters was not the welfare of the
borough, but the increase of the revenue. The liberties of
the people, for the most part, flowed not from the spon-
taneous fountain of the royal bounty, nor were they even
won by the valour of barons and soldiers, but were purchased by merchants, who paid their wealth into the
exhausted coffers of the monarch, as the price of their
privileges and rights.

We find Windsor, in the thirtieth year of Edward I., returning two burgesses to parliament. Who the electors were in this and similar boroughs at that period, is a question of some obscurity, and has been frequently agitated. That a few of the inhabitants only exercised the franchise, may be readily granted ; but that they alone possessed the right is scarcely to be admitted. It is evident from the first charter of Windsor, that the whole body of the inhabitants formed the corporation of the town ; and the consent of the whole community is expressly stated in the election returns from many of the ancient boroughs. The power of returning members to parliament in those times, it is well known, was deemed in some cases rather a burden than a benefit, and towns were very often glad to shake it off as an incumbrance. In the list of returns from Windsor, none are inserted from the seventh of Edward II. to the twenty-fifth of Henry VI., a space of one hundred and thirty-three years. It is probable that during that period no returns took place, and the inhabitants perhaps considered themselves as thereby favoured with a most desirable exemption.

A Windsor election then, was far different from what it is now. No humble addresses were sent round to the electors by the aspirants after parliamentary honours. There was no indefatigable canvassing by the candidate, attended by a party of his friends and supporters. The returning officer of that day dreaded to receive a writ, from the difficulty there was in executing it. Slowly did a few of his neighbours obey the summons to meet around the market-cross. Anxiously did each man watch the countenances of the rest, and if one saw the eyes of his fellow-townsmen turn on him, with a glance indicating that he was to be put in nomination, it was as when the lot fell on Jonah to be thrown into the sea. Main force had sometimes to be exerted to keep " the man of their choice," " the gentleman whom they had placed in the proud position of one of their representatives," from rushing in haste out of the assembly to give them chase like a stag hunted by a pack of hounds. In some cases he would elude their pursuit, and either a new member was elected, or the disconcerted sheriff had to make a return of his inability to execute the writ. This indisposition of some of our ancestors to avail themselves of the elective franchise, or to serve in parliament, has been represented as if it proceeded from their confidence in the wisdom and justice of their superiors, and an unwillingness to take part themselves in the legislation of affairs. But the fact seems to be, that as parliaments in those early times possessed but little of a legislative character, and were summoned chiefly for the purpose of levying taxes, the people shrunk from a parliamentary election as from a prelude to a pecuniary burden, not considering how important it was that they should hold the strings of their own purse. But though some towns might be indifferent to the exercise of the elective franchise for members of parliament, they seem to have valued highly the privilege of municipal self-government, and to have esteemed their charters as extremely precious.*

The bridge that unites Windsor to Eton is noticed in early documents, whence it appears that the right of pontage or levying tolls was granted soon after the institution of the borough ; not only people passing over had to pay, but the boats passing under, too. The watermen sometimes complained of the erection. It was broken down by

* It was stated in the " Windsor Express," January 7th, 1854, " that the town clerk took occasion to observe that when the corporation seal had been conveyed to the British Museum for the purpose of an impression being taken from it, that it had been discovered it was the original seal of Edward III., whose likeness, with that of Queen Philippa, it bore."

the Duke of Ireland, in 1387. Bridgekeepers are named, and it seems that the College of Eton had a right to pass toll free.

We find that though no parliamentary return was made from the 7th of Edward II. to the 25th of Henry VI. ; after that period, the towns-people regularly availed themselves of their electoral privileges. A fresh breeze of the spirit of political liberty would appear to have fanned the bosoms of the inhabitants, and to have awakened them to the exercise of their dormant rights. " It were a strange misrepresentation of history," says Mr. Hallam, " to assert that the constitution had attained anything like a perfect state in the fifteenth century ; but I know not whether there are any essential privileges of our countrymen, any fundamental securities against arbitrary power, so far as they depended on positive institution, which may not be traced to the time when the house of Plantagenet filled the throne."

During the fourteenth century Windsor must have possessed but a small population, for so late as the year 1555 it did not contain more than a thousand inhabitants, and it is fair to conclude that from the beginning it went on gradually increasing, as it was not exposed to those commercial fluctuations which materially affected the population of many towns in the middle ages. Some idea of its general state and appearance may be formed from the accounts we have of the domestic structures, the mercantile pursuits, and the social habits of the people of that period. Besides the castellated mansion of the prince and the noble, there were in different parts of the country manorial residences, and in commercial cities the dwellings of rich merchants were of a superior description; but neither of these were likely to be found in Windsor. Houses of a better class in the country, even farmhouses, had a large chamber or hall; and it is curious to read in a roll among the queen's remembrancer's records at Carlton Ride, how Master William sold to one William de Combe, one of the king's cooks, a hall with two chambers annexed, a granary with a gateway built over it, a stable and two barns, in the manor of New Windsor. But the dwellings in the town were no doubt chiefly, if not entirely, of the humble class, consisting of cottages of a single room, without division of stories, and a few shops, which were then little better than stalls or sheds, scattered here and there beside the road which led to the entrance of the castle. No public building for civic purposes existed, except a plain market-cross, which was erected in the year 1380, to which we shall here-after have occasion to refer. Cottages were then built of clay or timber, and in some cases of wood as to their frame-work, showing all the main piers in the walls, but filled up with stone or mortar, intersected by horizontal or diagonal beams grooved into the principal timbers. A chimney sometimes crowned the summit of these houses, but in many of them only an aperture was left in the roof for the escape of the smoke. A glazed window was a great luxury, and most dwellings received the light of day through open-ings of lattice-work. These notices of the domestic archi-tecture of the fourteenth century will assist the reader to form an idea of the appearance of Windsor at that time; and if he will call to mind the style of costume which then prevailed—the long coats, with hoods, worn by the men of the middle rank; the dresses of rich material and magni-ficent embroidery, with sleeves terminating at the elbow in long streamers, and the shoes of monstrous length, with pointed toes, worn by fashionable gentlemen; and the gowns thrown over a kirtle, worn by the ladies—he may easily imagine himself walking on a bright summer's morning on the banks of the Thames, strolling into the royal little town, and meeting many a group of artizans, tradesmen, and courtiers, as he winds his way up to the drawbridge and gate at the entrance of Edward's castle.

It may here be noticed, that scarcely any communication existed at that time between Windsor and London. The roads were so bad that Eleanor, the queen of Edward I., used to journey from the one place to the other by water, as she was not a good horsewoman, and the roads were impassable by the cumbrous vehicles in which even royalty was then accustomed to travel.

The architectural appearance of the town in the fifteenth century differed but little from what it had been during the previous one. Some indications of advancing taste might, however, be found in the ornamental woodwork of the over-hanging gables of the houses, and perchance in some oriel windows here and there adorning the better kind of residences. The town was by no means thickly populated, and the dwellings of the inhabitants were in many instances no doubt separated from each other by neat little gardens, blooming with roses and fragrant with honeysuckles. The furniture and domestic habits, even of the most influential persons in the place, were of a simple order. " The gentry of that period drank but little wine, had no foreign luxuries, rarely kept male servants, except for husbandry, and seldom travelled beyond the county in which they resided. We have reached in this age so high a pitch of luxury, that we can hardly believe or comprehend the frugality of ancient times, and have in general formed mistaken notions as to the habits of expenditure which then prevailed. Sir John Fortescue speaks of ' five pounds a year as a fair living for a yeoman'— a class of whom he is not at all inclined to diminish the importance."* The dresses, however, which were worn in

* Hallam.

the fifteenth century were not in keeping with the simplicity
of domestic conveniences and habits; for however plain our
ancestors might be in their arrangements at home, they made
a decidedly dashing appearance when they came abroad.
The long-toed shoes were, during the period of which we
speak, longer than ever, till in the vagaries of fashion they
changed their form and expanded vastly in breadth; whereupon parliament in its legislative wisdom restricted the
breadth of a man's shoe to six inches.　The tippets of the
hoods reached to the ground; high caps with feathers were
also worn, and low robes trimmed with fur, in some cases
having sleeves, in others simply arm-holes, were deemed
exceedingly graceful.　The ladies were fond of lofty head-
dresses adorned with horns, and robes not unlike the riding-
habits of the present day, with trains, which, in walking,
were thrown over the arm.*　Many a gentleman and many
a dame, thus attired in the costume of the age—a Justice
Shallow and a Mrs. Ford, for instance—are seen by the eye
of fancy enlivening the picture of the Windsor of that day,
walking along the streets or sitting under the shadow of a
noble elm on a summer's afternoon.

The earliest existing Windsor charity was a grant, in
1501, of four tenements and gardens in Shere-street, for
eight poor persons to dwell in, according to the intention
of William Paynall, then deceased.　And about the same
time numerous instances occur of obits in the parish church.
Records of sums occur in parish accounts paid for lights in
the parish church, "our lady lyght," light of the Holy
Trinity, St. Thomas', St. Stephens', the rood light, and
many others, all probably extinguished by Edward VI. "A

---

* A gown was a costly article.　In the privy purse expenses of
Elizabeth of York, wife of Henry VII., when a workman's wages
were sixpence a day, we find 15½ yards of black damask, for a gown,
charged 7s. per yard.—" Paston Letters," vol. i. p. 1.

paire of organs," and chalies, and altar-cloths, and coverings of the rood, and towels, and curtains, and rings, appear in the church inventory. And 47*s.* 10*d.* is noted as remaining in the box for the "alms-houses" abovementioned, situated in Sheet-street. The corporation accounts show payments for numerous purposes, including "repairs of the bridge," "making a cucking stool," "writing all the year," and "upping the swans." A number of similar illustrations are supplied in the "Annals of Windsor."

During the rebellion of 1536 in the north of England, an unhappy butcher residing near Windsor somewhat sympathised with the insurgents, and prevailed upon a priest whom he knew to espouse their cause and preach in their favour. So said report. In proof of the butcher's treason, it was alleged that when he was serving his customers with mutton, and some economical gentleman or dame beat him down in price, he would say, " Nay, I had rather the good fellows of the north had it, and a score more of the best I have, than I would so sell it." That was enough ; the priest and butcher were accused, " while the king was lying at Windsor," and having confessed to the crime, were adjudged to death ; the priest being hanged on a tree at the foot of Windsor bridge, and the butcher on a new pair of gallows erected before the castle-gate.*

* A record appears in the Borough accounts for "nayles for the galowes," and for watching "them that were hanged two nights."

CHAPTER II.

MARTYRS IN THE REIGN OF HENRY VIII.

ISTORY tells us of some different characters in Windsor, from those mentioned in the foregoing chapter, who fell victims to Henry's ecclesiastical tyranny. Their story is worthy of remembrance so long as there are human hearts to execrate the spirit of persecution, and to sympathise with sufferers for conscience sake.

It was in the year 1544 that Robert Testwood was added to the choir of the Royal Chapel; he was a man who, in addition to his musical talents, seems to have possessed no small share of vivacity and wit. His professional qualifications and his conversational powers appear to have recommended him to the high favour of the dean and canons, at whose tables he was often entertained. But circumstances soon occurred which brought Testwood into no small trouble. He had imbibed some of the principles of the Lutheran Reformation, at that time deemed by the heads of the church in England extremely heretical, and in the course of his conversation with the clergy, he ventured to express his views. Having declared his opinion in favour of the ecclesiastical supremacy of the king, just before it was established by act of Parliament, and while the authority of Rome was still deemed paramount by the canons of Windsor, he exposed himself to the censure of the church, if not something worse ; but before they could complain of him to the dean, who happened then to be absent, the act of supremacy was passed, and when they thought to bring Testwood into difficulty, to their no small surprise the dean announced to them the decision of Parliament, and commanded that the Pope's pardons, which hung about the chapel, should be brought to him into the chapter, when he threw them into the fire and burnt them before their faces. "Whereat," says honest John Foxe, "the canons were all stricken in a dump." But Testwood did not again thus escape ; nor were his offences in the eyes of the clergy always so trivial. Windsor was at that time the resort of pilgrims ; multitudes from the most distant part of England flocked to the shrine of the "good King Henry," to offer their gifts of candles and waxen images, and repeat their prayers to the saintly monarch. Along the southern aisle of the choir they might be seen crowding together to enjoy the privilege of kissing his holy spur, and having his sacred hat, that cure for the headache, placed upon their brows. Behind the high altar, also, there stood an alabaster figure of the Virgin, which was another point of attraction, and was surrounded by large groups of worshippers, who devoutly touched and kissed the holy image. It happened one afternoon as Testwood was walking through the church, seeing the people round Henry's shrine, that his spirit was stirred within him, and he could not refrain from expostulating with such misguided devotees ; some of whom were so convinced by his arguments and appeals, that they promised they would return on these pilgrimages no more. Animated by his success with them, he approached the party round the Virgin, when, in the warmth of his zeal, he lifted up his key and broke off the nose of the image. This created no small excitement, and a lawyer in the town, of the name of Simons, picked up the broken nose, put it in his pocket, saying, significantly, "That shall be a dear nose to Testwood some day."

"Now," says Foxe, "many were offended with Testwood, —the canons for speaking against their profit; the wax-sellers, for hindering their market; and Simons, for the image's nose; and more than that, there were men of the canons who threatened to kill him." Still Testwood was little intimidated; for soon after, on a relic Sunday, when every man appeared with a relic in his hand, this chorister had none. "Take this," said the sexton, and gave him Becket's rochet, but the chorister refused to take it; again came a verger with St. George's dagger, and would fain have put it into Testwood's hands, but again he declined to accept any relic. Testwood then went up to one of the canons, who was arrayed in a golden cope, and pointing to a certain Mr. Hake, waggishly remarked, "Now if he had his horse and St. Martin's cloak, and Mr. John Shorn's boots, with King Henry's spurs and his hat, he might ride where he would." Nor did Testwood stop here. At that time a paper was put up at the door of the choir, extolling the merits of the Virgin. Just before the commencement of service one day, as the dean was going in, and crossing himself with holy water, this incorrigible chorister passed by, and tore down the paper. "Testwood," said the dean, calling him to his stall, "how dare you be so bold as to pull down that paper?" "Master," said the undaunted Testwood, "how could you suffer such a paper to be put up? be not offended with what I have done, for I shall stand to it."

On another occasion, when a hymn to the Virgin was sung by one of the choir, this indomitable opponent of the worship of the saints rather indecorously expressed his disapprobation, by introducing in the counter verse the opposite of what had just been repeated. All this could

not fail to rouse the indignation of his ecclesiastical superiors, whose vengeance, as we shall soon see, fell in a fiery
shower on his devoted head. There were others in Windsor
who sympathised with Testwood in his antipapal notions
and feelings. The churchwarden of the parish was of this
class, and he loudly complained of idle tales about the
Virgin which the vicar told in his sermons. A preaching
priest, named Anthony Pearson, was another of these early
Protestants; and so was Marbeck, the organist of the
Royal Chapel, and the composer of the solemn and venerable notes for responses, still in use in our cathedrals.
The Book of Common Prayer noted by him still
exists, printed in 1550, by Richard Grafton, the king's
printer. He was also the first man who made a Concordance of the English Bible. Of the latter undertaking
he gave an account to the Bishop of Salisbury, by whom
he was examined on the charge of heresy. Foxe thus records it in his "Acts and Monuments":—

"When Thomas Matthew's Bible came first out in print,
I was much desirous to have one of them; and being a
poor man, not able to buy one of them, determined with
myself to borrow one amongst my friends, and to write it
forth. And when I had written out the five books of
Moses, in fair great paper, and was entered on the book of
Joshua, my friend, Master Turner, chanced to steal upon
me unawares, and seeing me writing out the Bible, asked
me what I meant thereby; and when I told him the cause,
'Tush,' said he, 'thou goest about a vain and tedious labour;
but this were a profitable work for thee, to set out a Concordance in English.' 'A Concordance,' said I, 'what is
that?' Then he told me it was a book to find out any
word in the whole Bible by the letter; and that there was
such an one in Latin already. Then I told him I had no
learning to go about such a thing. 'Enough,' said he, 'for

that matter, for it requireth not so much learning as diligence ; and seeing thou art so painful a man, and one that
cannot be unoccupied, it were a good exercise for thee.'
And this, my lord, is all the instruction that ever I had,
before or after, of any man."*

Poor John Marbeck may be regarded as the first to lead
the way in a humble but useful walk of English Biblical
literature ; and his diligence in the study of the sacred
volume presents a beautiful instance of the avidity with
which the common people, at the time of the Reformation,
availed themselves of the means of scriptural instruction.

The above-mentioned persons, and some others whom
Foxe names, were the fathers of Protestantism in the town
of Windsor ; and Testwood, Pearson, Filmer, and Marbeck
were, in the year 1544, all committed to the town gaol to
take their trial under the act of six articles, or "whip with
six strings," as it was called, and bloody strings they were.
St. Anne's day was fixed for their trial, and because a sufficient
number of Papists in the town could not be found willing
to fill up the jury, the farmers occupying the dean and
canons' property were summoned to attend. The accused
were all found guilty, and condemned to the stake ; but
Marbeck was afterwards pardoned. "All night long," says
the martyrologist, "till dead sleep took them, were they
calling on God for his aid and strength, and praying for
their persecutors, which of blind zeal and ignorance had
done they wist not what, that God of his merciful goodness
would forgive them, and turn their hearts to the love and
knowledge of his blessed and holy word : yea, such
heavenly talk was amongst them that night, that the
hearers watching the prison without, whereof the sheriff himself was one, with divers gentlemen more, were constrained

* Foxe, vol. ii. p. 463.

to shed plenty of tears, as they themselves confessed."*
They were condemned on the Thursday, and on the following Saturday were conducted from their prison through the
town to a field just by where Travers' College now stands ;
and having expressed at the stake sentiments of the utmost
confidence and hope, though in that quaint language which
was the fashion of the day, they meekly yielded to their
fate, and so in a car of fire ascended to the skies. "Many
who saw their patient suffering," says Foxe, "confessed that
they could have found it in their hearts to suffer with
them."

Their enemies, it appears, encouraged by their death,
prepared to give information respecting some other sus-
pected heretics, but in this they overshot the mark, and
brought down retribution on themselves. For as the king
was one day hunting in Guildford-park, he met with the
sheriff and Sir Humphrey Foster, and inquired how the
laws were executed at Windsor. They told him the tale
of the execution of these poor men, and said that it went
much against their consciences to condemn them ; when
Henry, with how much sincerity we do not undertake to
say, exclaimed, "Alas ! poor innocents !" and on his return,
caused Simons and one Dr. London, who were extremely
active in searching out heretics, to be apprehended. In
consequence of this, they were convicted of perjury, and
sentenced to ride round Windsor, Reading, and Newbury,
with papers on their heads, and their faces towards the
horses' tails. The circumstance of Henry's causing these
Papists to be punished for their zeal against Protestantism,
after he had approved of the act of six articles, is strikingly
illustrative of his capricious temper ; which was, in truth,
a two-edged sword, inflicting wounds on both parties, and

* Foxe, vol. ii. p. 467.

M 2

glutting itself in the blood of friends as well as foes.   That spot where the martyrs fell is holy ground, and strange it is, that in all the histories of Windsor, among all the splendid associations of royalty and chivalry, and love and poetry, which its name calls forth, no allusion, until very recently, as far as we remember, should be made to those men, who, though humble in their day, are now, we doubt not, saints in heaven, with crowns more radiant than the princely owners of that castle ever wore.

CHAPTER III.

AGE OF ELIZABETH.

NO doubt, during the long and gorgeous reign of Elizabeth, Windsor sometimes witnessed those quaint spectacles which were the fashion of the age. The readers of Sir W. Scott's "Kenilworth" will remember the numerous shows that distinguished her memorable reception at the Earl of Leicester's palace, and most persons will have read of those progresses which the maiden queen made through divers parts of the kingdom, and of the entertainments given to her by her subjects, both citizens and nobles; and though, perhaps, no exhibitions equal to them graced the courts and parks of Windsor, for we have no accounts of any, yet, probably, revels of a somewhat similar description did sometimes enliven, with gaudy glitter, the walls and environs of the castle. And surely the loyal men of Windsor and Eton, in those days, were not lacking in loyal demonstrations any more than the men of these times; and if the queen's tradesmen did not illuminate their houses, erect triumphal arches covered with dahlias, and give dinners in the long walk, with the appurtenances of balloons, and crowds of Eton boys running beside the royal carriages, yet we may safely indulge in the idea, that on some grand occasions, Windsor and Eton put forth all their energies to welcome royalty: and as we see Elizabeth's great state-coach rolling along, we can fancy the houses decorated with tapestry, and pictures, and flowers, and groups of allegorical figures, with giants and dragons here and there stationed to meet her highness; and boys and girls starting forth from some grotesque kind of concealment to repeat their verses and present their offerings; while the firing of cannon, the beating of drums, the ringing of bells, and the huzzas of the people, rend the air. The propensity of the English at that time, to indulge in the last of these demonstrations, is noticed by Hentzner, and leaves no doubt as to the noise with which they would greet her majesty's entrance into the royal town; for, says the worthy traveller, "the English are vastly fond of noises that fill the ear, and it is common for a number of them, that have got a glass in their heads, to get up into some belfry, and ring the bells for hours together for the sake of exercise."

Two relics of the loyalty of the age, the one belonging to Eton College, the other to the town of Windsor, may here come under our notice. The Eton Memorial, belonging to the year 1563, consists of a collection of Latin speeches, to the number of seventy-three, a few in prose, but most of them in verse; several of them acrostics, ingenious but ridiculous; and all of them redolent of that spirit of flattery which marked everything addressed to the eye or ear of royalty. One boy addressed the queen as a blooming rose, and the light of the world, without whom the whole earth would perish :—

"O rosa, lux mundi, sine quâ terra peribit."

Another praised her beauty, wealth, and wisdom, as the united gifts of Venus, Juno, and Minerva :—

"Te Juno, princeps, copiis
Explevit ornatissime,

Sapientiam Pallas gravem
Reliquasque virtutes animi
Clarissimas plene dedit :
Corpus sed erectum Venus
(Ut pulchritudinis Dea est)
Formam decoramque addidit."*

All the rest of the speakers followed on the same side.

But Windsor has also its memorial of loyal speech-making. It is preserved in the following form :—

"An oration, conteyning an expostulation, as wel with the Queens Highnesse faithful subjects, for their want of due consideration of Gods blessings enjoyed by means of Her Majesty ; as also with the unnatural Englishe for their disloyaltie and unkindnesse towards the same their sovereign ; at the first pronounced upon the Queen Majestys birthday (Sept. 7th, 1586), in the Guildhall of the Burrowe of New Windsor, by Edward Hake, of Grays Inne, Gent., then Mayor of the same Burrowe ; now imprinted this 17th Nov., 30th Year of the Queen Highnesse most happie reigne.

"TO THE READER.

" Aut quam minima aut quam dulcissima."

Then follows the oration, occupying sixteen closely-printed pages.

The orator begins with a lamentation over the ingratitude of the English people, and compares it with the thankfulness of the ancient heathen for their social privileges. He goes through the history of Mary's reign, showing its inglorious character, and the persecutions of the people ; and then bursts forth into the warmest eulogiums on the accession of Elizabeth, and points out the advantages enjoyed under her administration, particularly mentioning

---

* Nicholls' " Progresses of Queen Elizabeth."

the preaching of God's word, and "worldly and external peace." Then he expostulates, in the most impassioned style, with the disaffected part of the nation, and concludes his speech in the following words :—

"Last of all, to you, my brethren and neighbours, the inhabitants of this town of Windsor ; if it be an universal benefit, far passing other temporal benefits, even to all the people of her highness's dominions, that her majesty, in the midst of these evil days, sitteth prosperously and peaceably in the seat of her royal kingdom, preserving the same from all annoyance, to the no less admiration than high commendation thereof in all foreign countries ; again, if not only the participation of so high a benefice in common with others, but also to ourselves ward, an assured hope to stand free from her majesty's displeasure, and in lieu thereof, a settled persuasion of her princely favour towards us, be now seen among us by means of her gracious presence —oh, how much have we to rejoice and, in the Lord, to boast ! We, I say, the inhabitants of this borough ; the rather, for that while many thousands of her majesty's dear subjects can only say and speak by the report of others, of the prosperous health of their most natural and loving prince, we can say and see the same, to our unspeakable comfort : while others do hear her majesty (I must say most lovingly) speaking unto them by laws only, we have not only the fruition of her laws, but also her most amiable and royal person, at this time, as at sundry other times, speaking unto us."

The long oration is followed by "A short speech of the same mayor unto her majesty when he received her highness at Windsor, and presented her with the mace, 10th of August, 1586 :—'With that sincere and faithful obedience, most renowned queen—not which law hath commanded, but which love hath procured—we, your poor townsmen, inhabiting this your ancient borough of Windsor, do here present ourselves before your highness, offering up unto the same, not only this small piece of government, which we sustain and exercise under your majesty, but ourselves also, and all that we have, freely, not coarctedly, joyfully, not grudgingly, to be for ever at your gracious disposing; wishing, and from our hearts praying, the King of kings, that your majesty may long live a queen to enjoy the same; and that we, your subjects, may never live a people to deny the same.' The mayor presented her highness with a petition in writing, in behalf of the said town of Windsor; and at her departure, eleven weeks after, she sent her gracious thanks for this, and for the speech on the birthday."

No doubt this worthy mayor of Windsor (and, to speak the truth, he really was a man of eloquence and learning, albeit a little pedantic) had a large meeting to hear his speech — that speech, which, of all the hundred speeches spoken in the old hall, has thus come floating down to us on the stream of history, a solitary specimen of Windsor eloquence in the olden time. No doubt he had a fitting audience to listen to his effusion, and was greeted with thunders of applause, as indeed he deserved; nor would it be too much to conjecture that a corporation dinner followed such an exhausting effort, with other entertainments characteristic of the age. And when he met the queen with the mace! We can see him with his cloak and chain, and doublet and hose, with the worthy bailiffs and corporation in his train; they bow and kneel, and the gilded mace is reverently presented, and her majesty, standing there as we see her now in her picture, looks on with wondrous condescension. They were great men in their day, looked up to in the town, no doubt; but all, save Mr. Hake, are gone into oblivion.

Let us now yield to the gentler influence of natural
scenes and objects connected with Windsor in the days of
Elizabeth : and first, let us go down to Eton. "In the
precincts of Windsor," says Paul Hentzner, "on the other
side the Thames, both whose banks are joined by a bridge
of wood, is Eaton, a well-built college. As we returned to
our inn, we happened to meet some country people, celebrating harvest-home : their last load of corn they crown
with flowers, having besides an image richly dressed, by
which perhaps they would signify Ceres : this they keep
moving about, while men and women, men and maid-
servants, riding through the streets in the cart, shout as
loud as they can, till they arrive at the barn. The farmers
here do not bind up their corn in sheaves, as they do with
us, but directly as they have reaped or mowed it, put it
into carts, and convey it into their barns." These are
pleasing images of rural simplicity ; and we confess, those
well-loaded carts, winding along the village of Eton, then
of agricultural appearance, with the merry maidens and the
farmers' servants singing their songs of glee, and shouting
harvest-home, while the setting sun throws his slanting rays
over the college chapel towers, and the well-reaped fields
around it—all calm and silent, save when interrupted by
those joyous shouts—we confess, these sights and sounds
have, to our eye, ear, and heart, a beauty far transcending
all the pomp and pageantry of proud Bessy's court.

And now, crossing the wooden bridge, and walking
through Datchet-lane, and entering the park by the Thames,
let us cross it, and look for Herne's oak.

> "There is an old tale goes, that Herne the hunter,
> Sometime a keeper here in Windsor Forest,
> Doth all the winter time, at still midnight,
> Walk round about an oak, with great ragg'd horns;
> And there he blasts the tree."

Many an oak, as fine and finer than Herne's, has been cut down and never thought of; or stands, the survivor of storms that have beaten round it for a thousand years, and is passed by unnoticed; but this oak of Herne is what Carlyle would call "a world-famous" oak. There is a wondrous spell in genius—how it immortalises the spot on which it lights! the objects it has embalmed with its descriptive pen live in immortal renown! It creates objects which have no existence but in the imagination, and associates them with certain spots by a power so magical, that we strive to identify the localities which have been so touched by the wand of genius, as if the persons and events described had really existed there. Hence, as we walk by the Thames, beside Windsor Park, we look for the shore which "was shelvy and shallow," where "the rogues slighted" the unfortunate knight into the river: and, deluded in a similar way by the poetry of Scott, we search along the romantic borders of Loch Katrine for the very spot where—

> " From underneath an aged oak,
> That slanted from the islet rock,
> A damsel guider of its way,
> A little skiff shot to the bay,
> That round the promontory steep
> Led its deep line in graceful sweep;
> Eddying, in almost viewless wave,
> The weeping willow twig to lave,
> And kiss, with whispering sound and slow,
> The beach of pebbles bright as snow."

Genius equally immortalises the place where it first enters the world. What multitudes has it drawn round the places it has thus hallowed! Crowds go to Stratford, pilgrims of all lands and ages; and they go to see—what? A little low-ceiled room, with four whitewashed walls, and an old piece of wainscot—that is all!—but Shakspere was born there! In that humble garret-looking place, did one of the greatest minds that the Divine Being ever sent into the world, first look through its infant eyes upon a mother's smiles and tears; there lay that winged genius in its callow down, nestling at its parent's bosom—destined to sweep through the regions of thought with an eagle's pinion. There he was born; and this fact sheds a splendour over the old walls more dazzling far than tapestries, mirrors, pictures, golden hangings, velvet couches, and all the pride and pomp of kingly palaces could ever do. Genius has a kingship of its own. It needs no mantle, orb, or sceptre,— it is its own regalia; and before its inherent majesty crowned heads have done and are doing homage, as the walls of that house at Stratford, written over with the names of princes, even now bear witness.* The spell of beauty which genius casts over objects but little interesting in themselves—over such things as blasted oaks and humble time-worn cottages—shows how mind has the superiority over matter; how the associations of intellect can ennoble the meanest forms of materialism; how the spirit of man can create, out of the perishing elements of earth, undying memorials of itself, thus revealing its noble nature, and giving indications of its immortality.

Mr. Charles Knight states that the real Herne's Oak was cut down some fifty or sixty years ago, not by order of George III., but to his deep and lasting regret; and, in support of this opinion, relates the following anecdote :— About the year 1800, Mr. Nicholson, the eminent landscape draughtsman, was on a visit to the Dowager Countess of

---

* And here it may be interesting to state, that, in the same spirit in which so many noble and literary pilgrims have visited Stratford-on-Avon, his majesty the King of Prussia, soon after his arrival at Windsor Castle to attend the baptism of the Prince of Wales, sought the remains of Herne's Oak, and plucked from the ivy which still mantles it a leaf, which he preserved as a relic.

Kingston, at Old Windsor; and his mornings were chiefly employed in sketching, or rather making studies of the old trees in the forest. This circumstance one day led the conversation of some visitors at Lady Kingston's to Herne's Oak. Mrs. Boufoy and her daughter, Lady Ely, were present; and they were very much with the royal family. Mr. Nicholson requested Lady Ely to procure for him any information that she could from the king, respecting Herne's Oak, which, considering his majesty's tenacious memory and familiarity with Windsor, the king could probably give better than any one else. In a few days, Lady Ely informed Mr. Nicholson that she had made the inquiry he wished of the king; who told her that, when he (George III.) was a young man, it was represented to him that there were a number of old oaks in the park, which had become unsightly objects, and that it would be desirable to take them down. He gave immediate directions that such trees as were of this description should be removed; but he was afterwards sorry that he had given such an order inadvertently, because he found that among the rest the remains of Herne's Oak had been destroyed.*

On the other hand, Mr. Jesse considers that Herne's Oak is still standing in the avenue beside the path leading to Datchet; and he states that King George III. frequently asserted that he had cut down an oak tree close to the present one, because many persons confounded that with the tree still in existence, and called it Herne's, which, he said, it was not. This statement Mr. Jesse makes on the authority of Mr. Davis, the king's huntsman, who has heard the king frequently assert that he had cut down the suppositious Herne's Oak, and heard him say so when his mind and body were in a perfectly healthy state. Mr. Jesse

* " Pictorial Shakspere," Merry Wives of Windsor

further remarks, that the king placed the present tree under the care of Mr. Engall, telling him that it was Herne's Oak ; and that George IV. often affirmed that the true oak was not cut down by his father.

There are aged persons in the town and neighbourhood of Windsor who state that tradition is in favour of an oak cut down ; but, as Mr. Jesse mentions, there are some other persons, particularly a lady in her ninety-fourth year, who report that they and their fathers always had the existing oak pointed out to them as Herne's. Mr. Knight observes that this oak is of small girth, and appears to have suffered premature decay, and that when he first knew it the trunk was not bare ; but Mr. Jesse considers that the present appearance of the tree by no means indicates that it is not of that ancient date which would carry it back to the time of Herne the Hunter.   The size of the trunk not being so large as some other oaks, may be easily accounted for by the fact that they are pollards, while this is a maiden oak.

These are the chief arguments which have been adduced on each side of this controversy.   Great diligence has been displayed in the collection of evidence, and much ingenuity and taste exhibited in conducting the argument ; but the point in question is by no means easy to determine. Opposite traditions are the main witnesses, between whose conflicting testimonies and pretensions to credibility it is difficult to decide.   We shall rest content with having simply stated the case and summed up the evidence, leaving it to our readers to form a jury and return a verdict.

We must now leave Herne's Oak, and look at the town of Windsor in the sixteenth century.

"The Windsor of the time of Elizabeth," says Mr. C. Knight,* " is presented to us as the quiet country-town,

* Referring to Shakspere's " Merry Wives of Windsor."

sleeping under the shadow of its neighbour, the castle. Amidst its gabled houses, separated by pretty gardens, from which the elm, the chestnut, and the lime throw their branches across the unpaved road, we find a goodly company, with little to do but gossip and laugh, and make sport of each other's cholers and weaknesses. We see Master Page 'training his fallow greyhound,' and we go with Master Ford 'a-birding;' we listen to the pribbles and prabbles of Sir Hugh Evans and Justice Shallow with a quiet satisfaction, for they talk as unartificial men ordinarily talk, without much wisdom, but with good temper and sincerity. We find ourselves in the days of ancient hospitality, when men could make their fellows welcome without ostentatious display, and half a dozen neighbours 'could drink down all unkindness' over a hot venison pasty."

Of the external appearance of the town during the fifteenth century, the period to which Shakspere's comedy refers, this may be taken as a tolerably correct description ; but judging from Norden's map of Windsor, made in the early part of the reign of King James I., the town in the time of Elizabeth must have presented a different aspect, the houses being represented in that map as built close together on both sides the street, leaving no space for 'such gardens as Mr. Knight so poetically describes. A house at the bottom of the Hundred Steps, destroyed in 1860, was supposed by some to have been in the thoughts of Shakspere as the abode of Mrs. Page in the " Merry Wives of Windsor." Tradition, too, assigned a house opposite the White Hart to Mr. Ford, but all this is very chimerical. There is more sense in looking after the house of " mine host of the Garter." Such a hostelry existed in Shakspere's time, as appears from the corporation records. It may be identified by looking at Norden's map. These two inns

are seen at the top of Thames-street, with their signs far
projecting into the highway. That nearest the end of
Peascod-street is, no doubt, the Garter Inn. It is curious
to find that the landlord, Richard Gallys, or Gallis, in
1562 was Member of Parliament for the borough. He
served the office of mayor three times.

It should not be forgotten, when we picture to ourselves
the Windsor of the sixteenth century, that the internal
arrangements of English houses at that time were anything
but comfortable. Erasmus, who visited England in the
reign of Henry VIII., complains of the doors and windows
of the houses being badly contrived, and of the dilapidated
state of the walls in many instances, which being full of
chinks freely admitted the wind and weather. "The
floors," he says, "are, for the most part, of clay strewed
with rushes, which are often renewed, fresh layers being
placed over the old ones, and the whole remaining for
perhaps twenty years, so as to form a solid pavement, including deposits of fish-bones, spittle, fragments of meat,
and other filth not to be mentioned."

Judging from Norden's larger map, the town of Windsor
consisted, in the early part of the seventeenth century, of
rows of straggling houses, lining Thames-street, High-street,
and Peascod-street. There are very few marked at the town
end of Sheet-street. The houses about the church and
behind the town-hall seem almost as numerous as at present. A building on pillars, with two crosses at the top,
stands opposite Peascod-street ; and the stocks hard by at
the south end.*

---

* In the "Annals of Windsor" it is remarked that in neither of
Norden's drawings is there anything indicating the position of the
high cross, which probably stood at the junction of the four streets,
Thames-street, High-street, Peascod-street, and the Castle-hill. It
was erected in the reign of Richard II., was restored by Dr. Goodman, Bishop of Gloucester, in 1635, and was finally removed after

the present town-hall was built. The authors distinguish between Norden's building on pillars, with the two crosses at the top, and the market or high cross. But why? In Norden's larger map of Windsor, the site of the building which Messrs. Tighe and Davis call the corn-market is identical with their account of the site of the cross. They think the cross had been destroyed before Norden's map was made; but this is impossible, as Dr. Goodman, in 1635, refers to it as "our old cross in the heart of our public market-place;" and again, as "ready to fall." It must then have been in existence thirty years before. I cannot believe that Norden would have left out of his plan such an important public building as the high cross, near to, but distinct from, the edifice he represents. The land on which the cross was built was leased to John Sadler for that purpose in 1380, which shows the building must have been of some considerable extent; and what Dr. Goodman did to the cross was, according to the mayor's letter to him at the time, only to erect "a new crucifix, where never was any before, in the heart of our public market-place." The Doctor speaks of it as something that could "in an instant be blotted out and defaced." Pote describes him as causing "a statue or picture an ell long, of Christ hanging on a cross, to be erected in colours," and on the other side "the picture of Christ rising out of the sepulchre." It is plain that what Goodman did was only to repair an old edifice, and to add these carvings or paintings. I can find no contemporary allusion to a cross and a corn-market house as distinct buildings. Items of repairs of the cross cease when we come to items about repairing the corn-market; which is easily explained by recollecting that the Commonwealth's men, who abhorred crosses, would object to give that name any longer to the building which had borne it before.

CHAPTER IV.

INDSOR shared largely in the political excitements of the seventeenth century. Mr. Bagshaw, of Windsor, informed the House of Commons, the 14th of January, 1641, that as he went to Windsor the night before, " he saw several troops of horse, and there came a wagon laden with ammunition thither ; and that he was informed there were about four hundred horse in the town, and about some forty officers." Mr. Taylor, member for the town, was expelled from the House in May of the same year, for declaring that Lord Strafford's Bill of Attainder was a judicial murder. The cross in the market was demolished in 1641. " Scandalous monuments and pictures" were, by order of Parliament, 1643, to be destroyed in the churches and chapels of Windsor and Eton. Soldiers committed depredations in the park, killing the deer and burning the pales ; and one Alexander Hayne, Gentleman Usher of the Black Rod, who had a house at Windsor, complained, in 1644, of the burning of a hay-stack of his, worth one hundred pounds. Windsor was fixed upon, in 1642-3, as the head-quarters of the Parliament army; and the townspeople from the beginning took the Parliament side of the struggle. In 1648, an ordinance was presented to the House of Lords, " for appointing three ministers to preach at Windsor, and to have one hundred pounds yearly a-piece for their maintenance." Under the proper date, the parish register contains a curious record of the monarch's execution in the following words, " King Charles in y° Castle." The organ in the church was taken down in 1650 ; and in the same year appears an item in the churchwardens' accounts, illustrative of irregularities in the supply of the parish pulpit—" Paid for one pint of sack given to a marchant of Brisstell wch preached in the p'ish church by William Myelles Mare his appointment, 8*d.*" A new hour-glass was frequently purchased; and for preservation, the church-plate was delivered over to the custody of the mayor and corporation, who placed it in the town-hall. No account is preserved of rejoicings in Windsor at the Restoration, but on the 7th of August, 1660, a petition was presented to the House of Commons, from the mayor, aldermen, and burgesses, on behalf of the poor men and women who were "commanded out of the castle." Portions of the royal edifice had been appropriated to the use of certain needy people, who were now dismissed, and thrown upon the town for support. An odd entry, in 1662, of 8*d.* paid " at town halle when the commissioners were there, to purge y° corporation, as they said," refers to the ejectment of certain old parliamentarians from the corporation ; and at the same time a form of declaration against the solemn league and covenant was imposed. Glimpses of a royal visit are caught in a charge of £4 7*s.* 6*d.* "for cleansing and mending the streets against the king's coming in ;" and of a grand civic visitor, in the item of 1*s.* 3*d.* " for twelve quarts of Rhenish wine and a sugar-loaf given to the Lord Mayor of London, and paid at the Garter."

Many of the items in the town records refer to the period of the civil wars, whence it appears that the jovial ways of the Windsor corporation went on at that time just as usual, suffering no interruption from the terrors of intestine strife : so little are the social habits of a people altered by national calamities, and so quietly often does the stream of domestic cheerfulness flow on through the obscure nooks of society, while the tempest of political discord is beating with violence on its lofty eminences.

There is a name of frequent occurrence in the municipal accounts during the Commonwealth, and afterwards, of whom tradition tells an amusing story, and who, for his whimsical loyalty, deserves to be put upon the historic record. It is the name of William Davis, blacksmith both to the king and the corporation. He had performed various works in the castle in the reign of Charles I., and was afterwards patronized by Oliver Cromwell. But this independent tradesman, though he continued to do the castle business for the sake of the veneration which he cherished for the edifice, would not touch a shilling of the usurper's money in return. And, in further demonstration of his attachment to the royal family and his indignation at a republican interregnum, it is said that he wore a hat from which the crown had been cut off, alleging as a reason for so doing, that he could not think of wearing a crowned hat, as there was in England in those days no crowned head. Brave William Davis—a worthy royalist and a self-denying worshipper of his king ! Few successors of a like spirit, we apprehend, has he left behind him ; few indeed whose loyalty would lead them to work for nothing, and to walk the streets with a crownless hat.

A very important question was agitated during the latter half of the seventeenth century, as to the parties in whom was vested the right of electing members of Parliament. On the one hand, it was contended to be in the corporation, on the other, in the inhabitants. Sometimes returns had been made by the mayor, bailiffs, burgesses, and inhabitants ; at other times by the mayor, bailiffs, and burgesses alone. In 1640, it had been resolved by the Long Parliament that all the inhabitants had votes. This broad basis of electoral privilege, however, was removed by Parliament on the restoration of Charles II., and upon the report of Serjeant Charlton on an election petition, it was resolved "that the mayor, bailiffs, and burgesses, not above thirty in number, have only the right to elect." Still the inhabitants were determined to contend for their right to the suffrage, and at several successive elections double returns of representatives were made. The corporation assembled in the town-hall, and there elected the men whom they wished to serve them in Parliament ; and at the same time a party of the inhabitants, sometimes to the number of two hundred, assembled in the market-place, and resolved upon returning to the House of Commons the men of their choice.* In 1678, Parliament decided that the inhabitants at large had the right of election, and that their representatives were duly elected ; but in 1689 the decision was reversed, and the narrow basis of representation was again adopted. It is interesting to remark that Sir Christopher Wren was often a candidate returned by the corporation,

* In connexion with these struggles, the name of William Taylor, or Tayleur, appears, who was a popular candidate returned by the townspeople in opposition to the candidate returned by the corporation. Between him and Lord Mordaunt, the constable of the Castle, there was a mortal feud. The former accused the latter with having unlawfully ejected him from his residence, and falsely imprisoned him, and with offering insults to the honour of his family ; all of which, with other charges, were made ground of for the impeachment of Lord Mordaunt by the House of Commons in 1668. The trial excited great interest, and is noticed both by Evelyn and Pepys. The proceedings were terminated by adjournment of Parliament, but Lord Mordaunt was soon afterwards removed from his office of constable of the Castle. In the "Annals of Windsor," vol. ii. 332, 349, there is a full account of the impeachment.

to be unseated on a petition from the inhabitants. No election for several Parliaments occurred without a struggle between the corporation and the townspeople, till, in the year 1737, it was finally resolved—"that the right of electing members for the borough of New Windsor is in the inhabitants paying scot and lot."

From a perusal of corporation papers and records relating to the period now under review, we have been enabled to catch some glimpses of the condition of the town at that time, and of the character and habits of the people. The following document, being a letter from Mr. Matthew Day, an alderman of the town, relating to the erection of a wall round the pest-house, exhibits the Windsor of the seventeenth century, and brings before us vividly the miseries of the plague which had often visited the town before :—

"Mr. Maior,—My sarvis presented unto you, and to the brotheren of your sosictie; I haveinge bine a member thereof; and onely remaine alive of those your predcsessors whoe are named in your charter; meake bould to put you in remembrance of the frugall care they had of the improveing of the rates and revenues of this corporation, which I doubt not but that your bretheren, now sucscedinge, will indevor to continew, if not to augment to the succeeding bretheren of the sosiety; and what they did for the generall good of the inhabitance of this towne in the buildinge and making of a pest-house, the benefite thereof hath bine found to have been much for the saftie of the towne, in the time of visitacions.

"For before there was a pest-house thay weare necessetatid to make small cottages and hutches for such as were visetid, for the better saftie of the towne (in the fildes); and notwithstanding there care in buildinge of a pest-house, the want of a wall about it was found to be defective, for that I have knowne some infectid have, in the anguish of theire desese, broke out of the pest-house, and came naked in to the towne, and were forced back in to the pest-house.

"Whereuppon it was conceved that of necessety a wall was to be meade about the ground belonging unto the pest-house, for the better securetey of those whoe weare infectid, for cominge into the town, and for the comfort of those visetid peopell, for taking of the ayre (without offence to others).

"Uppon which consideracions the wall about the ground of the pest-house was buellt, which was not done at the charge of the maior and his bretheren onely, but by the gift of several of the inhabitans that lived in the towne, and other well-afected to the good of the towne, whose names and giftes I have a perticuler.

"And if their be anie defect in the wall it wold not be neclecid to be repaired, for we know not how sone it maye pleasse God to send a visitacion, and in the repairing of it, to imetate the cowst that your predecessors take, which I doubt not but will be a good helpe for the doinge of it.

"Yours to sarve you,

"MATHEW DAY.

"From my house, this viiith of March, 1659."

As we read the quaint epistle, we have a fearful light thrown on the "visitacions" of which he speaks; and though the plague did not desolate Windsor to the same extent as it desolated London, when the death-cart went its rounds, and the dead were thrown from the windows to receive a dishonoured burial, yet the thought of those "hutches" in the fields, for the reception of the unhappy victims of disease; of the pest-house and its gloomy associations; and of the infected inmates, in the anguish of their pain, rushing naked into the town, and being forced back to the pest-house, fills us with horror: and while the sad epistle

makes us sigh over the calamities which befel our fathers,
it excites the warmest gratitude to Divine Providence, who
in the present day spares us these awful "visitacions."

There are other records connected with Windsor about
that time, which exhibit the town under a very different
aspect, and which show that, notwithstanding the calamities
of the period, the townspeople pursued their usual habits,
and availed themselves of all opportunities of regaling
themselves with the good things of this life; for ever and
anon, as the eye runs down the columns in the old account
books of the Windsor corporation, does it light on an item
relative to the provision of some hospitable cheer for the
corporation worthies, in the pursuit of their municipal
vocation.   Entries for quarts of sack and loaves of sugar
are as frequent as were, no doubt, the sips those gentlemen
took of the delicious beverage.   When any corporation
business was done, it seems to have been the invariable
custom to crown it with refreshments at the " Garter," or
" White Hart," both which inns are repeatedly mentioned.
When Mr. Mayor and several others met about a petition
concerning soldiers' pay, they adjourned to the " White
Hart," and spent six shillings and threepence.   When Mr.
Mayor and some of his company went to Colonel Venn, on
his leaving the castle, there was a bill run up for a gallon
of wine and four loaves of sugar; and when Mr. Mayor and
Sir Richard Braham met, they could not separate without
having beer and tobacco.   Sometimes a little more substantial fare was provided for these municipal worthies, and
"baking of venison pasties" is charged for in the town
account.   The inferior entertainments, especially the cup of
sack, seem to have been of almost *daily* occurrence.   Not
a bill could be paid without another being incurred with
" mine host of the Garter" or some other host; and after
two or three little bills are mentioned, we find an item like

this—"for drink at these several payments." Other entertainments of a higher order occasionally occurred, and beef
and bacon, and veal and mutton, and pullets, and a hundred other things for the table, are minutely specified and
charged for. Nor were these viands tossed up for the table
without elaborate culinary preparations, for we find charged
in one instance "to four women to help the cook for fourteen days against the prince's coming."

The habits of tippling cherished by the corporation
appear to have been the fashion of the townspeople at large,
for no less than seventy public-houses are mentioned as
existing at the same time, besides several from which the
licences were taken away. This was a great number, considering the size of the town, and it shows how much such
places of resort must have been patronized. The taste of
the inhabitants for public-houses, sack, and beer no doubt
furnishes an explanation of the numerous entries in the
town books relating to the repairs of the town-hall windows, the hasps of the market-gate, and other matters
which had suffered damage from violence.

Sometimes grand rejoicings took place in Windsor, the
charge of which was borne by the corporation. Mention is
made of beer, ale, and wood for a bonfire, upon the news
of the marriage between the Prince of Orange, afterwards
William III., and the Princess Mary, the daughter of
James II.; and it appears that the municipal dignitaries,
in catering for the amusement of the populace, sometimes
introduced bear-baiting, the favourite amusement of the
period—as we find among the corporation accounts "charges
for a rope and bear." Frequent entries also occur relating
to gratuities presented to the members* who represented

* Such gratuities were common at that period; and in the case
of Andrew Mawell, at least, who represented Kingston-upon-Hull,
the custom still continued of paying the representative.

the town in Parliament, and to the steward of the borough,
of which the following is a specimen :—

For three hogsheads of ale, sent one to the Earl of Hol-
    land, one to Mr. Wynord, and one to Mr. Cornelius
    Holland, burgesses of the Parliament of this borough,
    with the charge of land and water carriage .   . £4 15 4

   We select a few other entries as illustrative of the times:

For six quarts of sack, when the peace was proclaimed
    between the Dutch and us £0 12 0
For padlocks, keys, and mending locks, for a chain and
    staple for the whipping post 0 5 0
To the crier for giving notice to keep the hogs out of the
    street 0 2 0
Male pillions and straps, to go to 'sizes 0 2 6
Paid at town-hall when the commissioners were there, to
    purge the corporation, as they said .   .   . 0 3 8
To Mr. Frith, for fetching part of the ducking stool,
    which the water had carried away*   .   .   . 0 2 0

In the corporation accounts towards the close of the
seventeenth century there are numerous items of sums paid
in discharge of bills connected with the erection of the
town-hall. This edifice was built from a design by Sir
Thomas Fits, surveyor of the Cinque Ports, at an expense
of £2006 14s. 4d., and was paid for out of the corporation
funds, exclusive of £680 7s. 6d. which was raised by private
contribution. The original architect died in January, 1689,

---

   * "The cucking stool was an engine invented for the punishment
of scolds and unquiet women, by ducking them in the water, after
having placed them in a stool or chair fixed at the end of a long
pole, by which they were immerged in some muddy or stinking pond.
Blount tells us, that some think it a corruption from ducking stool,
but that others derive it from choaking stool. Though of the most
remote antiquity, it is now, it should seem, totally disused."—
Brande's "Popular Antiquities," vol. ii. p. 442.
   "There is an order of the corporation of Shrewsbury, 1669, that
a ducking stool be erected for the punishment of scolds."—"History
of Shrewsbury," p. 172, 4to. 1779.

and the works were completed under Sir Christopher Wren. In the year 1707 the corporation, in order to evince their loyalty to the reigning sovereign (who, as Pote observes, constantly made Windsor her summer residence), erected a niche at the north end of this building, in which they placed a wooden statue of the queen, with an inscription, which, though intended as an exquisite compliment to her majesty, was in reality a stupid satire.

ANNO REGNI SUI VI.
DOM. 1707.
ARTE TUA, SCULPTOR, NON EST IMITABILIS ANNA;
ANNA VIS SIMILEM SCULPERE? SCULPE DEAM.
S. CHAPMAN, PRÆTORE.

In the niche at the opposite end of the hall there was placed a statue of George, Prince of Denmark, attired in a Roman habit, with an inscription beneath scarcely less absurd than the former :—

SERENISSIMO PRINCIPI
GEORGIO PRINCIPI DANIÆ,
HEROI OMNI SÆCULO VENERANDO.
CHRISTOPHERUS WREN, ARM.
POSUIT MDCCXIII.

It would seem, however, that there were some of the townsmen who were sadly wanting in loyalty; for it is curious to find in the hall book in the year 1706 that there were members who said " the corporation was not twopence the better for the queen's coming to Windsor," which words, it was added, "do not agree with the grateful sense the corporation hath and ever shall have of her majesty's most gracious favour in affording them so much of her royal presence and the benefit they receive thereby." The delinquents were called to account and required to beg the queen's pardon.

We find no incidents of any interest in the history of the

town during the eighteenth century, and it only remains
briefly to indicate the alterations that have taken place of
late years. There are here and there still remaining in
Windsor portions of houses which belong to the seventeenth
century. The Duke's Head is said to have been the house
of Villiers, Duke of Buckingham. Behind the shop of
Mr. Lester, confectioner, in High-street, there is a staircase
of the time of the Stuarts, if not earlier. The Free School
near the Church, the Bank, and a house inhabited by A.
Moore, Esq., close to the bridge, are said to have been designed by Sir Christopher Wren. The last contains some
beautiful wood carving, attributed to Grindling Gibbons.
But the town has been so much altered of late that some
parts of it would hardly be recognised by those who have
not seen it for the last thirty years. Changes began to
take place much earlier than that. For example, the
borough gaol used to stand in St. Alban's-street, near the
Castle-hill; but it was removed by George III., who built
a new one in George-street, since pulled down. It is said
the monarch was annoyed by the prisoners, who would look
at him through the bars of their cells as he came down
from the castle, and used to cry, "God save the king—we
wish your majesty would let us out." At that time, and
as late as the year 1824, a gateway in the Italian style,
called Queen Elizabeth's gate, crossed the Castle-hill by
St. Alban's-street, and the left as well as the right side of
the hill was covered with houses and shops. Near the
Castle gate, and within the Castle domains, were three
lodges—the first, called the Queen's Lodge, and erected in
1782, at a cost of £44,000, from plans by George III.; the
second, called the Upper Lodge, an old building used by
Queen Anne, and by George III. in the earliest part of his
reign, and afterwards by some of the princesses; and the
third, or Lower Lodge, once St. Alban's House, but after-

wards purchased by the king for the younger branches of
the royal family. The former two are destroyed, the latter
remains as part of the royal mews, and is the building
nearly opposite the riding school, occupied by some of the
royal servants. Buildings, until within the last few years,
continued to line Thames-street on the east side down to the
entrance to the Hundred Steps, leaving the roadway very
narrow. The new bridge was built in 1822. Victoria-street,
the new road by Bachelors'-acre, by which, on a now unoccupied piece of ground, the royal mews stood, and
Clarence-crescent, with some adjoining thoroughfares, have
all been made within about thirty years. A road to Old
Windsor and Datchet used to run through Frogmore by
the side of the park walls, now pulled down. In lieu of the
old roads, enclosed now in the royal domains, the present
new ones were granted by the Crown.

The old parish church* was in a very dilapidated state
previously to its being pulled down for the erection of the
present edifice in 1820. It is a curious fact, stated on
the authority of Mr. Secker, late town clerk of Windsor,
that formerly there was but one sermon on a Sunday, and
it was delivered alternately—morning and afternoon.
When there was no discourse at the parish church, the
people after prayers walked to St. George's Chapel, to hear
it there. This created great disturbance, to put an end to

---

* We are told in Boswell's "Life of Johnson" (Croker's Edition),
vol. i., 297, that "he was sometime with Beauclerk at his house at
Windsor, where he was entertained with experiments in natural
philosophy. One Sunday, when the weather was very fine, Beauclerk
enticed him insensibly to saunter about all the morning. They went
into a churchyard, in the time of divine service, and Johnson laid
himself down at his ease upon one of the tombstones. 'Now, sir,'
said Beauclerk, 'you are like Hogarth's Idle Apprentice.'" Perhaps
Windsor Churchyard was the scene of this incident. It might, however, be Clewer, or Datchet, or Old Windsor.

which George III. allowed £50 a-year for a sermon in the church every Sunday. The new church on the road to the cavalry barracks, used as a military chapel, was built in 1844. The congregation of Independents now worshipping in Victoria-street Chapel, opened in 1833, formerly assembled in the small Presbyterian Church in High-street, which originally was a theatre, and was appropriated to sacred purposes when the present theatre was built in Thames-street. The Independent congregation is the oldest body of Dissenters in the town. It originated in the latter part of the last century, and at first, being very small, occupied a building not far from the present one, and called "the Hole in the Wall." An inconvenient place of worship was afterwards fitted up in Bier-lane, where the good people were occasionally disturbed in divine service. The Wesleyan denomination, at a much later period, built a small chapel in the same Lane, on the opposite side, but removed in 1836 to the edifice in Peascod-street. The Baptist Chapel was opened in 1839.

PART II.

DESCRIPTIVE.

CHAPTER I.

THE ROYAL PRECINCTS.

E never approach Windsor by the South-Western Railway, without thinking of Heidelberg. The favourite castle of our English monarchs—planted on a hill, its terrace crowning lovely slopes of garden ground and woods — calls to mind the once cherished home of the Electors Palatine, which, in like manner, rests in lordly magnificence on a declivity covered and enlivened by masses of foliage. The battlemented ridge here peeping above the tree tops, with faces looking down on field, and road, and river, is very much akin to that which surmounts the orchards there—where we have seen English tourists rejoicing in one of the most glorious of landscapes ; and have talked with them of the fortunes of poor Elizabeth of Bohemia, who, as Ferdinand the Elector's wife, and our first James' daughter, is a connecting historical link between the two edifices. Nor are the positions of the towns and bridges of Windsor and Heidelberg, in relation to the kingly halls and haunts—so long their chief attraction—much unlike. But, as in many other cases, when some few features of resemblance have struck the mind on a first survey, the comparison leads to a contrast ; so, the similarity between these two places is accompanied by many points of difference. We miss at Windsor the noble heights of Heidelberg, ascending behind the palace. We miss the valley. We miss the hanging woods and vineyards. Nor is the royal borough internally at all like the German university town. And then, moreover, and so for ages may it be, while Heidelberg is a crumbling ruin, deserted of her princes, Windsor is in the perfection of its strength and beauty, its lawns ringing with the laugh of merry children round their royal parents,* who there find a magnificent retreat and a happy home.

Opposite the entrance to the railway station is Travers College, standing near the spot where the martyrs were burnt in the reign of Henry VIII. We walk up the town till we reach the gateway which bears his name. It was erected in the first year of his reign, and the rose, portcullis, and the fleur-de-lis still decorating the front, are memorials of the Tudor origin of this stately piece of architecture. Once it was used for judicial purposes, for Stow calls this gate *the Exchequer of the honour*, where had been, and yet continued, a monthly court, kept by the clerk of the castle for the pleas of the forest. Here, tradition says, he came out to meet Anne Boleyn, when she entered the castle in the sunshine of his fickle favour, to be created, in the old presence chamber, a peeress of the realm, to wear the coronet of a marchioness, preparatory to putting on the diadem of a queen.

The appearance of the gateway shows the recent restoration of the masonry, and so do all the adjoining buildings. On the left-hand side is the guardhouse, and at the corner is the Salisbury Tower. A row of houses for the military knights on the Le Maire and Crane foundations till lately stood before the wall between the Salisbury and Garter Towers. On this site, buildings are now being erected for the use of the garrison, and the outer wall is being

* This, alas! is now no longer so.—January, 1862.

pierced with windows. Within the Garter-tower there has just been discovered an old stone staircase, with a roof of curious construction, something like complicated steps reversed. The military knights occupy the buildings on the right-hand side of the ward. In the midst of them is the Tower where the Governor lives. The Garter-house, with that symbol over the door, is now the residence of the Master of the Queen's Household. In the drawing-room of the latter is a carved mantelpiece of the time of James I.

St. George's Chapel is built in the Perpendicular style, and is one of the finest examples of it in the kingdom. There are, however, still remaining a few fragments of earlier date.

On walking round the exterior of the chapel at Windsor, the attention is immediately arrested by the fine windows in the aisles, and especially by the noble western window lately restored. "Like those in Henry VII.'s Chapel, and King's College Chapel," (observes Mr. Britton), "it fills up the whole width of the nave, and like the former is divided into three large compartments, each of which is again sub-divided by smaller mullions into five lights. Horizontally it consists of six tiers of lights, each with a cinquefoil head, and filled with ancient stained glass. Every transom has internally and externally an embattled moulding. The west window of Henry VII.'s Chapel contains only three transoms, and that of King's Chapel only one. The latter is divided into nine lights by vertical mullions." The western door-way, which has nothing to recommend it, exhibits the square outline and spandrel. The entrance to the cloisters at the east end of the chapel, between that and the tomb-house, is full of grace. "It has neither sculpture nor foliage of any sort to aid its effect, but it is nevertheless singularly appropriate and beautiful." As the eye passes along the elegant pile, the flying buttresses, yielding their light and ornamental supports to the clerestory, produce a pleasing effect. Yet the buttresses here are very plain compared with some erected in the same age. This part of the edifice is a striking example of the combination of utility and ornament, which is so important a principle in Gothic architecture. Of all the external features of St. George's Chapel, the battlements are the most elaborately ornamented. They are carried round the roof, forming an elegant mural crown, and afford a choice specimen of the taste of that period. Adjoining it at the east end is the royal tomb-house which Cardinal Wolsey intended to be his mausoleum. The history of that appropriation has been already given. It is a late instance of Perpendicular architecture, retaining " its propriety and elegance of design." It displays " neither any admixture of other styles nor any of the extravagance of German or French art of the period." Passing through the beautiful gateway between the chapel and the tomb-house, you enter the dean's cloister built by Edward III. and lately restored. The south wall is a fragment of the chapel of Henry III., and in the first arch is a curious painting of a crowned head—probably that of the royal builder. This relic was discovered behind the plaster while the restorations were going on in 1859. A projecting window on the opposite side belongs to a room said by some to have been occupied by Anne Boleyn. Beyond are the canons' cloisters, leading to the Hundred Steps, which have just been entirely rebuilt, and now bear no resemblance to what they were when we began to climb them thirty years ago.

On the left-hand side is a passage by the porch and doorway leading to the Chapter House. The rubbish by which this was concealed has been lately removed, and the groined roof and curious panelling are well worth examination. Crossing the passage to the outside of the chapel, you have a view of the northern aspect of the edifice. Some buildings connected with the canons' houses opposite have been recently removed, including the relics of John Denton's foundation. A part of the wall of the Domus Regis is thus thrown open to view, with the remains of a door in the wall of the second story, perhaps an entrance to one of the original royal apartments constructed by Walter de Burgh in the 24th of Henry III. Some brick pilasters and ornaments of the time of Inigo Jones appear on a wall just by these ancient relics. Proceeding westward we come to the Dean and Chapter's Library on the right-hand side, and on the left the old Horse-shoe Cloisters, so called from their being in the form of a fetter-lock, one of Edward IV.'s badges. To the left is the entrance to the bell tower, with the chimes of which the inhabitants of Windsor and the visitors there must be sufficiently familiar ; seeming at the summer's noon hour to be merrily telling of home joys, and of nature's pleasant gifts ; and on a winter's night—floating clear and strong through the frosty air, as the snow crackles under the pilgrim's foot—to be wailing out the dirge of departed generations. Norden's plan, drawn in James I.'s time, represents this tower with its surmounting cupola very nearly in its present state, and any one who will take the trouble to enter the tower—and it is well worth the trouble—will find the lower story in its pristine state, twenty-two feet in diameter, vaulted on plain stone ribs, with recessed arches terminating in loopholes, and showing the walls to be no less than twelve and a half feet thick. The whole is constructed with chalk, faced and arched with free-stone. The numerous inscriptions on its time-worn sides, seemingly hewed by unhappy prisoners, suggest to the moralist many a lesson and reflection. The upper part of the tower, where the massive stone walls are filled in with an enormous network of timber, forming apartments inhabited by the keeper, is very curious.

Passing under the gateway at the end of the cloister we come again into the open ward.

Having completed the outer circuit, let us examine the interior of the building. Attention is immediately attracted by the roof. There is presented a triumphant display of art. The scientific visitor will notice how the difficulty of the flat central span resting on the four cones is met by using low four-centred arch in a way " which is the perfection of this kind of vaulting, and is, perhaps, the most beautiful method ever invented."* The arches springing from the summits of the rows of graceful columns like the branches of palm trees—the beautiful interweaving of these on the roof, like the fibres of a leaf, yet all arranged in perfect forms— and the lightness and elasticity of the whole, which seems as if supported by magic—mark the highest excellence in the construction and decoration of this essential part of an edifice. The whole reminds us of Milton's description of the Indian fig-tree :—

> " Such as at this day to Indians known,
> In Malabar or Deccan spreads her arms,
> Branching so broad and long that on the ground
> The bending twigs take root, and daughters grow
> About the mother tree, a pillared shade
> High overarched, and echoing walks between."†

" Each side of the nave consists of seven similar compartments, with corresponding piers, panelling over the arches, windows, and panellings in the aisles, upper tier of windows, also groining springing from the clustered columns. A fascia, or frieze of half angels, extends all round the interior of the building beneath the upper windows. An elegant ornament of lozenged-shape leaves, &c., a genuine mark of the Tudor style of architecture, is shown above

---

* Fergusson's " Handbook of Architecture," p. 83.
† " Paradise Lost," book ix. line 1102.

these heads, the bodies of which are displayed as covered with feathers. Each transom or horizontal mullion of the windows has an embattled moulding. The two western arches of the nave, between that and the aisles, are rather wider than the others."*

The roof of the chapel is further ornamented with various coats of arms and other devices. The arms of Edward III. and IV., of Henry VI., VII., and VIII., and of several noble families, may be distinctly recognised, as well as the rose, portcullis, and fleur-de-lis, the badge of the last two Henries.

The impression of loftiness, and hence the emotion of sublimity produced, when looking at the roof, is greatly aided by the vast number of details—by the multiplication of parts, instead of enlargement of the scale, as in the case of lofty buildings of the Grecian orders. The tracery deserves careful observation.

In the aisles on each side of the choir there are beautiful specimens of screen-work in front of the different chapels, and other objects of interest. Ascending the northern aisle on the left side is Rutland Chapel, where some of the Rutland family are interred ; and on the right is Hastings Chapel, in which there are grotesque paintings of the Martyrdom of Stephen. Two children of Edward IV. and Queen Elizabeth Widville are buried in this aisle. Also the Duchess of Saxe-Weimar, niece to Queen Adelaide. At the east end is the entrance to the Chapter House, which contains the portrait and sword of Edward III. A curious iron lock, a richly worked grating, and an escutcheon on a door, in this aisle, should be particularly noticed ; and passing round at the back of the altar, another beautiful piece of ironwork will be seen on the door leading to the tomb-

* Britton's "Antiquities," vol. iii. p. 39.

house. In the south aisle, at its eastern end, is Lincoln
Chapel, once Sir John Scone's. Near to this is the
memorial niche of Beauchamp,* Bishop of Salisbury ;
opposite, a black-letter Bible is chained. In this aisle
Henry VI. is buried. There is on the right side a
chapel, dedicated to John the Baptist by John Oxenbridge, a canon of this church. It was erected in
1522. The screen is a beautiful piece of workmanship ;
but the paintings, intended to represent the history of
the Baptist, are extremely grotesque. Next to it is the
screen which belongs to Urswick Chapel, removed here
when that chapel received the Princess Charlotte's cenotaph.
The inscription, requesting prayers for the souls of King
Harry VIII., Christopher Urswick, and all Christian souls,
is an odd mixture of Latin and English. Adjoining, on the
same side, are four ancient paintings of Prince Edward,
the son of King Henry VI., Edward IV., Edward V., and
Henry VII. Underneath them is the monument recently
erected by the Queen in memory of the Duchess of
Gloucester, with good bas-reliefs of the "acts of mercy," by
Mr. Theed. Opposite is Oliver King's Chapel. The door
bears the following inscription :—

DE SURSŪ EST   UT DI-S-CĀ.

In the blank space is introduced the carved figure of a
volume, chained. The sense of the whole seems to be—
"This book came from above, for our instruction." Oliver
King was secretary to Henry VI., Edward IV., Edward V.,
and Henry VII. ; and, after being a canon of Windsor for
some time, was, in the year 1492, raised to the see of
Exeter ; and in 1495, translated to that of Bath and Wells.

---

* Mr. Britton, quoting Mr. Gough, says that Beauchamp was
buried within his own private chapel or oratory at Salisbury.

He built the Abbey Church at Bath, the latest example of a cathedral edifice in this country. He died in the year 1503, and is supposed, though there are some doubts on the subject, to be buried in this little chapel. At the end, near the south door, is Bray Chapel.

The founder of this chantry had so much to do with the chapel that he deserves special notice, and we are glad to introduce the following paragraphs from Mr. Britton's "Architectural Antiquities" (Vol. iii. p. 33) :—

"That the Chapel of St. George, at Windsor, owes much to the skill, as well as to the munificence of Sir Reginald Bray, there can be no doubt. His arms, sometimes single, sometimes impaling those of Huse, whom he married, and his device of a flax-breaker, are in so many parts of the ceiling and windows, that they could not have been placed there without a more than ordinary claim to the situation.

"The chapel on the south side, still called Bray's Chapel, was built by him to receive his body, as appears by his will, which is dated August 4, 1503, and he thereby directs that his body shall be buried in the chapel on the south side of the church of our Lady and St. George, in the Castle of Windsor, which he had made for that intent, and also in honour of Almighty God, &c. He wills that his executors, after his decease, should, with his goods and the issues and profits of his lands, make and perform the new works of the body of the said church, and thoroughly finish them, according to the form and intent of the foundation, in stone-work, timber, lead, iron, and glass, and all other things necessary ; that they should cause a tomb to be made for him in the said chapel ; and he gave forty marks a-year to the Dean and Canons to distribute thirteen pence every day to thirteen poor men or women, at the door of the said chapel.

"He died the next day, and in the November following his will was proved in the Prerogative Court of Canterbury.

"No tomb was erected, but his body probably lies under the stone which is placed over Dr. Waterland; for Mr. Pote, in his account of Windsor, tells us, that on opening the vault for that gentleman, who died in 1740, a leaden coffin of ancient form was found, which by other appearances was judged to be that of Sir Reginald, and was, by order of the Dean, immediately arched over with great decency.

"From the expression in the will as to finishing this church, it may fairly be inferred, not only that great works had been carried on at his expense, but that he had a share at least in the designing them. After seeing what he did here, it may not, perhaps, be too much to conjecture that he had also a share in the design of Henry VII.'s Chapel at Westminster, where he assisted in laying the first stone."

In the Bray Chapel there is a tomb to the memory of William Fitzwilliam, who died October 13, 1659. "This tomb corresponds in design and material with that of Chaucer in Westminster Abbey Church, which Gough says was 'the work of Mr. Nicholas Brigham, of Caversham, in Oxfordshire,' and erected by him in 1556. The design and mode of workmanship show the decline—the last struggle—of the Tudor style of church architecture, and is therefore worthy of preservation." In the Bray Chapel there is a monument to Dr. Giles Thomson, Bishop of Gloucester, and one of the translators of King James's Bible, besides others that we have not space to mention. Indeed, we have passed over several in our rapid walk round the chapel, which the visitor, of course, will see, but with regard to which there is not much of artistic or antiquarian interest to observe. We may, however, perhaps pause for a moment, just to say with regard to the chan-

tries we have hastily passed, that the one bearing the Rutland name was founded at the expense of Sir Thomas St.
Ledger, for the interment of the Duchess of Exeter, sister
of Edward IV., in 1475. In the centre is the altar tomb
of Lord Ross, ancestor of the Duke of Rutland. Hastings
Chapel was built by the wife of William Lord Hastings,
Chamberlain to Edward IV. Lincoln Chapel contains the
monument of the Earl of Lincoln, who was High Admiral
of England for thirty years, and died in 1584. It was
erected by his widow. The Oxenbridge Chantry and that
of Oliver King have been particularly noticed. And now it
only remains to walk down the aisle to the west end to
view the Beaufort Chapel with its tomb and statues to the
memory of the Earl, who died in 1526, and the elaborate
monument to the Duke, who was buried here in 1699. It
is here, too, that the remains of the Marquis of Worcester,
who died in 1646, repose. The cenotaph of the Princess
Charlotte, in the opposite aisle, by Wyatt, with its gilded
canopy—of the whole of which we leave the visitor to form
his own opinion—occupies the room of what was originally
Urswick's Chapel.

An old iron alms-box stands by the entrance to the
choir. The interior is very magnificent. A few years ago,
the roof was richly tinted, and the oak carving carefully
cleaned and polished.* Some of the windows were about

* After examining the carved seats in the choir, it is amusing to
turn to a letter by Horace Walpole, written to Lady Ossory, on
the 22nd of July, 1788 :—"You may know, perhaps, that in days of
yore the flaps of seats in choirs of cathedrals were decorated with
sculptures; sometimes with legends; oftener, alas, with devices at
best ludicrous, frequently not fit to meet the eye of modesty. Well,
madam, two new stalls being added in the Church of St. George at
Windsor, as niches for the supernumerary knights that have been
added, the custom has been observed and carried on in the new flaps
—not to call up a blush in the cheek of mother church, but in the
true catholic spirit. One of the bas-reliefs I do not know, but pro-

the same time admirably reglazed with painted glass, so as
to make more conspicuous the tastelessness of those painted
in George III.'s time, from West's designs. The heraldic
ornaments on the stalls of the Knights of the Garter, and
the overhanging banners, add to the general effect.
Henry VIII. and Charles I. are buried in the choir; and
at the altar steps is the entrance to the royal vaults, where
are interred George III., George IV., William IV., Queen
Charlotte, and Queen Adelaide. Beside them are the Dukes
of York and Kent, Prince Alfred, the Princesses Amelia
and Augusta, and the Princess Charlotte.

Looking at St. George's Chapel in its present state, it is
curious to read the following letter from Mr. Francis
Pigott, a correspondent of the "Gentleman's Magazine."
It is dated the 20th of June, 1786.

"From Eton I adjourned to the Chapel of St. George
at Windsor. Here a new scene presented itself; an elegant
and neglected Gothic chapel, perhaps the first in the world
for beauty and splendour, but dirty, and disregarded to
such a degree as to become a nuisance to the eye and a
reproach to the sexton, who I am told receives daily hand-
some donations for showing it, yet is regardless to the
greatest degree of shame, not so much as dusting the
monuments or washing the chapel. An elegant monument
of the Beaufort family is at this moment tumbling
into ruins, some of the principal figures thereon being
supported by common cords or ropes; another, of the
Lincoln family, totally in ruins; others of the Rutland

bably the martyrdom of St. Edmund the King; the other is the
ineffectual martyrdom of George the King by Margaret Nicholson.
The body-coachman is standing by, to ascertain the precise moment.
If you had not heard of this decoration, I will not say, madam,
that I had no news to send you; at least I may subscribe myself
your ladyship's humble clerke and antiquarie, H. W."—(" Letters to
the Countess of Ossory," vol. ii. p. 334.)

and Exeter families, alike ruinous, certainly for want of a report to those noble families to whom they belong. This royal chapel is, I am informed, now shut up for divers repairs and ornaments, which his majesty has condescended to bestow upon it, particularly the window so much talked of for the east end, and the celebrated window by West. This is a season, therefore, for all persons whose ancestors are there interred to give their particular directions for the repair of these sepulchral monuments. And I flatter myself we shall see the pews, heretofore used in the sermon time, and the old pulpit, removed. The pavement of this royal chapel would be disgraceful to a barn ; perhaps his majesty, whose monument, from his munificence, it will become, may direct a new pavement to be laid down, as he takes great delight in this very beautiful temple. Or if the Knights Companions of the Garter were to contribute thereto, and to ornament the windows in the aisles with their arms, or other painted glass, it would add great solemnity and magnificence to the whole."*

Leaving St. George's Chapel, we pass the deanery to the left, adjoining the tomb-house. Just beyond, are the castle store rooms, with the Winchester Tower rising above them, and facing the north terrace. There is the inscription *"Hoc fecit Wykeham."* Corresponding on the south side is King Henry III.'s Tower. Across the space here, and dividing the lower ward from the middle ward, there was formerly a wall and gateway, as shown in Norden's map. The buildings attached to King Henry III.'s Tower are the architect's offices,† from which there runs a path between walls to St. George's Gate. Proceeding to the left

---

* "Gentleman's Magazine," vol. lvi. p. 449.

† Several curious fragments of Henry VII. buildings, dug out from under Queen Elizabeth's Gallery and the Royal Chapel, are at the present time ranged on the wall near the office.

by the side of the dry moat of the Round Tower, we reach the Norman gateway with its machicolations and portcullis, passing under which, there is an entrance on the left, by Queen Elizabeth's Gallery, to the north terrace, and on the right to the covered stairway which conducts to the top of the Round Tower, where, on a fine day, we are told, twelve counties may be seen. Sir Jeffrey Wyatville raised the Round Tower thirty feet, exclusive of the Watch Tower, which was twenty-five feet more. Descending to the terrace, and proceeding to the east end, a line of iron rails is found dividing it from the east terrace, which, with its garden, extends far beyond its original limits. Before Sir Jeffrey Wyatville's additions, the terrace was confined to the narrow raised walk along the east front of the castle. At the end of the north terrace was a sun-dial, close to which were steps leading down to the open park. The public had free access to all that portion of the royal domain. By Mother Dod's Hill, as it was called, there was a pleasant walk to Datchet, and all the way boys trundled their hoops and flew their kites at liberty. Returning along the terrace, and re-entering the upper ward, we now find the quadrangle or upper court carefully enclosed, and wearing the appearance of a majestic solitude ; but in the days of George III. it was all open for people to walk and loiter wherever they pleased. Some still living can remember playing at boyish sports within these royal precincts, and making the old walls ring with their merry shouts and cries. The equestrian statue of Charles II. then stood in the middle.

Pausing here for a moment to look round, and remembering the present palatial appearance of the castle on the north terrace, it is interesting to read the following passage from Mr. Poynter's Essay, prefixed to Sir Jeffrey Wyatville's " Illustrations of Windsor Castle :"—

" The only original trace of the architecture of the four-teenth century, now to be discerned, on the exterior of the upper ward, occurs in the principal gate adjoining the keep, where the whole of the archway, and the machecoulis which overhangs it, display a character not to be mistaken. The gateway which occupied the north-eastern angle of the upper court, taken down in the late alterations, exhibited similar machecoulis ; and Hollar's general view indicates the same in that occupying the place of the present state entrance. None of the towers appear ever to have borne this striking characteristic of the castellated architecture of the fourteenth century ; but the formal repetition of square outlines, so offensive to the eye, previously to the operations of Sir Jeffrey Wyatville, was broken by lofty and picturesque turrets, most of which disappeared in the alterations of the seventeenth century. To the south and east, the castle presented a stern aspect of defiance. The ditch extended throughout those two sides, the curtain walls were blank and unbroken, except by buttresses, and the only apertures were the gateways and loopholes in the tower. The apart-ments were of course lighted altogether from within. The three small areas on the side where the buildings are double, since known as Birch Court, Horn Court, and the Kitchen Court, seem to indicate that the north front originally bore the same character as the rest ; but of this there is no representation until buildings of late date had supervened."

The Grand Staircase and the Waterloo Gallery now occupy the sites of these three courts.

But it is time to enter the State Apartments. Those which are at present open to the public are fewer than they used to be. They are situated in what was called the Star Building of Charles II., and you approach them now by a Gothic porch next to King John's Tower. On the narrow staircase is a portrait of Sir J. Wyatville. The first room shown is the QUEEN'S AUDIENCE CHAMBER, still retaining its original name. The ceiling is covered with allegorical paintings, by Verrio, and the walls are ornamented with tapestry illustrating the history of Esther. The whole-length portrait of Mary Queen of Scots is very curious. There are also portraits of Frederick Henry, Prince of Orange, and William II., Prince of Orange. All the frames are by Gibbons. Next is the VANDYKE ROOM, formerly the old Ball Room. Here are portraits of Henry, Count de Berg; King Charles I. and his family; Mary, Duchess of Richmond; Thomas Killigrew and Thomas Carew; Henrietta Maria, Consort of Charles I.; Anastasia Venetia, Lady Digby; George Villiers, Duke of Bucking-ham, and his brother, Lord Francis Villiers, full length, as boys; Thomas Francis of Savoy, Prince of Carignano; Henrietta Maria, Queen Consort of Charles I.; Beatrice Con-stance, Princess de Cantecroye; Children of King Charles I.; King Charles I., front, profile, and three-quarter face; Henrietta Maria, Queen Consort of Charles I.; Lucy, Countess of Carlisle; Sir Kenelm Digby, Knt.; King Charles II. when a boy; Sir Anthony Vandyke; Henri-etta Maria, Queen Consort of King Charles I.; Three Children of Charles I.; Mary, Countess of Dorset; King Charles I., on horseback, accompanied by M. de St. Antoine, his Equerry, on foot; portrait of a Gentleman, unknown.

We have no space to relate anecdotes respecting the per-sons represented in this unrivalled collection of Vandykes, nor to give criticisms on the pictures. We would, however, observe that in this room the finest and most celebrated picture is the King Charles on horseback.* It is a world-

* " In Smith's Catalogue it is said that King Charles presented a duplicate of this picture to Sir John Byron, of Newstead Abbey,

known picture, a *chef-d'œuvre* of the artist. Among other pictures interesting and beautiful, may be mentioned Lady Venetia Digby, and the half-length of Henrietta Maria, the face seen in three-quarters. What can exceed in youthful grace the two young Villierses and the group of the royal children? The picture of Charles and his family is very beautiful. "The arrangement of this picture has all the quiet elegance of Vandyke; and in the painting, more particularly in the figure of the little prince, in front, we see the result of his Venetian studies, in the warm depth of the tone, and the mellow touch; the hands are, as usual, very fine. It is hardly possible, remembering the sorrows and the troublous times which afterwards burst on this devoted family, to look without an emotion of pitying complacency on this representation of domestic happiness, security, and royal dignity, set forth in all the enchanting illusion of art."

The QUEEN'S STATE DRAWING-ROOM, which still goes by the old name, though more frequently called the Zuccarelli Room, from paintings by that master, contains, beside the Meeting of Isaac and Rebecca, the Finding of Moses, and seven Landscapes, by that artist, portraits of Henry, Duke of Gloucester, the three Georges, and Frederick, Prince of Wales. These landscapes are fair examples of Zuccarelli's style, "of which the great and unredeemable fault is insipidity."

The STATE ANTE-ROOM, formerly the State Bedroom, and. earlier still, the King's Public Dining-room, retains Verrio's ceiling, and some good carvings by Gibbons. The

which is now in possession of Lady Warren, of Stapleford; and that another duplicate, or copy, is in possession of the Earl of Warwick. There exist, in different collections in England and on the Continent, thirty-six portraits of King Charles by the hand of Van Dyck."— MRS. JAMESON.

stained glass portrait of King George III. is conspicuous enough. The Grand Staircase, with Chantrey's colossal statue of George IV., conducts to the grand vestibule, furnished with trophies and armour, and a curious clock.

THE WATERLOO CHAMBER contains portraits of the following great men of Europe during our wars with Napoleon:—Amand Emanuel Sophie Septimanie Duplessis, Duc de Richelieu, President of the French Council, and Minister for Foreign Affairs from 1815 to 1822 ; General Overoff, one of the Russian Adjutants-General ; H. R. H. Adolphus Frederick, Duke of Cambridge ; the Right. Hon. Robert Banks Jenkinson, second Earl of Liverpool, K.G., Prime Minister from 1812 to 1827 ; King William IV. (by *Sir David Wilkie*) ; King George III. (by *Sir William Beechey*) ; King George IV. ; the Right Hon. Robert Stewart, Viscount Castlereagh, K.G., Secretary of State for Foreign Affairs from 1812 to 1822 ; H. R. H. Frederick, Duke of York, K.G. ; Karl Wilhelm, Baron von Humboldt, Prussian Minister of State and Plenipotentiary at the Congress of Vienna ; the Right Hon. George Canning, Secretary of State for Foreign Affairs in 1807, and again in 1822, Prime Minister in 1827 on the death of Lord Liverpool ; the Right Hon. Henry Bathurst, third Earl Bathurst, K.G., Secretary of State for the Colonies in 1815 ; Ernst Friedrich Herbert, Count Munster, Plenipotentiary from Hanover at the Congress of Vienna ; Ercole Consalvi, Cardinal, Plenipotentiary from Pope Pius VII. at the Congress of Vienna ; Karl August, Prince of Hardenberg, State Chancellor of Prussia ; Frederick William III., King of Prussia ; Francis I., Emperor of Austria ; Alexander I., Emperor of Russia ; Charles Robert, Count Nesselrode, Russian Secretary of State for Foreign Affairs, and Minister at the Congresses of Vienna,

Aix-la-Chapelle, and Verona; Pius VII. [Gregory Barnabas Lewis Chiaramonte], elected March 14th, 1800; John, Count of Capo d'Istrias, Russian Secretary of State for Foreign Affairs, and Plenipotentiary at the Congress of Vienna; Clemens Wenzel Nepomuk Lothar, Prince of Metternich-Winneburg, Duke of Portella, Austrian Chancellor of State from 1813 to 1848; Rowland, Viscount Hill, G.C.B. (by *H. W. Pickersgill, R.A.*)—his Lordship commanded a Division of the British Army at the Battle of Waterloo; Charles X., King of France; Karl Philip, Prince of Schwartzenberg — he commanded the Allied Forces at the memorable battle of Leipzig, Oct. 18, 1813; Karl Ludwig, Archduke of Austria, second son of the Emperor Leopold II., and brother of Francis I., Emperor of Austria, General Field-Marshal of Austria; Lieut.-Gen. Sir Thomas Picton, G.C.B., (by *Sir Martin Archer Shee, P.R.A.*)—commanded the fifth division of the British army at the Battle of Waterloo, where he was killed; Louis Antoine de Bourbon, Duke of Angouleme, son of Charles X., King of France; William Frederick, Duke of Brunswick-Oels (copied by — *Corden* from a miniature)— the Duke was killed at Quatre Bras, June 16, 1815; H. R. H. Leopold George Christian Frederick, Prince of Saxe-Coburg-Saalfeld, K.G., now King of the Belgians; General the Right Hon. Sir James Kemp, G.C.B., G.C.H. (by *H. W. Pickersgill, R.A.*)—commanded the fifth division at Waterloo, after the death of Sir Thomas Picton; Count Platoff, Hetman of the Cossacks; Arthur, Duke of Wellington, K.G.; Gebhard Leberecht von Blucher, Prince of Wahlstadt; Charles, Count Alten, G.C.B., and G.C.H. (by *Reichmann*)—commanded the third division of the British army at the Battle of Waterloo; Henry William Paget, Marquis of Anglesey, K.G., G.C.B., &c. (by *Sir Martin Archer Shee, P.R.A.*)—commanded the cavalry at the Battle of Waterloo ; Lieut.-General Count Czernitscheff, one of the Adjutants-General to the Emperor of Russia during the campaigns of 1813, 1814, and 1815 ; William Frederick George Lewis, Prince of Orange—commanded the Netherlands Troops at the Battle of Waterloo, and was severely wounded in that terrific conflict. He became King of the Netherlands on his father's abdication, October 7th, 1840.

After examining this collection of portraits,* of which those not otherwise described are by Sir Thomas Lawrence, most visitors will confirm the judgment of the artist, who considered himself most successful with the Pope and Consalvi. " If what I have done here in the portraits of the Pope and Cardinal be compared only with my own works, I have had complete success." The picture which ought to be best is one of the very worst—the portrait of Wellington.

Next is the PRESENCE CHAMBER, ornamented in the style of the period of Louis XIV. On the walls are specimens of Gobelins tapestry, representing the story of Jason and Medea. The west side of the room contains " The Marriage of Jason and Creusa," " The Combat of the Soldiers born of the dragon's teeth," and " The flight of Medea to Athens, after having murdered her two sons ;" the east

---

* Mrs. Jameson says, " I think it unnecessary to say anything of the portraits in the Waterloo Chamber; the attention of the spectator will probably be directed by his individual associations and predilections ; but without doubt the best picture is the portrait of Pius VII., and the worst that of the Duke of Wellington. The portrait of Prince Schwartzenberg, and several others, are in a bad state from the effects of a bad chill, which has rendered them partially invisible. In this room an opera-glass will be found useful ; some of the pictures are hung much too high ; and of one or two it may be said, that if they were hung out of sight entirely it would be no great loss: neither as pictures nor as personages do they figure advantageously here."

side, "Jason pledging his faith to Medea," "Creusa con-
sumed by the Fatal Robe," and "Jason carrying off the
Golden Fleece." The room also contains a MALACHITE
VASE, presented to the Queen by Nicholas, Emperor of
Russia; and two Granite Vases, presented to King
William IV. by Frederick William III., King of Prussia.

The present ST. GEORGE'S HALL comprises not only
the "St. George's Hall" as left by King Charles II. after
his reparation and restoration of the Castle, but also
the Private Royal Chapel; which latter, however, becoming
comparatively useless and to a great extent dismantled,
after the erection of the Grand Staircase by King
George III. in 1800, was entirely removed by Sir Jeffrey
Wyatville, and with the space thus gained the present apartment was formed. Its ceiling is decorated with
the arms of the knights of the order, from the institution to
the present time; and its walls exhibit the portraits of the
Sovereigns of the Order, from JAMES I. to GEORGE IV. At
the east end is placed the Sovereign's Throne, behind which,
on twenty-four separate shields, are emblazoned the arms
of each Sovereign of the Order, from Edward III. to King
William IV. The names of the several knights are painted
between the panels of the windows on the south side of
the Hall, to each of which is affixed a number corresponding to that attached to the arms on the ceiling, commencing
with those of Edward III. and the Black Prince, over the
gallery at the east end.

THE GUARD CHAMBER adjoins St. George's Hall. Some
whole-length figures are clad in the armour of the personages whose names are written on the brackets upon
which they are respectively placed.* These consist of suits
of armour, once belonging to a Duke of Branswick, 1530;

* The accuracy of the statements is more than doubtful.

Lord Howard, 1588 ; Earl of Essex, 1596 ; Henry, Prince of Wales [eldest son of King James I.], 1612 ; Charles, Prince of Wales [Charles I.], 1620 ; and Prince Rupert, 1635. At the south end is a portion of the foremast of the VICTORY, Lord Nelson's flag-ship at the battle of Trafalgar, completely perforated by a cannon-ball. Nelson's bust, by *Sir Francis Chantrey*, is placed on the top of it.

Close to these are two field-pieces selected from the captured Sikh artillery by Viscount Hardinge.

Next, there are, or were, two small pieces of brass ordnance, apparently of French manufacture, formerly belonging to Tippoo Saib, Sultaun of Mysore, and taken at the capture of Seringapatam. Both are mounted on mahogany carriages of English manufacture.

Here are also the busts of JOHN CHURCHILL, DUKE OF MARLBOROUGH, copied from *Rysbrach* by *Sevier;* and ARTHUR WELLESLEY, DUKE OF WELLINGTON, by *Chantrey;* with the small banners presented on the anniversaries of the battles of Blenheim and Waterloo, as the tenures on which their estates voted by Parliament are held.

Over the fire-place is the shield said to have been presented by Francis I., King of France, to our Henry VIII. on " THE FIELD OF THE CLOTH OF GOLD." The following is a translation of the inscription :—

" This circling border though but small itself, contains within its circuit vast ambition ;—ambition which overturns Kingdoms and lays low Empires. It abolished from amongst men the life and glory of Pompey, and raised on high the empire of Cæsar. The mild clemency of Cæsar is extolled to the skies, but to Pompey it was at length destructive. The ring and severed head of Pompey draws tears from Cæsar, whence it was clearly seen, how upright he was. Then the garment sprinkled with gore during the sacrifice, prophetic of evil, certified that such would be his fate. If you should therefore contemplate the power of ambition, you would not discover an evil more pernicious."*

Two other relics here may be noticed. A chair made from an oak-beam, taken from "Alloway's auld haunted kirk," a little, obscure, roofless ruin in Ayrshire, described in Burns' tale of "Tam o' Shanter."

The other chair is made from an elm-tree which grew on the battle-field of Waterloo. In the upper portion of the back, over a carved representation of the village and church of Waterloo is a Latin inscription by the late Marquis Wellesley. It reads thus in English :—

> THIS CHAIR,
> CARVED FROM THE WELLINGTON ELM
> WHICH STOOD NEAR THE CENTRE
> OF THE BRITISH LINES
> ON THE FIELD OF WATERLOO,
> IS HUMBLY PRESENTED TO
> HIS MOST GRACIOUS MAJESTY
> GEORGE THE FOURTH.

From the Guard Chamber the visitor enters the QUEEN'S PRESENCE CHAMBER. The ceiling is by Verrio. The walls of this room are decorated with Gobelins tapestry, representing other portions of the history of Esther and Mordecai, in continuation of those mentioned before.

Over the doorways are portraits of two princesses of the House of Brunswick, each surrounded by Gibbons' carving.

Over the chimney-piece, which is sculptured by Bacon, is a portrait of Henrietta Maria, Duchess of Orleans, by *Mignard*.

The children are her two daughters, Maria Louisa and Anna Maria. The first was married to Charles II., King

---

* Here, as well as in a few particulars we have described, we avail ourselves of the authorized Guide to the State Apartments.

of Spain, and the second to Victor Amadeus II., Duke of
Savoy and King of Sardinia.

Until recently, the Queen's Closet, the King's Closet, the
Council Room, the King's Drawing-room or the Rubens
Room, and the Throne Room, were shown to the public. In
the Queen's Closet is an admirable portrait of Thomas
Howard, Duke of Norfolk, by Holbein ; and there too
hangs the celebrated picture of "The Misers," by Quentin
Matsys. The King's Closet, amongst other paintings, has a
Head, by Parmigiano, the Woman of Samaria, by Guer-
cino, a St. Catherine, by Domenichino, and a Man with a
Gardener's Knife, attributed to Andrea del Sarto. The
pictures in the Rubens Room are of unequal merit, and
some were not wholly painted by that artist. Philip II. of
Spain is bad ; the Battle of Nordlingen, poor ; perhaps St.
Martin dividing his Cloak with the Beggar, a noble com-
position, has some colouring in it from the pencil of
Vandyke. There are two landscapes, Summer and Winter,
very charming.

The Council Room is adorned with pictures by A. Caracci,
Correggio, Rembrandt, Holbein, and Sir Joshua Reynolds.
The Throne Room, used for the installation of Knights of
the Garter, contains a picture of the First Installation, by
West, and portraits of the last three sovereigns. The
vestibule to the Throne Room has five pictures by West—
Edward III. at the Battle of Cressy, the Black Prince
receiving the King of France, Philippa at Neville's Cross,
Edward entertaining his Prisoners at Calais, and Philippa
pleading for the Citizens.

We have noticed the successive names and uses of some
of the State Apartments. Those who are permitted to see
the beautiful library, which is in the part of the building
erected by Elizabeth and Henry VII., will be interested in
learning the curious changes which have taken place in that

portion of the royal edifice. We enter King Charles's room, which runs across the building north and south. This used to be the queen's bedchamber. Proceeding to the continuation of the library in what is now termed Henry VII.'s room, we find ourselves where formerly was an ante-room, containing Sir Peter Lely's beauties of Charles's court, and where, next to it, stood the queen's dressing-room. Then ascending the steps, we come to what was Elizabeth's picture gallery, with the beautiful old mantelpiece of her reign.

The royal library, which thus occupies the rooms known as Charles II.'s and Henry VII.'s, with the Blenheim tower (in which is the room where Anne was drinking tea when the news reached her of the victory of Blenheim); and the Elizabeth gallery, contains about forty thousand volumes, the greater number of which are old and valuable works on history, geography, topography, &c., with those of the Greek, Latin, French, and other classical writers, and early printed books. Amongst the latter are a splendid copy of the famous Mentz Psalter, and a unique Caxton, on vellum. Charles I.'s Shakspeare is another of the treasures of this collection.

In connexion with the library, on a lower story of the Star buildings, is the collection of prints and drawings, which is one of the richest and most extensive in the country. The engravings consist of portraits, historical events, &c., and prints after all the great masters. Few collections of Hollar's engravings, Hogarth's works, and engravings after Sir Joshua Reynolds, can compare with those which are found here. And there are illustrated copies of Lord Clarendon's works, Grammont's Memoirs, Coxe's Marlbororough, &c., with a noble assemblage of Galleries, &c. &c., and works on the fine arts. There is also a very large collection of caricatures from the sixteenth century down to the present time. The drawings are contained in about two hundred volumes, and comprise some fine drawings by Raphael, a still greater number by Michael Angelo, a very numerous and most interesting series by Leonardo da Vinci, with others by Albert Durer, Canaletti, the Caracci, Carlo Maratti, Claude, Correggio, Domenichino, Guido, Holbein, Poussin, &c. &c., Kirby, the Sandbys, Bruce the Abyssinian traveller, &c. &c. There are here also the "Sobieski Missal," which is an exceedingly fine specimen of mediæval illumination and miniaturist work, and several splendidly decorated Oriental MSS. The collection of miniatures contains some of the finest examples of the works of Holbein, Hilliard, the Olivers, Hoskins, Cooper, Janet, &c. &c. Besides these, there are the great collections of State papers known as the "Stuart" and the "Cumberland Papers," and a vast assemblage of maps and plans illustrative of the military history of the last century before the French Revolution.

The armoury, arranged a few years ago by His Royal Highness the Prince Consort, is situated in the gallery between the Cornwall and Brunswick Towers. Besides curious weapons of various kinds—including eastern scimitars and other jewelled swords—the far-famed Tippoo Saib's tiger head, and the peacock with its tail of diamonds, are here preserved, as well as the ball which killed Nelson at Trafalgar. On the basement floor of the Prince of Wales' Tower, is the Plate Room, remarkable for costly table services and works of art—such as Flaxman's shield of Achilles, and a nautilus shell, set by Cellini. We might mention a number of other beautiful ornaments, but we have no room for description, and it is idle to give a mere catalogue. There are very few antiquities in the collection, owing to the circumstance of the royal plate having been melted down in the civil wars of Charles I. There is an ancient cup, reported to belong to him, and another said

to have been Henry VIII.'s. Nell Gwynne's bellows are
also preserved here.

In the Pages' Vestibule, on the upper floor, are several
charming paintings by Canaletti and Zuccarelli, and two or
three by the two artists jointly, or by Visentini and Zuccarelli ; one by Marco Ricci ; and a portrait of James II.
when young, by Dobson. The life-size statue of Penelope,
by Wyatt, also deserves attention.

But it is in the Grand Corridor, which runs along the
east and south sides of the upper ward of the castle, and
is 520 feet in length, that the most rich and varied
assemblage of works of art is collected. In spite of the
badly-arranged light, and the lowness of the ceiling, the
effect, when viewed from either end, or from the entrance
to the Queen's private staircase, whence it is extended in
both directions, is remarkably grand. Some of the finest
portraits ever painted by Lawrence catch the eye amongst
the first : Lord Eldon, Lord Thurlow, Pitt, the Marquis
Wellesley, the Duke of Devonshire, the Princess Charlotte
(a replica of the figure in the large picture of Queen Caro-
line, now in the Princess Royal's room), Dona Maria (the
late Queen of Portugal), Canning, Sir Walter Scott, and
Alderman Curtis. There is also a good copy of Reynolds'
portrait of the beautiful Duchess of Devonshire, by him.
Of Reynolds' own works. there are portraits of the Princess
of Gloucester, Lord Erskine, the Duke of Cumberland
(the Culloden Duke), the Earl of Eglinton, and Garrick as
Kitely, and a strangely quiet historical scene—the Marriage
of George III. Hoppner is well represented by his portraits
of the late Archbishops of Canterbury and York—Manners
Sutton, and Dr. Markham ; Admiral Keith, and the Duke
of Kent. Landseer's "First of May, 1851," which shows
the Duke of Wellington offering a birthday present to his
little namesake, Prince Arthur, in the presence of the

Queen and the Prince Consort, is here also. Of Gainsborough, there is only the picture of the Duke and Duchess
of Cumberland with Lady Luttrell ; but in the Queen's
Audience room there are some most exquisite portraits of
George III.'s family, by him.   The Viscountess Mel-
bourne, by Cosway, approaches Reynolds in gracefulness.
Kneller's George I. has little interest compared with the
two portraits of the Duke and Duchess of Marlborough.
A pleasing little picture by Nollekens, of Frederick Prince
of Wales and his sisters, is here ; and Hayter's portrait of
the Queen in her coronation robes ; and Sir David Wilkie's
last work, a portrait of the late Sultan Abdul Medjid.
Zoffany's two great groups, the Royal Academy, and the
Academy at Florence, are of especial interest.   Of the
same class, but of higher historical importance, are the
Ball at the Hague, by H. Janssens ; Queen Victoria's First
Council, by Wilkie ; the Coronation Communion of the
Queen, by Leslie ; the Marriage of the Queen, by G. Hayter ;
the Christening of the Princess Royal, by Leslie ; and the
Reception of Louis Philippe at Windsor, by Winterhalter.
Loutherbourg's two pieces of the Review and Sham Fight
at Warley Camp must not be overlooked ; nor Hogarth's
most characteristic scene in the Mall. And careful students
of art will particularly observe the picture of Federigo,
Duke of Urbino, with his Sons, by Melozzo da Forli.

But the greater number of pictures are by Canaletti,
whose works may be studied here with the greatest advan-
tage.   His finest views of Rome, Venice, and London, are
to be seen here.   And with them a goodly number of the
best examples of Zuccarelli's graceful but fanciful landscapes with figures.

The long array of busts, of the present and late Royal
Families, with almost all the famous statesmen, warriors,
and men of art, science, and letters of recent times, by dis-

tinguished sculptors, forms a very striking feature in the Corridor. Nor do the bronzes, some of them life-size busts, of Henry IV. and La Reine Margot, Charles I., Charles V., Philip II., and the Duke of Alva; others, fine and early copies of the antique statuary of Italy; the clocks, one of which is surmounted by a coffer of engraved crystal, and stands on a large musical box; the cabinets, particularly the huge cabinet of richly-carved ebony, which once belonged to Cardinal Wolsey; and a finely ornamented jewel-case with enamel portraits of the Queen and the Prince Consort, by Gruner, less assist in filling the eye, and producing upon visitors the impression of grandeur truly royal.

Through the glass doors leading to the Queen's private staircase, may be seen a statue of Edward VI., of life size, under an elegant canopy. The young king stands in an easy attitude, intently engaged in reading a book, which he holds in his left hand, while he appears to mark some passage, which has riveted his attention, with the sceptre which he holds in his right. On the page are to be seen the words, "Now Josiah." It was executed by the Baron de Triqueti, and placed here by the Prince Consort, as a means of keeping the pure fame of this best example of England's sovereigns before the royal children, from their earliest years.

The other Private Apartments which are open to visitors (by special orders from the Lord Chamberlain), are the White Drawing-room, where are portraits of the Queen, the Prince Consort, and the Prince of Wales when a child, by Winterhalter; and one of Queen Charlotte, with George IV. when an infant, by Cotes. Here also is a small table, which is a beautiful specimen of Florentine work.

The Green Drawing-room contains the magnificent collection of Sèvres porcelain, arranged in cabinets, which is of fabulous worth; and a huge but elegant porcelain vase of

Russian manufacture. Fine bronzes, after antique Italian statuary, are placed on the cabinets. Here also are Lawrence's portraits of the Princess Sophia and the Duchess of Gloucester. And on each side of the fireplace are bronze satyrs, holding their infant satyrs near the fire for warmth.

In the Crimson Drawing-room are portraits of the Duke of Kent and of the Duchess, by Winterhalter; a fine vase of Russian malachite; and several curiously inlaid cabinets.

And in the Dining-room is the celebrated punch-bowl or wine-cooler, of silver gilt, designed by Flaxman, the foot of which is fashioned into a succession of marine caverns, whilst the upper part is wreathed round with vines, amidst which infant Bacchuses gather clusters of grapes. The ladle is made in the shape of a Trochus shell.

Pictures and works of art, of every kind, and of conspicuous excellence, are also distributed in rich profusion through all the strictly private rooms of the Royal Family, the Royal Household, and visitors.

Before leaving the interior of the castle, it will be an interesting illustration of the extent of the edifice, and the variety of its provisions, to give the following particulars, supplied to us on authority:—There are seventeen State apartments; forty-eight rooms, comprising the kitchen—which is very spacious, and well worth a visit—with pastry, confectionery, vegetable, and other store-rooms; seventy-nine bedrooms; sixty-five sitting-rooms; and rooms containing 231 beds for servants. The length of passages is about 1700 yards; and there are fourteen furnaces in different parts of the building, connected with the heating apparatus.

The following is a list of the towers of the castle:—Round Tower, Winchester Tower, Powder Tower, Norman Tower, Blenheim Tower, King George IV.'s Tower, Entrance

Tower to State Apartments, Cornwall Tower, Brunswick Tower, Prince of Wales' Tower, Chester Tower, Clarence Tower, Victoria Tower, South Turret or Augusta Tower, York Tower, Lancaster Tower, Edward III.'s or the Devil Tower, King John's Tower, and Henry III.'s Tower. There are two towers at the north-east angle of the quadrangle which are named in Sir J. Wyatville's plan the Kitchen Gateway Towers, but this entrance is now converted into the Visitors' Entrance.

The outer towers include the Governor of the Military Knights' Tower, Henry VIII.'s Gateway Towers, Salisbury Tower, Garter Tower, and the Curfew or Bell Tower. There are three towers occupied by the canons, which have no names.

Leaving the castle for the parks, it is to be remembered these have undergone extensive alterations of late years. Much of the Home Park, containing 500 acres, was till lately open to the public, but was then less beautiful than at present. New walks and drives have been tastefully planned; and the Kennel, where there is a fine collection of choice breeds of dogs; the Dairy, which is a gem of architecture and elaborate decoration; the Aviary, stocked with domestic and foreign fowls; and the Model Farm, with its extensive buildings, and admirable arrangement for the live stock, are all additions more or less recent, which now add much to the interest of a walk over this part of the royal domain. Even the Slopes are comparatively modern. The charming little cottage which bears Queen Adelaide's name, shows it is not very long since it was erected; and all over this spot, once called Mother Dod's Hill, people still living, as was said before, played in their boyhood with kite and ball. Frogmore grounds, attached to the house in which her Royal Highness the Duchess of Kent breathed her last, has secluded walks by the side of a lake and amidst the shades of a wood, which none who are familiar with them would willingly forget. A mausoleum contains the remains of the illustrious Duchess; it is to receive a statue of the deceased lady by Mr. Theed. Beyond, towards Old Windsor, are the royal gardens, with immense conservatories. Going round by the new public road towards the Great Park, the visitor sees on his right hand the buildings of Shaw Farm. Coming in upon the Long Walk in this direction, a fine view is obtained of the castle. The trees which form the queen's ride were planted in the reign of Charles II. and William III.; about the same time the carriage road was made; it runs for two miles and three-quarters, with the York and Lancaster Towers of the castle at one end, and Snow Hill, surmounted by a colossal statue of George III., at the other. The undulations of the road produce a pleasant effect; and when the further end by the statue is reached, a view is obtained of a kind which has nothing equal to it in the world. The road which there crosses the end of the Long Walk at right angles, abounds in both directions with charming views, and a ramble down into the green glades under the glorious old trees will be found full of delicious pleasure. Not far off lie Cumberland Lodge, once the residence of the Culloden Conqueror, the royal lodge, now a small relic of the once famous cottage of George IV., and the Flemish Farm, a group of rustic buildings in red brick. Out into the forest by Blacknest Gate one finds green alleys and preserves, where hares and pheasants ever and anon cross your path; and in exploring the neighbourhood as far as St. Leonard's, noble trees and glimpses of fine views will well repay the wanderer. In the south-easterly direction is Virginia Water. The Lake, Chinese temple, Hermitage, Belvidere, ruins, and Cascade, we can merely mention.

NOTE,

Respecting the Royal Parks, compiled from papers in the Office of Woods and Forests, and communicated by a Gentleman in that Department.

DURING the Commonwealth, the whole of the landed property of the Crown and of the Prince of Wales, as well as considerable parts of the possessions of the bishops and ecclesiastical corporations, were sold by trustees appointed by the Parliament, to raise money for the payment of the soldiers who had been employed against the royal authority. The sales were chiefly made to persons having an interest in the lands as lessees or grantees for unexpired terms, and at very moderate rates of purchase. On the Restoration, the House of Lords, on the 16th of July, 1660, ordered—"That the King's Majesty shall be, and he is hereby restored to the possession of all his manors, &c., notwithstanding any sales, alienations, or dispositions made by any pretended authority whatsoever."

The authority of the House of Lords for making this order, or how it could be enforced, does not appear. The resumption was, however, acquiesced in by the purchasers under the Commonwealth, though many cases of concealment were connived at in favour of persons of influence, or who had contributed to the King's return. Among these, the officers employed in the army of the North, under General Monk, were secured in their possessions by a special declaration from the King; and the estates held by them were either confirmed, or full equivalents paid for those which were deemed necessary to be restored to the Crown.

The royal residences of Windsor, Hampton Court, and some others, had been reserved out of the powers of sale originally granted to the trustees by the Commonwealth Parliament; but at a later period the pecuniary difficulties of the Government, and the clamours of the soldiers for their arrears of pay, led to a very general allotment of both the Great and Little Parks at Windsor among the disbanded officers and soldiers as tenants at will, until their claims could be otherwise adjusted. The timber had been previously felled and sold, and the allottees forthwith proceeded to make their occupations as profitable as possible, by breaking up the virgin soil, and converting the park into tillage lands, dotting the expanse with such mean

Q

cottages and farm buildings as the slender means of such unthrifty tenants enabled them to erect. The marks of cultivation in ridge and furrow, so generally traceable throughout the Park, are probably to be referred to this period of waste. The scene which the royal domain must have presented at this period could not but have been deeply offensive to the great bulk of the community, who had gained nothing by the overthrow of the royal authority, and by the establishment in its place of an all-pervading ecclesiastical tyranny.

Immediately after the Restoration, the attention of the King was directed to these allotments; and early in the month of August, 1660, orders were issued, giving the several occupiers permission to remove their growing crops, but requiring them to quit possession forthwith. For the most part they obeyed these orders. A few refractory spirits remained till the following year; but the feeling of the neighbourhood was against them: their presence was deeply offensive to the royalist nobility and gentry, and no voice was raised for their protection. By the autumn of 1661 they had all removed, without giving occasion either for tumult or for legal proceedings.

It is probable, however, that the wasting cultivation for corn crops during this period proved very injurious to the subsequent productive power of the land. There are no indications of any suitable arrangement in laying the surface again down into grass. The subsequent spontaneously produced herbage was of the most unprofitable character, and much of it may still be rated as nearly worthless vegetation.

Some three or four of the officers who had been employed in the Lord Carlisle's regiment, and who produced certificates of good service from his Excellency the Lord General Monk, now Duke of Albemarle, were allowed to remain in possession of the allotments on which they had been placed by "the State." These allotments, which were then estimated at from 8s. to 12s. per acre, were on the sites now occupied by the Flemish and Norfolk Farms; but after remaining in the occupation of these favoured individuals for a few years, the tenancies were determined, and the whole of the Park reverted to the royal possession.

Some of these "officers" who were reported as having been in arms throughout the war, and against his late Majesty, but who nevertheless appealed to the royal clemency for compensation for their tillage and improvements, and for some reasonable term of years in their farms, were rebuked with no measured severity; and while possession was being taken of their holdings, they were informed that their malignity *entitled* them to punishment rather than to the favour of the sovereign.

In the meantime, however, a property of this extent and value could not escape the greedy vigilance of the court of the returned King, and a lease of the whole Park, then described as "disparked, inclosed, ploughed up, and turned into husbandry, with several houses erected there, so that it cannot be re-imparked without much cost and charges," and reputed to contain 3410 acres, was solicited by Secretary Nicholas, who desired to have it for a term of thirty-one years, without rent, in consideration of his long and eminent services—subject, however, to a power of reassumption by the King if he should be disposed to restore the Park, and again to make Windsor his place of residence. Such barefaced pillage was resisted by his Majesty. The lease was not granted, Secretary Nicholas was displaced, and the property having been fully resumed, measures were taken for the restoration of the Castle, and for a re-planting of the Park, giving it in the main the features which it now presents.

CHAPTER II.

THE NEIGHBOURHOOD.

THE town of Windsor, as distinguished from the castle, has in it scarcely anything worthy of a stranger's notice. The hall, which was begun by Sir Thomas Fits and completed by Sir Christopher Wren, was a few years ago restored. It is a little curious that the columns in the midst of the railed-in market underneath do not touch the building they seem to support. And, it is said, they were put up by Sir Christopher to content the corporation, who thought they were necessary ; but so put up as not to yield the least support. The churches and chapels in Windsor have no great beauty.

No space can be devoted to the history of Eton. Early notices of the town are very scanty, and only such as antiquaries would care to collect. The mention of a couple of mills in Domesday Book, a charter for a market, grants of tolls, commissions of inclosure, and such dry material we must leave. The college is the one object of picturesque beauty, and it alone gathers round it historical associations of value. On a summer's noon, as seen from the north terrace of Windsor Castle, rising above the trees, bathed in golden sunshine, it is one of those graceful forms of architecture which fixes itself at once in the imagination. Nor will the lines of Gray, however hackneyed, fail to give pensive pleasure as they recur to the memory :—

> " Ye distant spires, ye antique towers
>   That crown the watery glade,
>   Where grateful science still adores
>   Her Henry's holy shade.
>   And ye that from the stately brow
>   Of Windsor's heights, the expanse below,
>   Of grove, of lawn, of mead survey,
>   Whose turf, whose shade, whose flowers among,
>   Wanders the hoary Thames along
>   Its silver winding way.
>
> " Ah, happy hills ! ah, pleasing shade !
>   Ah, fields beloved in vain !
>   Where once my careless childhood stray'd,
>   A stranger yet to pain !
>   I feel the gales that from ye blow
>   A momentary bliss bestow,
>   As waving fresh their gladsome wing,
>   My weary soul they seem to soothe,
>   And redolent of joy and youth,
>   To breathe a second spring."

And no one who has rambled round the courts of Eton College, ascended the queer old staircase to the long sleeping-room, and peeped into that granary-like apartment with its rows of beds, now done away with, and visited the chapel, and wandered in the cloisters, or loitered in the playing-fields, will be likely soon to lose the impressions thus derived of one of the grandest old schools in England. Should he now approach the time-stained gateway out of school-hours, and see troops of fine-looking boys of every age and size rushing out to play ; should he watch them running round the trees, or leaning on the walls, buying cakes and oranges of those well-known vendors of small luxuries, who eagerly await the hour when school-work is suspended ; should he follow them in the green fields, amidst oaks and elms, to see them wielding the bat and hurling the ball; or, should he walk on to the bridge and see them rushing into their boats, and handling their oars with all the vigour, and feathering them with all the grace, of practised boatmen; if he has a heart that sympathizes with the energetic joyfulness of boyhood, he will feel no small amount of pleasure at the sight of so many happy faces; and if he has the feelings of an Englishman, he will be gladdened to think that these robust and genial youngsters —so full of daring, so ready for endurance, and so workful in their pleasures—are to be amongst the soldiers and sailors and statesmen of the next generation.

Eton has within its walls a curious kind of album. Many and many a boy who has afterwards become an illustrious man, has cut his name upon the forms and benches, or scratched it on the plaster. As we have stood and looked on them, deciphering the oddly marked characters, shades of the departed, some very grand and august, have passed before us, and we have felt that we do not envy people whose sensibilities are unawakened by mementoes of the mighty dead; who have no ears to hear, and no language in which to speak to them; who are untouched by the joy or the sadness, the peace or the strife, the work or the warfare, the achievements or the failures of those who have crossed before us over the broad fields of human life, and left behind them the deep footprints of their path. Not a few of those Eton boys, in notching their names with a sharp knife on a plank of wood, were mechanically rehearsing—albeit with little consciousness of doing so—the deeper moral impressions they were to make in after days upon a nation's mind. Strange emotions have boys felt when, as old men, they have revisited the school and playing-fields; and we have heard that Wellington regarded their youthful games as the discipline which prepared him and others for their manhood, and that he used to say of Eton, "That's where Waterloo was won." His words referred *generally* to the training of the English nobility and gentry, from whom the *officers* came.

Eton Montem has now become matter of history ; we have seen it more than once, and of all gay scenes connected with our youth, that was certainly amongst the gayest. How the bright sunshine used to usher in the day ! In what bravery of velvet and silk and broadcloth and gold lace did the *oppidans* come out ! How very, very smart were the uniforms of captain and marshal ! How smart, too, the whole host of the young undistinguished—obliged to be satisfied with blue jackets and white trousers ! How calm, but determined, the demand for salt by the gay bag-bearers, who stationed themselves by the toll-gate on Windsor bridge, where we remember seeing them stop the carriage of King William and Queen Adelaide, to receive the accustomed tribute ! How grand the procession was all around the quadrangle, and then through the gateway, up the Slough road to Salt Hill, where the graceful waving of the flag, amidst shouts of applause, concluded the ceremony. And then came the unceremonious proceedings in Botham's Gardens, and finally the walks up and down the play-fields in the evening, with somewhat damaged attire on the part of the chief heroes—now happier than ever in the smiles of fathers, mothers, brothers, and sisters.

We shall go into no critical inquiry about the origin of Montem, however tempted to do so ; but in the sentences which are to follow touching Eton College and town, with a forbearance most virtuous in an archæologist, confine ourselves to the poetical and the picturesque. Of course we think of Sir Henry Wotton, the provost of Eton and the friend of Isaac Walton, who has embalmed the worthy in his matchless " Lives."* There they are sitting in the library, looking into old black-letter books, or, after an abstemious repast, having a quaint and quiet chat about angling or higher themes, as on a summer evening they look out of the window on the green field and the noble trees. And early on a spring morning, there they go, attired in angler's gear, with rods and lines, and landing-nets and worm-cans, and all the other appurtenances of the gentle craft, to the river-side down to Black Pots, where they fish and listen to the birds and wisely and lovingly talk together.

Eton College was founded by the pious munificence of Henry VI. The charter of foundation is dated 1441, and the school is designated " the Kynge's College, of our Lady by Etone, besyde Wyndesore." We shall not weary the reader with extracts from the documents, nor from the builder's accounts, with entries about sand and chalk, flints and bushels of oyster-shells, timber and stone ; nor describe how the work went on, how provost and fellows were chosen, and how they met and worshipped in the building before it was finished, and how alms-houses were built, and the boys were at length gathered ; but we cannot resist the temptation to insert the following little bit out of an old MS. : " When King Henry met some of the students in Windsor Castle, whither they sometimes used to go to visit the king's servants, whom they knew, on ascertaining who they were, he admonished them to follow the path of

---

* In the Windsor Parish Register, under date 1636, we find, " Bapt. William, son of Mr. Isaac Walton, and Rachel his wife." Walton married Rachel Ford in 1626, and had three children, two of them boys, who both died. Biographers say they were born in the angler's house, Chancery-lane, a few doors from Fleet-street. It is plain from this entry that one was born in Windsor, where it would seem at the time Walton was a resident, perhaps that he might be near Sir Henry and angle in the pleasant river Thames.

virtue, and besides his words, would give them money to win over their good will, saying to them, 'Be good boys, be gentle and docile, and servants of the Lord.'"

There is the walk to Datchet, carried across the lower Home Park through a noble avenue, haunted by memories of the fat knight, who, in the muddy ditch at Datchet Mead, was shot out of the basket "hissing hot," into the water, "where, with a kind of alacrity in sinking, he had been drowned, but that the shore was shelvy and shallow." And there are green lanes from Datchet to Upton, passing by a fairy-looking cottage with a goodly lawn and a pool of water, and drooping willows in front. And there is Upton Church, once ruinous but now restored, with its ivy-clad steeple, which vies with Stoke in its claim to the allusion by Gray of the "ivy-mantled tower, where the owl does unto the moon complain." Crossing by what is now Upton Park, we pause by an old-fashioned straggling brick house, above which the famous telescope, aspiring to the heavens, used to indicate the abode of the great astronomer Herschell. And going somewhat a-field on the other side Slough, one may ride to Stoke church-yard, and think of Gray and his mother. Close by there is the mansion of Mr. Granville Penn, with a piece of the tree under which his ancestor, the Quaker founder of Pennsylvania, formed his treaty with the Indians. The estate has now passed into the hands of Mr. Labouchere. Farther on, you reach Burnham Common and Beeches, one of the noblest collections of trees in England, where Burke used to meditate, and which Gray thus describes :—" I have at the distance of half a mile, through a green lane, a forest (the vulgar call it a common), all my own ; at least as good as so, for I spy no living thing in it but myself. It is a chaos of mountains and precipices ; mountains, it is true, that do not ascend much above the clouds, nor are the declivities quite so amazing as Dover Cliff; but just such hills as people who love their necks as well as I do may venture to climb, and crags that give the eye as much pleasure as if they were more dangerous. Both vale and hill are covered with most venerable beeches, and other very reverend vegetables, that, like most other ancient people, are always dreaming out their old stories to the winds;

> " ' And as they bow their hoary tops, relate
> In murmuring sounds the dark decrees of fate;
> While visions, as poetic eyes avow,
> Cling to each leaf, and swarm on every bough.'

"At the foot of one of these I squats me, (*il penseroso*), and there I grow to the trunk for a whole morning; the timorous hare and sportive squirrel gambol around me, like Adam in Paradise before he had an Eve; but I think he did not use to read ' Virgil,' as I commonly do there."

Stoke Pogis is worthy of being visited for its own rural beauty, as well as for its memorials of Gray. The picturesque church, with its "ivy-mantled tower," and the churchyard, with its "yew-trees' shade," its "rugged elms," and the quiet tombs, beneath which "the rude forefathers of the hamlet sleep." remain much as they were when the poet wrote the Elegy. The "shapeless sculptures" are there, upon which his eyes may have rested, and many a holy text is still strewn around,

> "To teach the rustic moralist to die."*

On a slight eminence, commanding a fine view of Windsor and Eton, a monument was erected in 1799, in memory of "the great lyric and elegiac poet," the inscription bearing that "he died in 1771, and lies unnoticed in

---

* The Author has here made use of some passages in a paper contributed by him some time ago to " The Leisure Hour."

the churchyard adjoining, under the tombstone on which
he piously and affectionately recorded the interment of his
aunt and lamented mother." In that tomb "sleep the
remains of Dorothy Gray, widow, the careful, tender mother
of many children, one of whom alone had the misfortune
to survive her." A more recent inscription under the
adjoining window runs thus :—" Opposite to this stone, in
the same tomb upon which he has so feelingly recorded his
grief at the loss of a beloved parent, are deposited the
remains of the author of the Elegy."

> " Hark, how the sacred calm that breathes around,
> Bids every fierce, tumultuous passion cease ;
> In still small accents whispering from the ground,
> A grateful earnest of eternal peace ! "

NOTE ON THE SALLYPORT NEAR THE YORK TOWER.

In an early part of the book notice is taken of a subterranean
passage lately discovered. I beg to subjoin a fuller account of
it, furnished by my friend, Mr. Turnbull, clerk of the works at
Windsor Castle.

" This passage is below the basement floor of the castle, a little to
the east of the York Tower, and extends from about twelve feet of
the front wall of the corridor towards the south, and terminates in
what was anciently the castle ditch.

" The length of the passage as it now exists is one hundred feet.
There is about twenty feet of this passage which has rubble walls
with stone-pointed arch, and two semicircular doorways with splayed
and moulded arches, one of which has still the iron hooks for the
door ; the remainder of the passage is cut through the solid chalk
rock ; the width is about five feet, and height from six to eight feet,
and the floor of the passage is twenty-two feet below the ground
level of the Quadrangle."

INDEX.

PAGE

ADELAIDE, second wife of Henry I.. 5
———— Queen of William IV. 231
Anne, Queen, at Windsor 139
———— wooden statue of 187
Anne Boleyn 70, 194, 196
Antiquities of Windsor 1
———— plea for their preservation 44
Armour, suit of 16
Arthur, King 2
Ashmole, the Historian of the Garter during the reign of
Edward VI. 76
Astrological studies—horoscope of Edward III. 17
Astrology—skill of Henry V. in that science 45

BANQUET in St. George's Hall 33
Banquet in the fifteenth century described 50
Baronial residences 23
Barons 13
Bear, White, kept in Tower of London 11
Beauchamp, Richard, Bishop of Salisbury 51, 54
Beaufort, Joanna, niece of Richard II.. 40
Bedford, John, Duke of 45
"Black Book," or Register of the Garter 2, 44
Blenheim, Victory of 140
Bramber, Lord of, and his wife 7
Brandon, Charles, Duke of Suffolk 76
Bray, Sir Reginald, architect of St. George's Chapel . . 52, 201
Burdon, William, the painter 24
Burford House, residence of Eleanor Gwyn 130

CARLTON'S, Sir Dudley, description of James I. at Windsor . 93
Castle:
   Additions of Henry III. 9
   Appearance of, in the reigns of the Norman Sovereigns . 14
   Appearance of, in the time of Edward III. 22
   Hunting seat of William the Conqueror 4
   Investiture of, by the Barons 8
   Old Castle taken down 18
   Rebuilt in the reign of Edward III. 17
   Rebuilding of, by George IV. 147
   Residence of William the Conqueror 3
   Taken by the Parliamentary Army 101
   Apartments, Private 221
   Apartments, State 208
   Apartments, number of 222
   Armoury 218

Castle—*continued.*   PAGE

   Bakehouse, formerly in Pescod-street 84
   Banqueting-house; new one in 1576 82
   Buildings, Star 62
   Busts . . . . 214—220
   Chapels :
      Bray's 201
      Edward the Confessor's 6
      Edward IV.'s 51
      George's, St. 62, 195
      Henry I.'s 5
      Henry III.'s 9
      Henry VII.'s 195
      John the Baptist's 200
      King's College 195
      Lincoln 203
      Wolsey's, reflections upon 69
      Urswick 200
   Cloisters 196, 197
   Corridor, Grand 219
   Courts 83, 207
   Fountain, Queen Mary's 90
   Galleries :
      Elizabeth 62
      Waterloo 207
   Gates :
      Queen Elizabeth's 188
      St. George's 205
   Gateway, Norman 206
   ———— of Henry VIII. 65
   Houses :
      New Commons 63
      Garter 195
      Chapter 199
   Kitchen 222
   Library, Dean and Chapter's 197
   Lodges 188
   Objects of interest :
      Armour, suits of 213
      Arms of Edward III., IV., &c. 199
      Bronzes 221
      Cabinets—Cardinal Wolsey's . . . . *ib.*
      Chairs, curious 215
      Clocks 221
      Ornaments, heraldic 204
      Screen-work, beautiful specimens of 199
      Shield, presented by Francis I. to Henry VIII. . . 214
      Sword of Edward III. 199
      Porcelain Sèvres, magnificent Collection . . . 221
      Tapestry, Gobelin 212, 215
      Throne, Sovereign's 213
      Vases, Malachite and Granite . . . . *ib.*

Castle—*continued.*   PAGE
   Offices, Architect's 205
   Paintings, by Vandyke, West, Zuccarelli, &c. . . 209, 216
   Portraits, by Canaletti, Gainsborough, Lawrence, &c.
                    208, 210, 216, 219, 220
   Prints and Drawings in connexion with the Library . . 217
   Parks, extent of, in the seventeenth century 91
     Home 223
   Road, Carriage, through Long Walk 139
   Sallyport, near the York Tower 235
   Staircase, Great, painted by Sir James Thornhill . . . 139
   ———— of the time of the Stuarts 188
   Store-Rooms 205
   Statues :
     Anne, Queen 187
     Charles II., equestrian of 206
     Edward VI. 221
     George IV. 210
   Terrace, North, raised by Elizabeth 81
   Towers 223
   Walks . . . . 138, 139—144
Cavaliers imprisoned in Castle 114
Cellini, Benvenuto 65
Chair, of great antiquity 24
Charles I., alterations he made in Castle 97
———— anecdote of the monarch and Colonel Harrison . 109
———— arrival of his Majesty as a prisoner at Windsor . 108
———— execution, curious account of, in Parish Register . 179
———— interment of the King 110
———— letters to Dowcett, his faithful servant 103
Charles, Marquis of Worcester, his loyalty and eccentricity . 115
Charles II. 24
———— alterations of Castle by him 123
———— anecdote of the King and Duke of Buckingham . 129
Chaucer, Alice, Dowager Duchess of Suffolk 47
Chaucer, Geoffrey, the poet 26
Chivalry, Spirit of 27
Concordance, first, of English Bible 161
Court, first held 5
———— fashions and furniture of, during reign of Edward IV. 56
Crewe, Bishop of Durham 134
Crisis in English History 98
Cromwell, his meetings for prayer at Windsor 115

D'ARBLAY, Madame. 146
David, King of Scotland 6
Davis, William, the noble Blacksmith 180
Demonstrations, loyal, at Windsor and Eton during reign of
   Elizabeth 165
Denton, John, the kind-hearted Canon 64
Dinner, complaint of, by Queen Elizabeth 84
Duke of Albany, Regent of Scotland 40

Durham, Bishop of, in 1095 5

Eagle and eaglets, Story of 7
Edmund de la Pole, imprisonment of 62
Edward the Confessor 3
Edward I., educated at Windsor 13
———— anecdote of 16
Edward II. . . . . *ib.*
———— III., christening of . . . . *ib.*
———— curious tale of 17
Edward IV., accession of 46
———— death and burial of 58
———— his coffin opened in 1789 . . . . . . *ib.*
Edward, Duke of Buckingham, condemned for treason . . 66
Edward VI., proclaimed by Garter 75
———— Visit to Windsor in dead of night 77
Eleanor, wife of Edward I. 15
———— journeys from London to Windsor 155
Elizabeth of Bohemia 193
Elizabeth, Queen, amusements at Windsor 85
———— imperious temper of . . . . *ib.*
Engine for supplying water to Castle, curious account of . . 126
Eric, King of Sweden, a suitor for the hand of Queen Elizabeth 84
Eton College 122
———— founded by Henry VI. 232
———— Gray's lines on 229
Eton Memorial of 1563 described 166
Eton Montem, description of 231
Evelyn, extracts from his Diary 123
———— glimpses of Windsor before and after alterations of
   Charles II. 126

Ferdinand the Elector 193
Fire in the Castle, 1295 16
Fire-tax and the Londoners in 1386 38
Fits, Sir Thomas, Surveyor of the Cinque Ports 186
Fitzgerald, Lady Elizabeth 70
Fitzwilliam, William, tomb of 202
Fortescue, Sir Edmund 114
Foundations 194, 196
Fuller, the Historian, on rumours concerning death of Henry
   VIII. 73

Gallys, Richard, Landlord of Garter Inn, and M.P. for
   Borough 176
Garter, Order of the 27
——— Alterations in laws of, by Edward VI. 77
——— Costume of the Order 30
——— Feasts described 32, 49, 95, 121
——— Glory of the Order restored by Mary 80
——— Installation of Prince Henry in 1603 95
——— Institution, date of 31

PAGE

Garter, Knights, apartments for 147
——— Ladies at feasts of the Order 34
——— Order restored upon Charles's accession 121
——— Origin of the Custom of decorating Ladies 35
——————— symbol of the Order 28
——— Pageants, description of 67
——— Patron saints of the Order 29
——— Processions of the earlier reigns 94
——— Zeal of James I. for the Order . . . . ib.
Genius, its creative power 171
George III., his attachment to Windsor 145
——————— anecdote of King and the Messenger 146
——————— attacks of Insanity and final retreat in Queen's
    Lodge . . . . ib.
George, Prince of Denmark, statue of 187
Gibbons, his incomparable carving 127, 188
Grafton, Richard, King's printer, accused of heresy, 1550. . 161
Gray, the Poet, monument to 234
Grey, Lady Jane 76

Hake, Edward, Mayor of Windsor 167
Hanover, House of 144
Henry I. 5
Henry II. 6
Henry III. 9
Henry IV., plot to assassinate him and his sons 39
Henry V., the hero of Agincourt 44
Henry VI. 42
——————— insanity of 46
——————— violent death of in the Tower . . . . . . ib.
——————— removal of the body to Windsor in reign of
    Richard III. 47
Henry VII. and Elizabeth 52
Henry VIII. and Wolsey 68
——————— amusements of, at Windsor 66
——————— death and magnificent funeral 72
Henry V. the Emperor 5
Hentzner, Paul, his rural description of Eton in Elizabeth's
    reign 170
——————— his description of curiosities of Castle 82
Herne's Oak, arguments respecting 172
Herschell, the Great Astronomer, abode of 233
Holman, Lieutenant, the blind traveller 147
Hospital, Leper 13
Houses for Dean and Canons, erected by Edward III. . . . 26
——— English, discomforts of, in sixteenth century . . . 176
Howard, Catherine, her prison house 73
Hugh de Pudsey, Bishop of Durham 7

Irving, Washington 43
Islip, Archbishop of Canterbury 32

PAGE

JAMES I. of Scotland, imprisonment of 39
———— love of, for the Lady Jane 40
———— residence of the King occasionally at Windsor . . 93
James II., celebrating mass in Wolsey's Chapel 132
———— public reception of d'Adda, the Papal Nuncio . . 133
———— warned by the Spanish Ambassador . . . . . ib.
Joan, Queen 31
John the Baptist, church dedicated to 149
John, King of France, a prisoner at Windsor 32
Jousts of foreign knights at Windsor 28
———— in honour of Queen, 1384 31
Julius II. 48

KILLIGREW, Sir Thomas, his just reproof to the King . . . 129
King, Oliver, Secretary to Henry VI. 200
Knight, Mr. Charles, description of Windsor, in time of Elizabeth 174
Knights :
    Alms Knights 54, 55, 80
    Holy Sepulchre 27
    Military 31, 79
    Naval, college erected for, in the reign of George III. . 146
    Round Table 27
    St. John the Baptist . . . . ib.
    St. Lazarus . . . . ib.

LEICESTER, Earl of 165
Lodgings let in the Castle 144
London, Dr., punishment of 163
Longchamp, Bishop of Ely 7
Louis of Bruges, Lord of Grauthuse 56
Louis XIV., splendid Court of 124

MAGNA Charta Island 8
Mantelpiece of time of James I. 195
Marbeck, organist of Royal Chapel 161
Mark Antonio de Dominis 96
Margaret, Queen of Henry II. 47
Marlborough, Sarah, Duchess of, beautiful reply to Charles,
    Duke of Somerset 140
———— secret of her influence 139
Martyrs in reign of Henry VIII. 158
———— Cranmer, Ridley, and Latimer conveyed to the Castle 79
Mary, Princess, beautiful sister of Henry VIII. 76
Mary, Queen of Scotland, attempting to celebrate mass . . 132
Masham, Mrs. 140
Matilda, Princess 5
Maude, Empress 6
Monument for Henry VI. 48
Mordaunt, Lord, impeachment of, in 1688 181

NEVILLE'S Cross, battle of 31

PAGE

Nichol's description of Queen Elizabeth at Windsor . . . 84
Nicholson, the eminent landscape draughtsman 172
Norden's map of Windsor 175
Norman architectural fragments 6, 25
Northumberland, Earl of 5

OLIVIER, John, perplexed with the tribute of bear skins . . 145

PAMPHLET, curious, of 1642 100
Passage, modern, underground 26
Pearson, Anthony, one of the early Protestants 161
Penn, Mr. Granville, mansion of 233
Penns of Pennsylvania, their tribute to British Crown . . . 145
Pepys' Diary, amusing extract of journey to Windsor . . . 121
Philip the Fair, anecdote of 61
Philip, husband of Mary, made a knight 78
Philippa, Queen 31
———— dying words of 34
Poor, entertainment of 11
Protestantism, fathers of, in Windsor 162
Puritans 99

RAINBOW, phenomenon of, first accounted for 97
Ralph, Archbishop of Canterbury 5
Ramsay, David, the illustrious clockmaker 97
Rebellion of 1536 in the North of England 157
Restoration, Charles II., proclaimed at New Windsor . . 117
Richard I. 7, 28
Richard II. 34
———— parting from Queen Isabella 37
Roderic O'Connor, King of Connaught 7
Roger, Bishop of Salisbury 5
Roman bricks 1
———— road, remarkable specimen of . . . . ib.
Round Table, King Arthur's 28
Royal Touch, anecdote of 3
Runnymede 8
Rustat, Tobias, a faithful servant of Charles II. 136
———— fellowships and scholarships founded by him . ib.
Rutland, Earl of 39

SALISBURY, Countess of 28
———— Earl of 33
Sallyport of the time of Edward III. 26
Saxe Weimar, Duchess of 199
Saxon Kings, Palace of 2
———— Urns 3
Sepulchre, Royal, from the design of Charles I. 147
Seymour, Jane, death and burial of 76
Shorne, John, shrine of, in Lincoln Chapel 54
Sigismund, Emperor of Germany, created a Knight of the Garter 44

PAGE

Simon de Sudbury, Address of, to the King 38
Somerset, Duke of, and James II. 133
———— Protector, sent to the Tower 78
Stephen, King 6
Storm in 1251 14
Stow, John, his relation of the removal of the body of
    Henry VI. to Windsor 48
Subterranean passage 12, 25
Surrey, Earl of—verses when a prisoner at Windsor . . . 71

Testwood, Robert, breaking the Image of the Virgin . . . 159
Thomson, Dr. Giles, Monument to 202
Throne—painted and gilt 11
Tournament in Edward I.'s reign 15
———— held on the feast of St. George, 1358 32
Tomson, Giles, Dean of Windsor 96
Tower of London, Queen's escape from 13
Town of Windsor, prior to the Conquest 3
Trial of Testwood, Pearson, Filmer, and Marbeck in 1544 . 162

Urswick, Dr. Christopher, associate of Sir Reginald Bray . 53

Verrio, a Neapolitan artist at Windsor, anecdote of . . . 125
Vespers, description of 50
Villiers, Duke of Buckingham, house of 188
Vineyard appended to Royal Palace 7
Virgin, Image of 10

Walter de Burgh 9, 197
Walton, Sir Isaac, notice of family in parish register . . . 232
Wardrobe of Castle—beds described 65
Wellington, at Eton 230
Westminster, Gift of Windsor to the Monks of 3
Whitelock, Lord Commissioner 117
Whitsuntide, Festivities of 4
Widville, Queen Elizabeth 199
William the Conqueror 3
William of Malmesbury 3
William Rufus 5
William of Scotland 6
William of Wykeham, facetious reply of 18, 22
William, Prince of Orange—invitation to England 134
William III. and Princess Mary—rejoicings at their marriage 185
Windows—stained glass 11
Windsor—why so called 89
———— changes in appearance 92
———— proposal to sell it by the Parliament 115
———— Town of 149
———— architecture, domestic 154
———— borough, when constituted 149
———— burgesses returned to Parliament in time of Edward I. 151

Windsor—*continued.*

                                                                    PAGE
Chapels in the town 189, 190
Church, Old Parish   189
Churchyard—anecdote of Dr. Johnson . . . . . .   *ib.*
Charity, earliest existing   156
Communication with London   155
Corporation of   150
    Accounts of   186
    Contest of Corporation and inhabitants   180
    Hospitable cheer of   184
    Seal of   152
Costumes of the people   154
Cross, High, site of   176
Cucking-stool   186
Election, described   151
Frugality of the people   155
Gaol, borough   188
—— prisoners annoying George III. . . . .   *ib.*
Hall, Town, expenses of   186
Houses, public, large number of   185
Inhabitants, number of, in 1555 . . . , ...   153
Inns : Garter, White Hart 176, 184
Market, columns of, by Sir Christopher Wren   228
Mediæval Windsor   149
Member for the town expelled from the House   178
—— —— gratuities paid to   185
Memorial, Windsor—oration and speech of the Mayor .   168
Neighbourhood of . . . .   228—235
Post-house—letter respecting   182
Pilgrims to King Henry's Shrine   159
Political excitements of 1641   178
—— liberty, revival of   153
Returns to Parliament   151
Wolsey, Cardinal—mausoleum he designed for himself .   68
Woodstock—tenure on which estate is held   140
Woodville, Elizabeth, wife of Edward IV.   56
——————— misfortunes and death of   59
Workmen *pressed* for rebuilding the Castle   18
——— wages of   20
Wotton, Sir Henry, Provost of Eton   231
Wren, Christopher, father of the famous architect   124
—— Sir Christopher, the architect 124, 181, 187
Wyatville, Sir Jeffrey de 25, 62

York and Lancaster, Houses of   46

THE END.

www.ingramcontent.com/pod-product-compliance
Lightning Source LLC
Chambersburg PA
CBHW030810020726
47499CB00006B/1849